Women's and Men's Liberation

Recent Titles in
Contributions in Philosophy

Women's and Men's LIBERATION _____

TESTIMONIES OF SPIRIT

EDITED BY
  LEONARD GROB,
  RIFFAT HASSAN, and
  HAIM GORDON

Contributions in Philosophy, Number 45

GREENWOOD PRESS _____
New York • Westport, Connecticut • London

Library of Congress Cataloging-in-Publication Data

Women's and men's liberation : testimonies of spirit / edited by
  Leonard Grob, Riffat Hassan, and Haim Gordon.
      p.   cm.—(Contributions in philosophy, ISSN 0084-926X ; no.
  45)
    Includes bibliographical references and index.
    ISBN 0-313-25969-0 (alk. paper)
    1. Women—Religious life.   2. Interpersonal relations.   I. Grob,
  Leonard.   II. Hassan, Riffat.   III. Gordon, Hayim.   IV. Series.
  BL625.7.W65   1991
  291.1'78343—dc20   90-47539

British Library Cataloguing in Publication Data is available.

Library of Congress Catalog Card Number: 90-47539
ISBN: 0-313-25969-0
ISSN: 0084-926X

First published in 1991

Greenwood Press, 88 Post Road West, Westport, CT 06881
An imprint of Greenwood Publishing Group, Inc.

Printed in the United States of America

The paper used in this book complies with the
Permanent Paper Standard issued by the National
Information Standards Organization (Z39.48–1984).

10 9 8 7 6 5 4 3 2 1

Copyright Acknowledgments

The editors and publisher are grateful to the following for allowing the use of material:

Marilyn Frye, *The Politics of Reality: Essays in Feminist Theory* (Trumansburg, N.Y.:
The Crossing Press, 1983).

Extract taken from *The Principal Upanisads* by S. Radhakrishnan, reproduced by kind
permission of Unwin Hyman Ltd. © 1953.

Contents

Part 1

Introduction

EACH NIGHT

What Scott Fitzgerald called the green breast
of the new world, I see when I look at you

each night you pull into our driveway
home from work, home to me,

holding in your look the sweetest dream
that's possible. Your face does that—

each night your smile is fresh, an innocence
that says this place is God's

and she is inside, waiting to receive me.
The pleasure of that expectation

on the roundness of your face never fails
to step into the light; each night it promises

I will be loved for being here and being me.

Belief is in our hug. Yet, in five minutes—
how are we betrayed? Your face goes flat,

my voice grates shrill; you
need TV and tire early.

I stay up to find my way
with someone in a book.

Myra Shapiro

1

The Quest for Dialogue between Men and Women: Introductory Remarks

LEONARD GROB

In a climate of continuing, but often fruitless, debate on issues of justice and equality for women, there is clear need to develop new initiatives in realizing a truly egalitarian society. In particular, there is need for such efforts to be inaugurated by those who have come to see the linkage between the liberation of women and that of men. This volume, containing writings by both men and women, is committed to the idea that only in the freedom of the other sex lies the possibility of the authentic freedom of one's own.

Although it is *necessary* for women and men to separate themselves *as* women and men from entanglement in patriarchal structures—how else can either sex begin to comprehend those forces that have created a society half of whose members have often been oppressed in the interests of the other half—such separation is by no means *sufficient* to realize the liberation process in its fullness. Such fullness manifests itself solely in that authentic dialogue between the sexes that forms the core subject matter of this book. This volume contends, throughout, that only in genuine encounter with all our fellow beings can we humans realize ourselves as human.

In stating the above, the editors of this anthology by no means imply that the situations of men and women in a fundamentally patriarchal society are *equivalent*. As individuals who carry their history with them, men and women do not begin the liberation struggle from the same or even similar points of departure; there is little question that men must take the lead in redressing the wrongs established in their name. Having granted this assymetry, however, we believe that both sexes bear (different degrees and kinds of) responsibility for giving new meaning to their (very different) histories in the course of realizing the healing work of dialogue.

What is the nature of this "dialogue" that forms the center of our concerns in the present volume? And how is it to be distinguished from those forms of communication that are mere pretenders to such status? According to the contemporary religious thinker Martin Buber, a major inspiration for assembling this collection of writings, dialogue occurs when two individuals refuse to remain content with subjecting one another to customary modes of objectification. Each partner to dialogue attempts to encounter the other with the fullness of her or his being. Each attempts to relate to the other as more than an instrument of his or her concerns, more than the embodiment of a role that we (inevitably) ascribe to her or him in our everyday interactions. My companion in dialogue is my co-subject, a being *on principle* beyond my appropriative grasp—in Buber's terms, a "Thou."

The contributors to this volume agree that in order to undertake new initiatives in fostering dialogue between the sexes, men and women must refuse to see one another *merely* as perpetrator and victim in a history of patriarchal oppression. Although men and women have indeed played (or been forced to play) these roles throughout the centuries, each sex must work to *transcend* its fixity of role. Only then can we realize that aspect of our humanity that the editors, following a long history of spiritual traditions, name the "divine." Men and women, we argue, must resist a reduction of our status to that of either victim or perpetrator, or even some combination of both. Rather, we must celebrate our embodiment of a dimension of transcendence that overflows any endeavor to ascribe to us a fixed role in any historical drama.

Such a "divine" aspect, moreover, is nothing to be posited or argued for by the powers of discursive reason; it finds expression in a process of dialogue to be *attested* to, to be *witnessed*. Hence the prevalence of the use of the term "witness" in Part II of the text. The "findings" reported in this book, are, in significant measure, those that emerge from personal experience with dialogue.

To say the above, however, is not to say that dialogue is some ecstatic or mystical event. Whenever and wherever I overcome my inclination to confine my partner within fixed schemas, there, in the midst of ordinariness, dialogue occurs. Nor does dialogue necessarily exclude conflict: "In a genuine dialogue," Buber claims, "each of the partners, *even when he stands in opposition to the other*, heeds, affirms, and confirms his opponent as an existing other."[1] Dialogue between men and women will not do away with confrontation between the sexes; rather it will allow for that form of confrontation in which both parties, for the first time, can heal their wounds in the course of acknowledging a sacred dimension of each other's being.

Furthermore, to see you, my dialogical other, as existing beyond any role that I might ascribe to you is not to predicate the existence of some ideal substratum lying at the foundation of your ordinary self. There is no "real" you apart from the self that appears in concrete interactions with others. To see you as *transcendent*, as transcending any category that I might apply to you, is not to see you as some idealized form. Buber's dialogical philosophy is no "vague idealism, but a more comprehending, more penetrating realism."[2] Thus my partner in dialogue is the most concrete of all beings: I face you not as a neutered ideal, but as who you are by and through your being this gendered individual, this man or woman.

The editors of this volume affirm the presence of dialogue, thus described, as the primordial ground of all human endeavor, including that endeavor of the liberation of both sexes that is our special concern. Buber claims that "in the beginning is relation," and it is this *ontological* primacy of dialogue that we wish to explore in relations between men and women. A history of oppression can only be overcome, in a "root" or radical sense, by a movement of *being*, a movement that is more than the mere exchange of ideas or feelings, more than an embrace of mutual interests in the name of compromise. Dialogue both requires and, paradoxically, brings about the ontological transformation of its participants: in Buber's words, "I become through my relation to the Thou; as I become I, I say Thou."[3] In dialogue, and in dialogue alone, can there be effected a truly fundamental or radical revolution in the relations between the sexes.

Much has transpired in the histories of both East and West to impede dialogue. And perhaps nowhere have roadblocks to dialogue been placed more firmly than in the major world religions. As many feminist theologians have argued, there is an inextricable linkage between the ways we envision the nature of the ultimate (the subject matter of religions worldwide) and our societal structures. If such ultimacy is framed within terms that are predominantly male, we stand little chance of realizing a society on earth in which women are accorded their full dignity as humans. If we reflect a male image of the divine—however "divine" is otherwise understood in the spiritual traditions—then men must, on principle, occupy a privileged position in everyday affairs of the society at large.

Having stated the above, we must now ask why a volume dedicated to a discussion of dialogue between men and women would turn to "testimonies of spirit" (the very subtitle of our work) as a central concern. How can spiritual traditions so steeped in patriarchy promote the dialogue of which we are in search? Why not abandon those traditions altogether in the process of inaugurating a search for some contemporary flowering of the spirit that is avowedly egalitarian in nature? Why have we chosen to reexamine five major traditions—Judaism, Christianity, Islam, Hinduism, and Buddhism—in the course of a search for a spiritual foundation for revolutionizing the relationship between the sexes?

The answer lies in our understanding that the ontological transformation we seek can never occur outside cultural contexts; we humans are situated firmly within history. And at the heart of all cultures, calling us to a concern with ultimacy, lie our spiritual traditions. The centrality of the religious quest across cultures is no mere accident of history. The questions posed and "answered" by these religious traditions are ones that echo with resounding force throughout time, challenging us to account for "who" we are and how we wish to be in our relations with others. Issues of the finite and infinite, the evanescent and the eternal, the just and the unjust, good and evil—all of these concerns lie at the heart of the traditions represented in this volume. If we are to grapple anew, and radically, with issues of justice and equality between the sexes, it is to these core teachings of major world religions that we must turn for guidance. Having rooted genuine dialogue between the sexes in an ontological event, we creatures of history must turn to our spiritual legacies for help.

To claim that we are immersed in history is not to say that we are *determined* by that history. The contributors to this volume are keenly aware of the ways in which the spiritual traditions have contributed to our patriarchal heritage; these aspects of our history, they contend, must be overcome. Yet all maintain that the traditions need not be abandoned wholesale; rather, they must be hallowed, renewed by their own purifying fires. Each believes that there are core teachings to be found in the traditions that can guide us in seeking to realize equality and justice for women; although so often disputed, betrayed from within, and covered over by dried-up institutional forms, they remain a source calling on men and women to initiate an authentic dialogue. Uncovering these core teachings enables us not to step outside of history, but to work to redeem it.

Our anthology is an attempt to sow these "seeds of redemption." Following a second introductory chapter, celebrating a spiritual odyssey of co-editor Riffat Hassan, five women "witnesses"—Tikvah Frymer-Kensky, Constance Parvey, Riffat Hassan, Kana Mitra, and Rita Gross—address their respective spiritual legacies. Each witness surveys her tradition's attitudes toward women and then proceeds to search for those teachings that would move men and women toward true dialogue. All speak from a theoretical perspective grounded in the praxis of their lived journeys (as women) toward faith.

This common endeavor to uncover teachings-toward-dialogue in five spiritual traditions does not imply any "homogenizing" of the individual efforts. Just as dialogue between individuals allows for, indeed *requires*, preserving the uniqueness of each party, so the interreligious dialogue so central to this anthology must be rooted in a *listening* on the part of each witness to the distinct voice of every other. This volume, given over to the ideal of dialogue, attempts to be self-illustrating. In Buber's words, "When a man is singing and cannot lift his voice, and another comes and sings with him, another who can lift his voice, the first will be able to lift his voice too. That is the secret of the bond between spirits."[4]

Our text also attempts to exemplify the participation of both sexes in the common task of liberation. Hence Part III, in which co-editor Leonard Grob and Leonard Swidler respond to the challenges facing them as, in Buber's terms, "partners in the living event" of liberation sketched by the women contributors in the preceding section. Like their female predecessors, these male authors incorporate elements of their personal histories into their discussion; all strive to overcome any fixed dichotomy between the personal and the academic.

A volume dedicated to offering new initiatives in dialogue between men and women cannot conclude without reference to concrete modes of educating our own and future generations toward dialogical practice. Part IV contains chapters by co-editor Haim Gordon and Betty Cannon, each examining educational practices in home and classroom that would spur these efforts. Both chapters endeavor to translate the ontological claims uncovered earlier in the text into pedagogies that encourage the realization of the liberation process. The authors celebrate the engagement of the spirit in the hands-on work of educational practice. What they suggest summons us to work ever harder to overcome our proclivities to objectify the other by limiting her or him to a fixed gender role. In Buber's words, "where the dialogue is fulfilled in its being, between partners who have turned to one another in truth, who . . . are free of the desire for semblance, there is brought into being a memorable common fruitfulness which is to be found nowhere else."[5]

This anthology is an endeavor, throughout, to realize the fruits of dialogue between men and women.

NOTES

1. Martin Buber, *Pointing the Way* (New York: Harper & Row, 1958), 238.
2. Ibid., 227.
3. Martin Buber, *I and Thou,* trans. Ronald Gregor Smith (New York: Collier Books, 1987), 11.
4. Martin Buber, *Ten Rungs: Hasidic Sayings* (New York: Schocken Books, 1947), 84.
5. Martin Buber, *The Knowledge of Man* (New York: Harper & Row, 1965), 86.

2

"Jihād Fī Sabīl Allah"*: A Muslim Woman's Faith Journey from Struggle to Struggle to Struggle

RIFFAT HASSAN

"We want you to be the ideologue of our movement." The earnest faces looking at me out of a world unutterably grim and dark . . . the earnest voices speaking to me in the deathly stillness of an hour of despair when one is afraid to hear even the throbbing of one's own heart. . . . I saw and heard the angry, tearful, fearful, defiant, despairing, determined, struggling, suffering women from one of the most active women's groups in my native Pakistan, and was spellbound . . . overwhelmed . . . transformed. In that moment of truth I knew with absolute clarity that I had arrived at a point of destiny . . . it seemed natural—inevitable— that the strange paths I had trodden in my life should have led me here, though I had never dreamed that I would be called upon so suddenly—so unexpectedly— to become the theoretician for a movement involved in a life-and-death struggle in a country that was mine by birth and unbreakable bonds of love, from which I had chosen to exile myself in order to be able to do my life's work. For years I had lived a hard and solitary life in an alien world, striving to become free and whole—returning periodically to my "homeland" only to find how alienated I was from "my people" in so many ways. Even as I saw and heard the women who wanted me to dedicate myself to their struggle for self-identification, for self-preservation, I knew how many worlds separated us. The mere fact that I lived alone with my young daughter, in a foreign land, earning my livelihood by the sweat of my brow, using every free moment of my work-filled life to pore endlessly over words, sacred and secular, to find a way to liberate millions of Muslim women from the unspeakable bondage imposed on them in the name of God, created a wide gulf between me and these women who addressed me.

---

*Jihād fī Sabīl Allah: striving or exerting in and for the cause of God; this is a Qur'anic imperative for all Muslims.

Would any of these women be willing to give up their lives of affluence and ease to share a day of my toil-filled life? I would have been surprised to find even one who would—and this thought saddened me. However, it did not affect my deep response to the call I had received. Whatever the distances, the differences that existed between these women and me, I knew in the hour of trial that they were my sisters and that our bond was indissoluble. I was grateful that the work I had done over so many years out of my own passionate quest for truth and justice had become profoundly relevant to the lives of my sisters. I had not hoped to see this day in my lifetime. With a heart full of tears—of joy, of sorrow—I said a silent prayer to my Creator and Sustainer who had brought me to this historic moment. I offered thanks for the opportunity to participate in such a moment and asked for strength and courage so that I might not fail in the critical task entrusted to me.

As I stood on the threshold of a new beginning, a new life, scenes from my past flashed before my eyes. I paused—to cast a look backward at the passages through which my life-journey had led me to bring me to this point of destiny. I knew that tomorrow would usher in a new phase of toil and tribulation and that then there would be no time to look back. But today I could be alone with my memories—of places and peoples and moments that had made my life-journey significant. I did not like to recall many of these memories for they are painful, but I knew that in order for me to have a clear sense of where I was and where I was to go in terms of my inner journey, I had to remember where I had been. I do not believe that it is possible to go forward without going backward, since our future is born out of our past. I closed my eyes and went back to the old house where I was born, which stood at the end of a *galee* (narrow street) adjoining Temple Road in the ancient city of Lahore in what is now Pakistan. In this house my story had begun.

My memories of the house in which I was born, where I spent the first seventeen years of my life, are heavily shaded with darkness. Even now I cannot read a passage about the joy, the beauty, the golden sunshine of childhood years without a storm of tears arising in my heart. I wish I had had a different childhood . . . my own was a nightmare that has never ceased to haunt me. What I remember most distinctly about being a child was how utterly lonely I felt in a house full of people and how unspeakably unhappy, scared, and bewildered I was most of the time.

Objectively, there were many reasons why I should have considered myself and my five brothers and three sisters as very privileged children. We were born into an upper-class Saiyyad family, and the Saiyyads, being the descendants of the Holy Prophet Muhammad, are regarded as the highest caste of Muslims, even though Muslims constantly protest against the idea that Islam has any caste system! My father and mother came from among the oldest and most distinguished families in the city and were both ''good'' parents in that they took care to provide us with a high quality of life. We lived in a spacious *kothee* (bungalow) and had a glamorous automobile (when only a handful of people had any) and a household full of servants who performed all the domestic duties. We went to the best English-medium schools (which to this day are regarded as status symbols), where we received a sound British education. Children in our neighborhood envied us: we were the children of "Shaah Saahib," as everyone called my father, who was the patriarch of the area and greatly respected and liked by all; all considered it an honor to come to our house to play, even though they knew about my mother's temper-tantrums and the possibility that they might be told unceremoniously to go home at any moment.

Why, when we were so blessed, was my life so full of shadows? The major reason was undoubtedly the deep conflict between my parents. Not only did they have diametrically opposing views on most matters but also radical incompatibility of temperament and character. My father was very traditional in his ways and values. Through most of my life I hated his traditionalism, because I understood it almost exclusively in terms of his belief in sex roles and his conviction that it was best for girls to be married at age sixteen to someone who had been picked out for them by the parents. It took me a long time to see that in some ways my father's traditionalism had been pure gold. He truly believed in taking care of disadvantaged people, relatives and strangers alike, and responding to every call he received for assistance. He was genuinely kind and compassionate and took joy in solving other people's problems, whether they were personal, professional, or social. Anybody could call on him at any hour, and he would receive the caller with courtesy and goodwill. My mother's ways and values differed fundamentally from my father's, even though, in her own way, she responded positively to many who sought the assistance of the "Begum Saahiba," as she was called. Her nonconformism to traditional Muslim culture consisted largely of her rejection of the hallowed cult of women's inferiority and submissiveness to men. She herself was not submissive to her husband. She treated her daughters better than her sons (with the exception of one favorite son) and believed that it was more important to educate daughters than sons because girls were born into Muslim societies with a tremendous handicap. Pre-Islamic Arabs had buried their daughters alive because they had regarded daughters not only as economic liabilities but also as potential hazards to the honor of the men in the tribe. Islam notwithstanding, the attitude of Muslims toward daughters has remained very similar to that of their nomadic forebears. My mother's repudiation of the ideals and practices of patriarchal culture and her passionate commitment to the liberation of her daughters from the *chardewari* (four walls) of the male-centered, male-dominated household put her into the category of radical feminists, which made her strangely out of place in my father's house and in the society in which we lived.

Long before I began to understand the complexities and ambiguities of the Muslim value-system, I knew that my mother would not win in any popularity contest vis-à-vis my father. She had a protected place in society because she was the daughter of the outstanding and creative artist-poet, playwright, and scholar, Hakim Ahmad Shuja'—who had also been a highly regarded educator and bureaucrat—and my father's wife, but in her own person she was viewed as a dangerous deviant. The fact that she had a biting and brutal tongue, and that she could, at times, be ruthless and unscrupulous, did not help to improve her image in many eyes. However, to me, all through my childhood, my mother was a savior-figure who protected me from being sacrificed upon the altar of blind conventionalism. And my father, who was admired and loved by so many, seemed to me through most of my early life to be a figure of dread, representing customary morality in a society that demanded that female children be discriminated against from the moment of birth.

As a child I used to be greatly troubled by the fact that my subjective perceptions of my parents differed greatly from the way in which others perceived them. I remember feeling very guilty because I could not relate to my "good" father to whom almost everyone could relate so well. I also remember feeling very angry and perplexed as to why my father, who liked everyone, seemed so averse to me. I knew that what I perceived to be his negative attitude toward me had something to do with my being one of my mother's "favorites" and belonging to her "camp." Their respective camps were the centers from where my parents conducted their cold war campaigns that enveloped us all and poisoned our family life. My parents did not yell and scream at each other. My father was too much of a gentleman to do that, and even my mother, whom many regarded as a "shrew," was conventional enough not to engage in a vociferous exchange with my father. But though physical and verbal violence did not characterize the relationship between my parents, there was no disguising the fact that they had deep-seated resentments against one another that manifested themselves in all kinds of destructive ways. I remember how the way my parents interacted with one another reminded me of Milton's words: "For never can true reconcilement grow / where wounds of deadly hate have pierced so deep," and I often wondered as a child why they continued to live together. Now I understand the reasons that made it imperative for them to live under one roof— they both came from "old" families to whom divorce was anathema, and they had nine children to raise. But the one roof under which we all lived could not be called a "home," if one defines this term as a place of love, warmth, and security. Our home was a rough sea where tempests raged incessantly. I could only deal with the unremitting hostility that pervaded the atmosphere by becoming a recluse. Before I was twelve years old I had retired from the world.

I believe that it was because I withdrew from an outer to an inner reality that I was able to survive the seemingly unending crises and calamities to which I was exposed. A hypersensitive, painfully shy, and profoundly lonely child, I hated the ugliness that surrounded me and retreated to a world made up of a child's prayers, dreams, and wishful thinking. In this world I found three things that have sustained me through the heartbreaks and hardships of my life: an unwavering belief in a just and loving God, the art of writing poetry, and a deep love for books. Unable to relate at a deep personal level to either of my two parents—such dialogue, I see now, is virtually impossible in Muslim culture, in which human beings relate to each other mainly in terms of their "functions" or roles and not in terms of who they are as persons—I learned to talk to my Creator and Preserver, who at all times seemed very close. I often asked God to reveal to me the purpose of my life and to help me fulfill this purpose. Perhaps that was a strange prayer for a child. However, I was not just any child—I was a war-ravaged child. Born female in a society in which it is customary to celebrate the birth of a son and to bemoan the birth of a daughter, and growing up in a house lacking in love and trust, I could at no time simply take it for granted that I had the right to exist, to be. I had, at all times, to find a justification for living. A very ailing child, I came quite close to dying a few times and almost wished that I were dead, but somewhere, deep within my heart and soul, I always had the assurance that God had a special purpose for my life that justified my existence, and that so long as I remained faithful to God I would be protected from the dangers and devastation that threatened me.

Alone in my inner world I discovered that, like my mother and grandfather, I could write poetry almost effortlessly. This gave me great happiness and hope. I felt as if this was a gift from God given to me so that I could create a world free of shadows, of hate, bitterness, and pain. Looking at the first poem in "My Maiden," a book of eighty-five sonnets written when I was about thirteen years old, I can recall the earnest child who wrote:

> This humble work of mine do bless my God,
> My fervent message to the world proclaim,
> I do not covet wealth or power or fame,
> I just want satisfaction for reward.
> I felt it was Your Will that I should write
> Of Beauty, Love and Joy, Eternal Peace,
> Of Sorrow, Struggle that a Death does cease,
> Of Hope, its sweet illuminating light.
>
> I've done my duty with all faithfulness,
> I strove to do Your Will, without a rest,
> I pray I have succeeded in this test,
> If I have, I can scarce my joy express.
> I am sincere that You, dear God, can see,
> I'll do Your Will, however hard may be.

How many worlds have passed away since I wrote that poem, but what I said in that poem still remains true for me. I believed then, as I believe now, that God had chosen me to be an instrument in implementing a plan that I could see only in part and understand only dimly. Since I first experienced the presence of God—powerful, healing, comforting, directing—in the solitude of my inner world, I have regarded my life as a trust that must be spent in *jihād fī sabīl Allah* (striving in the cause of Allah). As a child, there were times when I wanted to share my strong sense of being a missionary for God with my close friends.

But I was afraid that they would not understand my calling and would ridicule me. I remember that once, not without trepidation, I mentioned to a friend whom I considered to be wiser than the rest that I believed God spoke to me in special moments and showed me the path I was to follow. I hoped that he would understand what I was trying to say, but he was shocked by what seemed to him to be pretentious words. I remember how his words "So you consider yourself a prophetess or something!" went through my heart like a dagger and left me speechless. After that I would not speak about what lay closest to my soul, though I would write when the burden of silence became too heavy to bear. It was in one such hour that I wrote another sonnet—perhaps my favorite in the collection—which reads:

> Oft times when loneliness I cannot bear,
> When all my consolation, hope has fled,
> In words when there is nothing to be said,
> My feelings, then, with you—my pen—I share.
> When I unburden all my heart to you,
> Tell you the secrets of my restless mind,
> When for my thoughts expression I do find
> In verse, contentment—sweet and deep and true—
> Steals on me, offers solace to my soul.
> And though there still is grief, there still is strife,
> I'm comforted; my poems do console
> Me; and I know as long as I can write
> I'll have the will life's battle great to fight,
> For 'tis the truth—that writing is my life.

Writing was my chief mode of communication during my childhood, and I wrote much. By the time I was seventeen years old, two volumes of my poems, short stories, and articles had been published, and I was a well-known "budding" poet-author in the world in which I lived. My famous grandfather spoke of me with pride and said that I alone among all his grandchildren had inherited his writing talent. I felt grateful for his recognition and encouragement, but undoubtedly the person who meant the most to me during my early teens when I launched my writing career was my cousin "Sunny Bhaijan" (as I called him), who was married to my eldest sister. Sunny Bhaijan was a remarkably talented person who could have become a first-rate poet, artist, or musician if he had had the passion to create. But he lacked passion and thus was not motivated to develop his talents. He recognized both my ability to write and my passion and became my first mentor. Sadly, many things happened that caused me to grow away from Sunny Bhaijan while I was not yet out of my teens, but I still feel indebted to him for encouraging me to write.

Besides writing, my greatest joy in life in childhood was reading. One day, looking through a dusty bookcase in my house, I found a torn and tattered copy of Palgrave's "Golden Treasury" of poems. Finding that book was one of the most important things that ever happened to me, for it introduced me to many poems I grew to love deeply, including some sonnets of Shakespeare. I loved to recite poems to myself, over and over, till I knew them by heart. There was something about the measured music of poetry that captivated my heart and spirit. Though poetry was my first love, I also liked to read novels and read many "classics" by Dickens, Hardy, the Brontë sisters, Jane Austen, and many others. Of all the novels that I read in my childhood, the one that made the greatest impact on me was Emily Brontë's *Wuthering Heights*. This book had a haunting quality, and it seemed suspended between the world of reality and the world of dream, nightmare, and fantasy. The bleakness and wildness of its landscape seemed to correspond to my own psyche, and I identified with its strange characters, especially Cathy and Heathcliff. Apart from my reading of English "classics," I was also an avid reader of Agatha Christie's books, from which I learned much about human nature.

Most of my childhood I spent alone, writing and reading. I do not remember studying much for school. Despite that, I was the star pupil in my class from the beginning to the end of my scholastic career and won every honor and award there was to win. Many people, including my classmates and their parents, were very impressed with my academic success and treated me as if I were rather special. But as a child, and even as an adult, I did not crave success—perhaps because one does not crave what one does or can have. What I craved was love and peace around me and within me. I was a super-achiever almost against my will. Toward the end of my high school career I became resentful of my own success and wanted to fail. My family never seemed to notice my success, or at least never mentioned it to me—I thought that perhaps if I failed they would pay some attention to me. Had it not been for a teacher who cared for me, I might have acted out my bitter, rebellious feelings, but I did not, and in future years was very grateful that I had not wrecked a record career. I learned very early in life that there is no necessary connection between success and happiness, but I have also come to know that, though many bright women are afraid to succeed, lack of success is not likely to lead to an enhancement of happiness, and I could not have found what I craved through underachieving.

The twelfth year of my life was a landmark year for me because during that year my struggle as an "activist feminist" began. Up until that time I had been a quiet child living for the most part in an inner sanctuary. But before I had turned twelve, all of a sudden the reality of the external world began to close in on me ominously, threatening to destroy my place of refuge. My second sister, who was sixteen, was married off to a man with a lot of money and very little education. She had tried to resist the arranged marriage but had succumbed, as most girls do, to the multifarious crude as well as subtle ways of "persuading" wavering girls to accept the arrangement in order to safeguard the family's "honor" and her own "happiness." Seeing her fall into the all-too-familiar trap I experienced total panic. I was the next in line. Four years later the same ritual would be reenacted, and this time I would be the sacrificial victim unless I found

a way of averting the catastrophe. I knew that my mother would try to protect
me from an arranged marriage, but I was not sure that she would succeed. I felt
that I had to learn to fend for myself, to take a stand against my father and his
rigid conventionalism. I had to learn to fight to survive in a society in which
women's refusal to submit to patriarchal authority is tantamount to heresy. At
twelve I had not learned how to fight. I had not wanted to learn to fight. I simply
wanted to be left alone in my dream-world where I could write my poems and
read my books . . . but I knew then, as I know now, that if one is born female
in such a society as the one I was born in and wants to be regarded as a person
and not as an object, one has no option but to fight. And so I learned to fight,
and the fight continues to this day, though many battles have been won and lost.
Battle-weary, I pray for the dawning of the day when it will not be required of
women like myself to spend their entire lifetime fighting for their freedom each
day of their life, but I also pray for strength to continue the fight until there is
justice and freedom, under God, for all my sisters.

My father, who had not seemed to like me much when I was a little girl hiding
in my room, liked me even less when I appeared to become an impossible
teenage rebel who disregarded his wishes. For instance, when I was twelve he
wanted me to withdraw from the coeducation school where I studied and enroll
in an all-girls' school. Thinking with the mind of a twelve-year-old, I believed
that if I said "yes" to him once, I would always have to say "yes" to him.
Therefore, I refused to comply with his desire and said that if I was forced to
leave the school where I had studied for a number of years (and where my
brothers still studied), I would not go to any other school. My father did not
force me to leave, but he upbraided my mother constantly for spoiling and
misguiding me. From the time that I was twelve until I went abroad to England
at age seventeen, my father never stopped being upset with me over the fact
that I studied with boys and played competitive table-tennis (of which I became
a provincial champion) with them. But he never reprimanded me directly—
perhaps because during most of that time, he and I were not even on speaking
terms with one another. I learned through those tense, silence-filled years how
dreadful cold war is, and how through the coldness of its silence it may inflict
deeper injury than the angriest of words. Looking back, I am stricken with
sorrow that the world in which we lived made it impossible for my father and
me to talk to one another through most of my life. Perhaps if we could have
communicated directly we could have resolved some of our differences, or even
learned to build a personal relationship with one another; but in Muslim societies
fathers and daughters seldom talk to one another as peers or persons until the
daughters have left the fathers' household and become part of another household.
I who have been looking for a father all my life never knew my own until the
last year of his life, when he had become a weak and ailing human being who
cried to see his children come and cried to see them go. Not until then did I
know for sure that he cared about me and wanted to see me happy, regardless
of how he had disapproved of me through my growing years. We had so little

time to get to know each other, but I am grateful that I was reconciled to him before he died. Such reconciliation does not, and cannot, of course, make up for a lifetime of deprivation, but at least it makes it possible for me to weep for my father and for what we missed.

While being alienated from my father left a deep imprint on my life, my intense and strange relationship with my mother left an even deeper one. For much of my life my mother was the most important person in my life. Feeling as I did that I lived in an arena of gladiators, I regarded my mother as my sole protector after God, and depended upon her for my emotional survival. Certainly my mother gave me much. She provided me not only with the best kind of education but also with the opportunity to become a "person." Considering marriage to be a necessary evil rather than an ideal state, my mother did not raise her daughters to conform to the very rigid, well-defined norms prescribed for female behavior and accomplishments in Muslim culture. She wanted her daughters to have what she herself had never had—a chance to be properly educated, to see the world, to experience freedom, to become self-sufficient, successful, and powerful.

Perhaps my particular tragedy lay in the fact that my mother regarded me as her Derby-winning horse who would actualize all her dreams of glory. My mother perceived me as the most gifted and single-minded of her children and believed that I had what it took to do what she had wanted to do in her life. She told me over and over, from a time when I was very young, that I was to become famous like Florence Nightingale and Joan of Arc. She did not want me ever to think of marriage, since marriage was bondage and a grave impediment to growth and advancement. For me the sky was the limit, provided I was strong and unwavering in the pursuit of my goals and sought always to be a winner.

Much of what I am today is due to my mother's meticulous schooling, but I could never become the ruthless superwoman she wanted me to be. Even as a child I could not accept the way she discriminated against many people, including some of her own children. My earliest battle with her was over my three younger brothers, whom she frequently treated unjustly and unkindly. I protested in their behalf, and in behalf of the other "disadvantaged" persons, like domestic servants, whom my mother mistreated. Strangely enough she did not mind my protesting—in fact, she was rather amused by it and called me "leader of the opposition." Perhaps she did not mind my taking a stand against her because she liked to see me fight, even though it was against her. But my efforts to make her review her own conduct never worked. She lived, and still lives, in a world dominated by the idea of will-to-power.

While my mother wanted me to succeed, she never patted me on the back for doing well. I know that she was proud of my achievements because she told others about them, but I did not hear her tell me that she loved me. In my society there were many stories of how a mother's love was superior to all other kinds of love because it was "unconditional." I wanted so much to believe that, but I could not, since I heard my mother say repeatedly to me: "I do not love you,

I love your qualities." Her words, which were meant to affirm my "qualities," made me feel very lonely and sad. I could not receive my mother's love simply because I was her child. I could receive her approval only if I proved myself worthy. I recall that as a child my mother's attitude toward me often made me very melancholy, but that as an adolescent it made me very angry. Part of this anger, which stayed with me for a long time, was directed at myself because I could not break loose of my mother's control over me. Regardless of how strongly I wished to resist her emotional manipulation, when confronted by her immensely powerful personality I felt myself relapsing into a state of juvenile behavior when I reacted to her instead of acting as an autonomous person. It took some devastating experiences to finally sever the chains that bound the little girl in me to my mother's power and make me free of the burden of living out her fantasies instead of living my own life. Free of the bondage, I have sought to reestablish the bond. I still find it very difficult to "dialogue" with my mother, and my feelings toward her remain ambivalent, but I feel a strong sense of duty toward her. My mother not only gave me life but also the strength required to live the kind of life I wanted to live, and for that I owe her more than I can give. With her egocentricity and eccentricity, my mother's indomitable spirit, reflected in her steadfastness of purpose, courage, and refusal to give up in the face of insuperable odds, makes her the most extraordinary woman I have ever known, and despite all the heartache and agony she has caused me, I am proud of the fact that I am my mother's daughter.

Returning to my parents' conflict over me, I remember how tense things became as I approached my sixteenth year. For me my sixteenth birthday had nothing to do with "sweet sixteen," it was D-Day. My father wanted to see me married by then, but he had not found a way to arrange this marriage. He and I were not on speaking terms, and my mother would not hear of my marriage. My father was displeased and troubled about the situation. Another year passed, and the conflict seemed to intensify. My increasing independence of thought and action seemed to threaten my father's notion of family "honor." At the same time he recognized that I had brought much "honor" to my family by my academic successes, especially by standing first among the 24,000 students in the whole province in the intermediate examination.

Terrified lest I fall somehow into the death trap of an arranged marriage, I wanted desperately to escape from the danger that stalked me. My eldest sister had gone to England on a scholarship, and I asked her to secure admission for me in her college. She did so. I expected my father to oppose the idea of my studying abroad, but he permitted me to go. Perhaps by this time he had begun to feel that I deserved to have the opportunity to study abroad. Perhaps he also hoped that once I left home I would be out of my mother's sphere of influence and he would have greater access to me. He never told me his reasons for letting me go, but he spoke to me after a number of years on the day on which my brother and I set out for England with my mother. I wept as he embraced me and felt the pain of saying good-bye to him. In that moment of farewell he was simply my father and not "the adversary."

My seven years at St. Mary's college, University of Durham, in England, were full of homesickness and hard studying. After three years I graduated with joint honors in English literature and philosophy, and then, at age 24, I became a Doctor of Philosophy specializing in the philosophy of Allama Muhammad Iqbal, the national poet-philosopher of Pakistan, whose work I had loved and admired since childhood. During my years in England, I did, in fact, grow closer to my father and more distant from my mother (who never liked the idea of my being on good terms with my father), but when I returned home after finishing my studies abroad, I found that I was alienated from them both in fundamental ways. I could conform neither to my father's norms nor to my mother's values. Since I was no longer a child, I did not experience a child's fears, but I felt unutterably, unbearably alone. Coming home after seven long years of exile, I was again an outcast, an outsider.

It was in that state that I decided to marry a man who seemed to need me intensely. Always having had a great need not only to receive love but also to give it, for me the heaviest part of the price I paid for being a rebel against patriarchal society was that I did not feel free to express the love I felt for my own family members. A rebel's gifts are not accepted, and no one seemed to need my love. But Dawar needed it, and for years I gave it to him—unconditionally, unreservedly. My family was not thrilled with the idea of my marrying an "unmade" man, but they did not oppose it. Perhaps they had learned from experience that opposition did not deter me; perhaps they were glad that finally I had agreed to be married at all. Anyhow, as I began my married life I was aware of the social problems my husband and I would encounter on account of the fact that I was more educated than he and had better wage-earning prospects. These were serious matters in a society in which the man must always be seen to be in control and ahead of the woman, but in my joy at having found what I had always craved I did not pay much thought to them. For me, love was God's greatest gift, a miracle in a world of hate, and I believed that it could accomplish anything and overcome any difficulty. In Dawar's eyes I saw what I had never had—the promise of sustaining love—and overwhelmed, I wrote:

> Beautiful, beautiful eyes
> beautiful as the myriad-tinted sun
> lighting upon the golden leaves of autumn
> which fall like rain upon the dark, deep waters
> of Wear, which guards the cobbled streets and spirits
> of an ancient, distant town.
>
> A stone-and-concrete wall.
> A wall of murky hate
> a hate born out of fear

a fear born out of knowledge
that the spirit too
will rot beneath the burden
of the tainted flesh.
All around a wall
to hide the helpless anger
of sin-infected cowardice
and knowing, growing shame.
All around a wall
which in the end must win
crowding out the light
crowding out the life
in an eternal gloom.

The soul is sick with sorrow
for the wall is everywhere.
But looking through the mist
of doubt and hurt and sadness
soft with tender caring
knowing and understanding
holding out a strength
that keeps the heart from breaking
are the beautiful eyes,
the beautiful, beautiful eyes.

My dream of love on which I thought our marriage was based was beautiful, no doubt, but it turned out to be a dream. Dawar was a typical product—victim— of the patriarchal society and had a compelling need to be the "head" of the family. He found it impossible to fulfill this need being married to a woman who was a superachiever, while he regarded himself as a loser. He was attracted by my strength but resented it at the same time. He wanted to utilize my talents but also to deny them. I tried to be a "good" wife, exemplifying the rebel's hidden desire to conform to tradition. For what seemed like a long time I was the model wife, selflessly devoted to her husband, living only for him and through him, but all my efforts to build up his confidence in himself only made him more conscious of what he lacked. A highly introverted person, he became even more withdrawn from life. I thought that perhaps if we left our complex-ridden, male-chauvinistic society and moved to a place where men were not under so much pressure to prove their superiority to women, our marriage would have a better chance of succeeding. We did, indeed, leave Pakistan and came to the United States, but the pattern of our relationship had already been set and it did not change. When I had married Dawar I had not known him well, but more importantly, I had not known myself well. Like many women through the ages I had thought that it was enough to give love without asking for anything in return, but I found out, after five years of constant giving, that I had nothing left to give. I was a hollow woman living in a wasteland. Never had my life seemed more empty, barren, or full of unspoken anguish. The times prior to my second exodus from my homeland (the first one having been for studying) and those which followed it were, in many ways, the darkest ones of my life. Much happened then that scarred me forever.

For me the decision to migrate from the land of my birth to a land I had never seen was one of the most difficult and heartbreaking decisions I have ever had to make. Through all the years that I had lived in England I had literally counted the days until my return to my beloved country. To serve "my people" had been a dream I had cherished since childhood. It is hard to describe the full measure of the disillusionment I suffered when I returned to my homeland and discovered that "my people" were enslaved by a corrupt government and that I could not live and work in my own country unless I was willing to renounce the ideals I most cherished. Torn as I was between love of my people and my commitment to God to work for truth and justice, I might have lingered in indecision had I not witnessed the dismemberment of Pakistan from very close quarters. As deputy director in the "brain-cell" of the federal information ministry, I had reason to believe that the tragedy that occurred could have been averted if the people in power had loved the country enough to let go of their own power fantasies. Traumatized by what I saw, I knew that the time for *hijrah*[1] had come, for my homeland had become the territory of the godless. Facing this truth with an exceedingly heavy heart, I wrote:

> Who knows what lies ahead?
> Upon the vast, impenetrable brink
> of that which we call Future, lost and scared
> I stand tormented.
> Pain, the gnawing pain
> beneath whose weight the spirit wilts away
> of making the irrevocable choice.
> "To be or not to be," unhappy question
> that ever—till the end—must vex our kind.
> Can one forfeit one's dreams just to be safe—
> safe from the agony of mystic quest?
> Or must one, like one banished, leave behind
> so much that is one's own, to start anew
> somewhere where one can learn to dream again?
> A cruel choice—but one which must be made
> before the desperate strength of fading courage
> dies 'mid the tyranny of conventional ways—
> A cruel choice—but one which has been made—
> God take care of the rest.

God did, indeed, take care of providing for us as we set out to build a new life in the United States, but soon after our arrival I received news from home that shook the roots of my being. My younger brother Vicky, the closest to me of all my family and the only one who was always on my side, was dying of cancer. Wild with grief I went back to Lahore to be with him even though I was pregnant and very unwell. My memories of the following months are still so shrouded with pain that I cannot dwell upon them. Seeing my beloved brother waste away in the prime of a glorious youth was the hardest thing I had ever had to bear. In the midst of this overpowering sorrow another devastating blow fell upon us: my eldest brother, the guardian of my father's home and the most caring of all my family, died of a heart attack at the age of thirty-seven. I was not with my brothers when they died and could not participate in their funeral rites, but with them a part of me also died. What remained alive was emotionally paralyzed for a long time when my only reason for living was my little daughter, who was born as all the skies were falling on my head. For me, my little Mona, as I call her, has always been a miracle of God's grace, a gift given to me to keep me alive. When I named her Mehrunnisa[2] I did not know that she would live up to her name, but she is, indeed, a child with a heart so full of love and sunshine that she makes me forget the sorrows of my life. Like all mothers I want my child to have a safe and happy passage through life, but I also tell her that she must understand what it means to be Mujāhida,[3] which is her second name. I tell her that *jihād fī sabīl Allah* is the essence of being a Muslim and that I want her to commit her life to striving for truth and justice. I tell her that though she has herself known no discrimination, she must not become immune to the suffering of millions of Muslim girls who are discriminated against from the moment of birth. I tell her that my prayer for her is that she should be strong enough to be a *mujahida* in the long struggle that lies ahead of us and to continue the efforts of her mother and grandmother.

In the last decade and a half of my life there have been other events and mishaps that have affected me significantly. Perhaps the most memorable of the mishaps was my extremely short-lived marriage to Mahmoud, an Egyptian Arab Muslim more than thirty years my senior in age, who persuaded me to marry him after I had known him only a few days, saying that he would take care of me and my child, and help me develop my talents in order to serve God better. Emotionally wrecked by the death of my brothers and the end of a marriage in which I had invested so much care, and frightened of living alone with a young child in an alien world, I was mesmerized by Mahmoud's powerful personality and believed him when he said that as a member of the Muslim Brotherhood movement in Egypt, he had suffered imprisonment and torture for the sake of God. Mahmoud called himself a man of God, but I learned very quickly that being a man of God had nothing to do with being kind and compassionate and loving. It meant only that Mahmoud could command me to do whatever he wished in the name of God and with the authority of God, and I had no right to refuse, since in Islamic culture refusal to do what is pleasing to the husband is tantamount to refusing to do what is pleasing to God. Short as the marriage was, I came near to total destruction, physically and mentally, at the hands of a man who was not only a male chauvinist par excellence but also a fanatic who could invoke the holy name of God in perpetrating acts of incredible cruelty and callousness upon other human beings. Had I not had a lifetime of struggle for survival behind me and a total faith that God was just and merciful, I could not have survived the three months I spent with Mahmoud or the three years I spent fighting the lawsuits in which he involved me in order to punish me for taking a stand against him. He ruined me financially and did serious damage to me in many ways. However, as good and evil are inextricably linked together in human life, I am grateful even for this soul-searing experience, for it was this experience more than any other that made me a feminist with a resolve to develop feminist theology in the framework of Islamic tradition so that other so-called men of God could not exploit other Muslim women in the name of God.

While my personal life has been filled with momentous crises and upheavals throughout the years I have lived in this country, by the grace of God I have done well professionally. I am now a professor and chairperson of the Religious Studies Program at the University of Louisville. My specialization is in the area of Islamic Studies, and it was due to this expertise that I became involved in various ways, and at various levels, in the discussions going on around the country regarding Islam, after the Arab oil embargo of 1973 and the Iranian revolution of 1979 convinced the Western world that Islam was a living reality in the world. While I found many of these discussions, in which I was called upon to explain "Islamic revival" to Americans, interesting and stimulating, it was in another setting—that of interreligious dialogue among believers in the one God—that I found the community of faith I had sought all my life. In this community of faith I have found others who, like myself, are committed to creating a new world in which human beings will not brutalize or victimize one another in the name of God, but will affirm, through word and action, that as God is just and loving so human beings must treat each other with justice and love regardless of sex, creed, or color. I have found in my community of faith what I did not find in my community of birth: the possibility of growing and healing, of becoming integrated and whole. Due to the affirmation I have received from men and women of faith I am no longer the fragmented, mutilated woman that I once was. I know now that I am not alone in the wilderness, that there are some people in the world who understand my calling, and that their prayers are with me as I continue my struggle on behalf of the millions of nameless, voiceless, faceless Muslim women of the world who live and die unsung, un-celebrated in birth, unmourned in death.

God willing, my book *Equal before Allah?*, the first feminist theological study of the issue of woman-man equality in the context of creation, discussed in the light of the Qur'an[4] and the most authoritative Hadith,[5] will soon be published. This book will present compelling arguments for affirming that God created man and woman equal, hence the inequality that exists between men and women in all Muslim societies is not God-made, but men-made, and essentially unjust. It is my hope that this book will give the activist feminists struggling against religious oppression and authoritarianism in Muslim societies something to fight with. It is my prayer that it will motivate some other Muslim women to join hands with me in preparing for the next round of the battle, which is bound to begin as soon as we have won the first.

And in the end, I send to all my sisters, all the women in the world, a gift of song, a poem born out of death-like experience that epitomizes the journey I have described in the foregoing narrative:

> I am a woman
> with the eternal heart
> of a woman
> who, like Othello,
> loved not wisely
> but too well.
>
> I am a woman
> with the eternal heart
> of a woman
> living in a world
> in which the rules
> are made by men—
> and where men can
> break all the rules
> and yet be gods
> saviors and saints
> martyrs and heroes
> but where if women
> break the rules
> made by men
> broken by men
> they cannot live
> without being shamed
> slandered and abused
> beaten and hurt
> scourged and stoned
> burned and buried
> alive and damned.
>
> I am a woman
> with the eternal heart
> of a woman
> born to love
> living in a world
> in which when men
> love—they are called
> princes and knights
> poets and mystics
> or at the worst
> —perhaps—lunatics;

but when women love
then love becomes
a mortal sin
for which they must
give up their life—
for when a woman
is guilty of
a mortal sin
—the sin of loving—
then she must die
so that the jealous
god of love
may be at peace.

I am a woman
with the eternal heart
of a woman
living in a world
in which there are
a number of men
and also some women
who cannot love;
and since love is
what makes us human
and gives us life
these men and women
are callous and cold,
cruel and cowardly
though they wear
the masks of sages
and madonnas
and cherubs;
and they are always
ready to strike
my eternal heart
because I dare
to live and love.

I am a woman
with the eternal heart
of a woman
who has endured
so many births
and so many deaths
so that the seed
of life and love
may not be
destroyed by those
who in the name

of god of love
who does not love
want to create
a loveless world
a lifeless world
full of tombs
where one cannot hear
the sound of life—
the laughter of
a little child
warm from the womb
who wants to live
and wants to love
and to whom
an eternal-hearted woman
is what god should be.

I am a woman
with the eternal heart
of a woman
the bearer of life
the nurturer of life
the protector of life
I can give life
because I am not
afraid of pain
for I know that love
is always pain
even joyful love
is ringed with pain
and no one can love
who cannot embrace
with heart and soul
the pain of living
the pain of loving.

I am a woman
with the eternal heart
of a woman
and I can suffer
again and again
the pain of loving
men and women
who do not love
who will tear
my heart and soul
to little shreds
and who will put
my life-carrying body

upon death's bed
in order to
placate a god
who says he is
the god of love
but who abhors
both life and love
and who demands
a sacrifice
—my sacrifice—
and says that I
must slaughtered be
just like an animal
helpless and trapped
whose blood is spilled
so that the sins
of those who kill
may be forgiven.

I am a woman
with the eternal heart
of a woman
and though I may be
tormented and abandoned
dishonored and disowned
scourged and flogged
stoned and burned
and buried alive
I will never
be a martyr
I will never
be a victim
I will never
be a loser
I will always
be a survivor
I will always
be a winner
I will always
be triumphant
for though I go
I will return
and though I die
I will live again
forever and forever
for I am a woman
with the eternal heart
of a woman

and since my heart
is made of love
and love is eternal
embodied in creation
leading to resurrection
though all else will burn
with the funeral pyre
in the flames of the fire
my eternal heart
will never to ashes turn
and like a phoenix I will rise again
and like a phoenix I will be reborn.

NOTES

1. *Hijrah*: emigration; in the Islamic tradition this term has particular reference to the emigration in 632 A.D. of the Prophet Muhammad from his hometown Mecca, which was controlled by polytheist Arabs, to Medina, where he established the first Muslim community.

2. *Mehrunnisa*: symbol of *Mehr* (meaning "sun" and "love") among women.

3. *Mujāhida*: a girl or woman who engages in *jihād* (striving).

4. *Qur'an*: the primary source of Islam, believed by Muslims to be the word of God conveyed by the angel Gabriel to the Prophet Muhammad, who transmitted it to the first Muslims without change or error.

5. *Hadith*: oral traditions attributed to the Prophet Muhammad.

Part II

Witnesses for a Spiritual Feminism

3

Woman Jews

TIKVAH FRYMER-KENSKY

Judaism is a religion, a thought-system, a tradition, a history, a community, and a way of life, all intertwined. The very richness of the tapestry makes it difficult to define or pin down the Jewish belief and practice system. There are many voices, many periods of history, many disputes and agreements to disagree. The story of women in Judaism is similarly complicated, constantly in flux, and even more so today.

We should probably begin to consider the experience of women in Judaism with the reflection that Judaism is a religion and lifestyle with a built-in "mommy-track." Ever since the beginning of Judaism, and doubtless long before that, it has been assumed that a woman's life would be occupied with bearing and rearing children, providing for their economic and spiritual well-being. The Biblical poem "A Capable Woman" (sometimes called "A Woman of Valor," Prov. 31:11–21) shows an appreciation of women in this role and an assumption that women will fulfill it. In this poem, the woman of the house, wise and intelligent, is mistress of all the many economic tasks of women and an expert in buying and selling land. Because of her many capabilities, her husband praises her as he sits in the town gate. At this gate, the site of communal deliberations and legal judgment, the community made its decisions and adjudicated its disputes. The capable wife was not there—she was taking care of her household. It was her husband, together with the other men of the community, who engaged in these public affairs, and it was the strength and capability of the women that enabled their men to attend to such matters. This division of labor was the ideal of the scribes and scholars who wrote the Biblical Book of Proverbs at the beginning of the second Temple. Later, the founders of Rabbinic Judaism further refined a system that had different expectations for women and men.

In many religions, one might ask: what do social arrangements have to do with *religion*? But in Judaism, society is at the core of religious thinking. The fundamental idea of Judaism is that there is one power, one will, supreme in the universe, and that this will, God, is in partnership with humanity to form a more perfect universe. The divine ruler demands our allegiance, fidelity, love, and commitment to the establishment of a righteous order. The way to do this is found in the Torah, the divine instruction, a term that refers both to the Pentateuch and the whole content of divinely inspired tradition. The Rabbis elaborated this central commitment into a series of *mitzvot*, ''commandments,'' which spell out the parameters of proper behavior. There are two kinds of *mitzvot*: negative *mitzvot*, meaning proscriptions of impermissible behavior, and positive *mitzvot*, prescriptions of actions that one is required to do. These are part of the system of *halakhah*, religious law, which prescribes and regulates all the details of life and society.

In this system, all girls become obligated to the performance of *mitzvot* at the age of twelve (when a girl becomes a *bat mitzvah*, ''daughter of the commandments''), and all boys at the age of thirteen (*bar mitzvah*). But the *mitzvot* to which they become obligated have not been identical for boys and girls. Everyone is equally obligated to observe the negative *mitzvot*, that is, to refrain from improper behavior. But there is a difference in the positive prescriptions. Females are particularly admonished to obey three commandments, sometimes known as the *hanah mitzvot* by the acronym of their names. The first is *hadlaqah*, the lighting of the Sabbath candles. The second is *niddah*, the observance of the system of menstrual taboos (avoidance of male contact during the first half of the cycle), and the third is *hallah*, a formal destruction of a small portion of dough in memory of the portion reserved for priests during the existence of the Temple. There are, of course, no penalties in Jewish religious law for failure to observe commandments. But these three have a special sanction: according to the Mishnah, failure to observe them can result in death in childbirth. Postmenopausal women are not exempted from these commandments. In fact, in the absence of women, a man is also expected to light Sabbath candles and, if baking bread, to destroy the *hallah* portion. But the three *mitzvot* are particularly singled out as the woman's *mitzvot*: taken together they define and sanctify the traditional woman's domain. Active in the household, she is to guard its purity by being scrupulous about menstrual laws, preserve its communal acceptability by not making the priest offering into food for the family, and make it into sacred space by ushering in the Sabbath through the lighting of the Sabbath candles. In doing these three, she perpetuates Judaism in the home and makes it possible to transmit it to the next generation.

At the same time, women have been exempt from commandments to which men are obligated. Of the 248 positive commandments, women have traditionally been exempted from fourteen (by other counts eighteen):

• recitation of the Shema (the central prayer of Judaism)
• the study and teaching of Torah (sacred law and lore)

- wearing of Tefillin on head and arm (2)
- wearing Tzitzit (Tallit)
- writing a Torah
- recitation of the priestly blessing by male priests
- counting of the Omer (the days between Passover and Shavuout)
- hearing the Shofar
- dwelling in the Sukkah (the festive booth of the fall holiday)
- taking and blessing the Lulav (a stalk made of four types of plants)
- procreation
- circumcision
- making one's wife happy during the first year of marriage.

These are very few *mitzvot*, but collectively they can make a big difference. In this system, the central *public* acts of Judaism (study and communal prayer), the visible symbols of the worship community (Tallit and Tefillin), and the central call to accept divine sovereignty (the blowing of the Shofar) all may legitimately take place without the required participation of women. For at least two millennia, the public life of the community was a life of men. Even the commandment to procreate is addressed only to men, despite the physical impossibility of male single-sex generation. There are many reasons for this, not the least of which was the fact that a woman could not be obligated to pursue a course of action that might very well end in her death. But essentially, the reason for exempting women from the law is not important. The message that the exemption of women from this commandment gives is the same as that conveyed by the other exemptions for women: the men who comprise the community have, or rather had, the obligation to perpetuate it.

The Rabbis of the Talmud, already faced with a group of commandments from which women were exempted, suggested as explanation that women were exempt from those commandments that are "time-bound" (i.e., that have to be done at a set time). Thus, the blessing after meals (which can be done any time after eating) is required of women, while the recitation of the Shema, which has to be done at set points of the day, is not. Of course, this rule about time-bound commandments does not really fit the pattern of exemptions: fringes on one's garment are not time-bound, yet women are exempt from wearing them; and nothing is more time-bound than lighting the Sabbath candles, which cannot be done after the Sabbath has begun. But this idea of "time-bound" commandments shows the understanding and assumptions of the Rabbis. Household work, particularly with children, was considered to be a woman's proper highest priority, and she was exempted, say the Rabbis, from anything that might interfere with this.

There were consequences to this exemption of women. Not being required to attend public prayer, they were not able to be counted as part of the quorum of ten men who constitute the minimal public community necessary to have the special elements of public communal prayer. Not being obligated, they could not serve as the prayer-leader whose prayer fulfills the requirement of all who hear and respond to him. Not being obligated, their action in performing these ritual acts was considered an act of self-gratification rather than obedience to divine command, and there was dispute about whether women should recite the blessing that accompanied the ritual acts.

The Rabbinic system assumed that a woman would be occupied in the private domain, and this domain began to occupy her. She was increasingly defined as essentially and inherently "private." It is on this basis, still popular in many Orthodox circles, that women were defined as essentially private persons, so that no number of them can constitute an official public assembly, which requires ten men. The pattern of the optional *mitzvot* changed subtly. In home-centered rituals, such as counting the Omer, taking the Lulav, and eating in the Sukkah, women gradually became participants in such numbers that Halakhic authorities began to consider that women—as a group—had obligated themselves. Thus the Magen Avraham, a Halakhic authority of the seventeenth century, argued that women had become obligated to counting the Omer, and others extended the argument to the Sukkot rituals (eating in the Sukkah, taking Etrog and Lulav). On the other hand, in public rituals the direction of change went in the opposite direction. In the case of study, which in Judaism is a central *devotional* exercise and not only an intellectual pursuit, the exemption of women developed into a presumption that women would not study, and then into a cultural pattern in which women were not taught. Public worship followed a similar pattern, with women increasingly shunted out of visible participation in the community. Even the obligation to light Hanukkah candles underwent change. Women had been obligated to do this, but the public/private distinction became so important that this *mitzvah,* which was a *public* demonstration of the Hanukkah deliverance (and was moreover done outdoors until recently), became performed by men *for* the women.

The absence of women from the public life of the community was intensified by rules of segregation and "modesty" that developed in the first few hundred years of the Common Era. Among these was the Mehitza, the physical barrier between men and women as they pray. By the fourth century, it seems, women were physically separated from men by being in balconies or behind curtains. The family did not pray together. The men congregated near where they could participate in the action (which was all being performed by men); the women were out of sight. All the men could see were other men. This system of separation, probably borrowed from the Greco-Roman world, was explained and justified on the principle that women were a sexual distraction that would take men's minds off prayer. As women became more private, as men had less opportunity to interact with women other than their wives, they thought of these other women primarily as sex objects, and the fear of sexual temptation loomed ever larger. The men of Israel told stories about how the sight of a beautiful woman could cause men to perform almost superhuman feats in their drive toward immorality. They developed laws to guard against opportunities for sexual misconduct, chief among them the Mishnaic law of *yihud,* which prohibits a man and a woman from being alone together. They protected themselves from lustful thoughts by decreeing that women should be dressed "modestly" (covered from elbow to toe), that their hair should be covered, and that their voices should not be heard. The women of Israel, out in public on their tasks and labors, should not attract attention: the goal of "modesty" regulations is the invisibility of women.

The community of Israel did not ignore women, nor consider them less than Jews, but it also did not see them as independent members of the community. All the active members of the public life of the Jewish community in synagogue and school were men. Each man, in turn, represented his household, his wife and children. In this way, the male of the household mediated the message of the community, the learning and heritage, to his family. His family, in turn (particularly his wife), encouraged his active participation in this public devotional life and did everything possible to enable the man to participate. The women had become "other," a separate group that intersected with the public Jewish community. They were the "wives and daughters of Israel" rather than woman Jews. The women enabled the men to live their lives in the divine presence and were praised and honored for this role. Judaism evolved through the millennia of our era into a sort of "benevolent patriarchy" a community of God-centered men prescribing respect and affection for the women who provided them with their opportunities of divine service.

Women have long found security and fulfillment in this type of a system, but it is archaic and maladaptive to contemporary ideas of the proper relationship between the sexes and the real identity of women. It also lends itself to abuse. If the husband is the head of the household, responsible to the community for maintaining it, the well-being of its members depends on the goodwill of the man and, failing that, the strength of communal persuasion. But if this should fail, what can a woman do? In traditional Judaism, the right to create and dissolve a marriage was the husband's. If the woman was dissatisfied in her relationship, she had to depend on the community's ability to persuade her husband to grant her a formal divorce. When community control was weak (as it is today), this could lead to husbands permanently shackling their wives, creating *agunot,* "anchored" women who were no longer living with their husbands but were not free to marry anyone else. Any system in which the women are individual satellites to the men who comprise the community contains within it vast potential for abuse.

WHY, THEN, AM I A JEW?

In truth, I have no real choice. There is no "me" that is not a Jewish "me," no "I" to stand outside the people and choose to belong or not to belong to the faith. When I was about thirteen, one of my teachers told me a story. He had just been to a celebration of Martin Buber's eightieth birthday at the Ethical Culture Society. As he told the story (the scholar in me knows that I have no independent verification), a guest speaker praised Buber, claiming that he was neither Jew nor Christian, but the "universal man." This was high praise indeed at the Ethical Culture society, and everybody was full of good cheer and fellow feeling. Except Buber. When he arose in response, he slammed his hand down on the lectern and said "I am not a universal man. I am a Jew. I feel it in my blood and in my bones: I stood at Sinai." That story has stayed in my memory, for Buber expressed something deep in the soul of many Jews—a sense of eternity and community, a deep experience of linkage and history.

I am not naive. A twentieth-century scholar, I know how I came to feel this way. Every year at Passover I remember the primal event of Judaism, the exodus from Egypt. Every year I read in the Haggadah, the liturgy recited at the Passover feast, that "in every generation a person must look at him/herself as if she came out of Egypt." Throughout the year, the signposts of the seasons carry me once more into my Jewish identity. In June, at Shavuout (Pentecost), the start of summer brings the revelation and the coming of the Law; in September-October, at Sukkot, the fragile hut in which I eat the season's harvest of fruits and vegetables recalls the desert journey of the Hebrews to the Promised Land. I sit and taste the food, and invite Jews from past generations to come to share this memory with me. In the spring, at Passover, I celebrate freedom, beginnings, and rebirth. To these three harvests of history, the Jewish calendar adds re-membrances of good times (Purim) and bad (Tisha b'Av), momentous happenings (Hannukah) and small (Fast of Gedaliah). Even in my lifetime, more days have been added—days to commemorate the horror (Holocaust day, Memorial day) and the glory (Israel Independence day) of Jews in our times. In the passing of the present, Jews see their past; in the marking of days we meet our history.

To these annual events, shared by (I hope) most Jews, I add the events of my own life. When I was a very little girl, my father took me to a rally. There I listened to the vote at the UN that established the state of Israel, and then I rose with a huge crowd to sing the Hatikvah, the song of national Jewish identity. I am not sure where that really was, perhaps at Madison Square Garden, perhaps at Yankee Stadium. I was four years old at the time, and my memory of this event, my first real memory, is more mythic than historical.

Israel, Jews, the Holocaust—all were an important part of my life. Zionist youth groups and summer camps, years in Israel, Hebrew songs, Hebrew dances, all enhanced my identification with Israel and with the Jewish people. They did not make me an Israeli. I am an American, and like other Jews in America I mark my years in two calendars, journeying also through the American civic remembrances by which our nation of immigrants transforms itself into a people. Every Thanksgiving, we rehearse the arrival of the pilgrims and retell the stories of Jamestown; every Fourth of July we are reminded of the Revolutionary War, of independence, freedom, and the ideals of our founders. We reinforce these journeys through time with visits to Philadelphia, Boston, Williamsburg, Valley Forge, Gettysburg, and our many other national monuments and historical sites. Holidays, pilgrimages, and our studies in school all help us internalize our history until it becomes a part of us, inseparable from our hopes and values. In the communal memory of past events we realize our identities as Jews and as Americans.

The heritage of Jewish history and modern Jewish events provides a deep sense of community and a rich feeling of connectedness to past and present. But this is only a small fraction of Judaism. I have always felt somewhat ill-at-ease with the same Buber story that had such an impact on me. When I first heard the tale in my teens, I wanted to change Buber's answer. "Why," I responded (in the innocent effrontery of adolescence), "didn't he say 'I *stand* at Sinai' "? I still feel the need for this philosophico-grammatical change. The synagogue in which I grew up had a verse inscribed in Hebrew above the holy ark: *da lifney mee atah omed*, "know before whom you stand!" This ark, the cabinet in which the Holy Torah scrolls are kept, is the focal point of Synagogue architecture. Throughout the service, as I looked at it, I was reminded of the presence of One I could not see. The ark, the Torah, and this verse all directed me beyond myself, even beyond the community in which I stood, to an eternity of time, space, and will.

This transcendent message is reinforced every year with great impact on the solemn High Holy days of September. In the majesty of Rosh Hashanah, the year begins anew with a joyous proclamation of creation and the sovereign authority of the Creator. God sits on the universal throne. Then, in the days that follow, we focus on us humans, on our deeds and misdeeds and the sense of responsibility that they engender. These "days of penitence" culminate in the solemn day of Yom Kipper, a day of fasting, penitence, and hope. These solemn High Holy days, the "Days of Awe," reinforce our sense of transhuman nexus in our lives. They speak of our connectedness and obligations to each other, to the universe, and to God. This, the central message of Judaism, has become part of my own essence.

For all these reasons, I am a Jew and always will be. Ecumenical modern American that I am, I know that there are many religions, that they all strive to give their believers a sense of belonging, responsibility, and fervor. I believe with fervor and conviction that there are many paths for the human quest. But as for me, I am a Jew. I can do no other, nor would I want to.

This being a Jew is a matter of destiny, education, and identification. Nevertheless, above all, it is also a matter of choice. The forces that make us a Jew do not *compel* us to be so. If Judaism were a misogynist religion, I could not continue to choose to participate. A Jew I might remain, by tradition and upbringing, but a Jew in rebellion or, even worse, a Jew in silence and solitude, alienated from the tradition and the community that give energy to the Jewish spirit. Instead, I study and learn (which are Jewish devotional exercises), I train students to be Rabbis, I send my children to Jewish day schools so that they too can learn to learn, and I not only belong to a synagogue, I go regularly to pray in community. To me there is no doubt that Judaism provides a home for my spirit, a faith that allows me to grow and contribute.

As a woman, I know that the wellspring of Judaism is not in conflict between my love of Judaism and my woman-ness. The classical Rabbinic tradition of women's separateness is foreign to my life and beliefs, and the systematic exclusion of women from the men's club of prayer and learning is a history to be mourned. Whenever I approach the ancient texts that heralded the domestication of women, I feel again the same anger that I felt when I first realized that I could never have lived my life of involvement with Jewish learning had I been born before my time. But the rage recedes before the realization that the past can be laid to rest. Rage seems to me only valuable as an incentive to change, so that one develops the determination to lead the type of vigorously Jewish and feminist life that will keep at least some groups of Judaism open and receptive to all their members. We need to grieve about the past, and, having grieved, set aside our grief in order to create a new order. This is easier to do in Judaism than in some other religions, for even though Judaism has been totally androcentric in its focus, it has not been anti-woman. There have been misogynist statements from time to time, but they are neither consistent nor dominant in the tradition. In many respects, Jewish tradition exploited women, but it did not malign them. The result has been that Jewish women are famously strong-willed and proud. The women of Israel never were Victorian maidens. The Rabbis knew that they were strong, assertive mistresses of their households, and they encouraged this, proclaiming that the woman was queen in her household and expecting her to be active in pursuit of her family's aims. The women of Israel were responsible for the moral character of the household, the religious home observances, and the well-being of family members. Their responsibilities often brought them into what we normally consider the "public" domain, not only physically into public space but actively as wage earners and businesswomen. Judaism has always had an often-expressed appreciation for women in their place. This approval, of course, was conditional on their staying in their place, and was an important incentive to women to accept their lot and the approval that went with it. Nevertheless, Judaism did not tell women that they were inferior, or evil. With the explicit approval of the men, the women were openly capable.

There is another reason for the strength of Jewish women. Beyond all the patriarchal concerns and attitudes, there has always been another, deeper message of Judaism, sometimes not acknowledged, but always there. Beyond the Talmud lies the Bible, always proclaimed the most sacred of all texts, held to be divinely originated and divinely inspired, celebrated and studied liturgically as part of sacred service. And the Bible simply does not depict women as sex objects, or weak, or reticent. Of course, the Bible, written for its time, never imagines egalitarianism. The Bible inherited a social structure that we could call "hierarchical" or "patriarchal," complete with inequities between rich and poor, slave and free, ruler and ruled, men and women, and never questioned the fundamental premises underlying such social divisions. Some of these divisions, indeed, have never been eradicated. Slavery was abolished in Jewish law in Rabbinic times, and in Western culture only in our recent past. Male-female distinctions are disappearing only today, painfully, in fits and starts. And the poor are still very much with us, with the inequalities between rich and poor in America growing enormously in our own lifetime. Probably, none of these divisions could have been eradicated in Biblical Israel. Certainly there could have been no gender egalitarianism. At a time when half of all women could expect to die in childbirth, when it took multiple pregnancies and births to produce one child who would survive past the age of five, and when women rarely lived past thirty, and men not much longer—how could egalitarianism or unisex life-styles be conducive to survival?

Biblical Israel never questioned the legal subordination of women to men. But the way that Israel *justified* its skewed social order has had important ram-ifications for the way Judaism looks upon women. The social order is legitimated by divine fiat (Gen. 3): husbands are to be dominant over their wives. This divine prescription is really a description of historical reality. Attributing this social order to God doesn't open the door for much argument or dissent, but it also removes the onus from women for their social position. Nowhere in the Bible are women considered inferior, less wise, less moral, or in need of keepers. They have the life they lead because God announced that it would be so—a theistic way of saying "it is so because it is so." Social subordination is not a reflection of a lesser character. In fact, the Biblical portrayal of women shows them to be much the same as men. Neither sexy nor weak, they have the same goals as the rest of Israel, and pursue them with the same strategies and powers as the out-of-power men who formed the bulk of the population.[1] There are no characteristics that we can call "feminine" in the Bible that men do not also share, no attributes of "masculinity" not manifested by women.

The metaphysics of gender unity finds expression in the creation stories. In Genesis 2, after God creates the earthling (Adam), Adam is lonely. God sets out to create other creatures to accompany Adam. But even in his earliest, most primitive naivete, Adam can not find suitable companionship in cows or chickens. So God creates "woman" and "man."[2] The significance of this story becomes apparent when we compare it to two tales from the Babylonians. In the beginning of the Gilgamesh Epic, Gilgamesh is oppressing his city and the gods realize that his arrogance results from having no peer. They rectify the situation by having the mother goddess create a new creature who can be a counterpart to Gilgamesh, and she creates Enkidu—another male. When the two meet, they recognize their suitability to each other and become close companions. The second tale, the Agushaya hymn, has a similar plot-line. Ishtar, most ferocious and "virile" of the goddesses, is terrifying to the gods. The god Enki realizes that she needs a companion to occupy her attention and creates Saltu—another ferocious female goddess. In these Babylonian stories, the closest bonding possible is between male-male and female-female. By contrast, in the Bible, the suitable companion for a male is a female and the male-female bond is proclaimed as the closest possible connection between humans: "therefore a man shall leave his father and mother and cleave to his wife and they shall become as one flesh."

The other story of the creation of human beings also delivers the same message of mutuality and equality between men and women. In Genesis 1, on the sixth day, God created humanity in the image of the divine, "male and female created he them." Once again, the implication is that male and female, both in the image of the divine, are essentially similar to each other and that all differences are secondary to this congruence. The separate creation of Pandora in Greek mythology, and the Greek concept of the "race of women" that it illustrates, are a sharp contrast to this Biblical message of homogeneity. Just as there is no plurality of divine powers in Judaism, so, in reflection, there is no multiplication of different types of humanity. In Genesis 2, one human being was created, and when the solitude proved too lonely, the one was divided, with the second coming directly out of the first. In Genesis 1, both humans were created at once, but they were each created in the image of the one God.

The Bible sends a double message, for alongside these creation stories is the divine fiat that men will rule their wives. Further reading of the Bible shows that the Court and the Temple (though not prophecy) were in the hands of men. But in the household, there is no echo of the divine fiat. Where is the woman who does what her husband or father says simply because he tells her to do so? In Genesis, in the stories of the matriarchs, the husbands have the right to control the succession. But women are not automatically assumed to be willing to follow their husbands and fathers in all their decisions. They are not obligated to move away from their home. Before she is sent off to marry Isaac, Rebekkah is asked if she will move to Israel (Gen. 34:57–58). Even Rachel and Leah, already married, must be asked if they are willing to move with their husband Jacob (Gen. 31:4–13). Nor are the matriarchs assumed to acquiesce in their husband's choices of heirs: Sarah persuades her husband to eliminate Isaac's rival (Gen. 21:8–14); Rebekkah tricks her husband into awarding his inheritance blessing to Jacob (Gen.27).

The law codes and the narratives of Samuel and Kings sometimes show different pictures of the position of women. The law codes tell us that a husband can immediately annul a wife's vow if he overhears it, presumably because he controls the goods that she is vowing to present to God. But women such as the great (wealthy) woman of Shunnem do not consult their husband before deciding to bestow gifts or offer hospitality (2 Kings 4–8). In fact, Biblical narratives abound in strong decisive women who act for the benefit of Israel: from Deborah and Jael through Abigail, the great woman of Shunnem, and the Wise Women of Abel and of Tekoa, the women of Israel act with strength and decisiveness. Throughout the millennia of Jewish history, the power of these narratives has gripped the Jewish imagination and helped form its expectations of human behavior.

The impact of these stories was particularly strong on Jewish women precisely because of the Rabbinic exclusion of women from serious study. While the men were studying the Talmud, with its worry about sexual temptation and its determination to create a pure and purely male system, the women were learning the Bible stories, with their subliminally revolutionary message that women are not sex objects, victims, or submissive and meek. Jewish women have had other strong role models: from the Talmudic period came Beruriah the scholar, wife of Rabbi Meir, whose learning was famed and respected, and Rachel, the self-sacrificing wife of Rabbi Akiba, who worked to send him to school; from later in history came figures of wealth and charity such as Donna Gracia Mendes and the Americans Rebecca Gratz and Henrietta Szold. Different stories have had their greatest impact at different periods. The story of Rachel, Akiba's wife, was particularly important when scholarship could only exist when some women were willing to shoulder both household and economic burdens; the story of Beruriah had a renaissance when women themselves were encouraged to study. But in all the stories, women were glorified for strength and determination, perseverance and achievement. With these models in mind, women were able to live under the Halakhah (the legal system that defined everything, including the proper patriarchal relations between the sexes) without being effaced by it.

Religions are never static: they always entail process and growth. Every generation learns from its past and adapts to its present. Consciously or unconsciously, each community chooses anew the foundation message of the faith and, in so doing, modifies it so that it can continue to live. With very few exceptions, religions cannot live only in the past: they must respond to the human ideas and needs of each present generation. There are differences between Biblical and Rabbinic Judaism. The world changed, and the religion, always faithful to its core, changed in response to new needs and new ideas. From the standpoint of today—in other words, according to the needs and ideas of the late twentieth century—some of these changes were "advances": the abolition of animal sacrifice, the increased emphasis on interior values, the abandonment of war as a means of expression or persuasion. Other changes aren't as appealing to us, particularly the establishment of separate spheres for men and women and the reinforcement of this separation by rules of "modesty" (invisibility). This separation is not Biblical: it is deeply influenced by Greek ideas about categorical differences and about the dangers of sexual attraction. It is also part of the great emphasis on the household by a society that had lost its institutions of Temple and Palace.

But the changes introduced by the Rabbis were not irrevocable. They were adaptive to their own situation, and helped ensure the people's survival then and throughout the medieval period, but they have no place in a postindustrial society. Judaism has changed and will continue to change on all sociological issues. The modern revolution concerning women has been underway a long time, long before we were actually aware of its magnitude. Women began to be educated seriously in Jewish studies a hundred years ago, in response to the new reality created by the industrial revolution in which there were women of leisure, ready to be educated and being educated only in non-Jewish matters. Some voted with their feet, opting to abandon the Jewish lifestyle and community. Others found that they had nothing in common with their Jewish-educated husbands, leading to disrupted home relationships. To ensure the continuation of the Jewish family, a leading and brave Halakhic authority, the Hatam Sofer, decreed that in the modern world women needed to be educated in Torah, thus paving the way for the establishment of the first religious schools for girls. The education of women in Judaism had great consequences, for it meant that they would no longer be quite as dependent on traditional male interpretations of the traditional sources. Another major change happened without any particular legal decision or authority. Jews in America in the Conservative movement began to pray with "mixed seating": men and women sat together, there was no women's section and no *mehitzah* barrier. And somehow services didn't become orgiastic, men didn't abandon fervor for frivolity. Slowly, mixed seating had a profound psychological effect: as the worshippers looked around at the congregation with which they were praying, they saw both men and women. The message delivered subliminally by an unsegregated congregation is that the Community of Israel is both men and women.

These new directions have turned into a fundamental sea-change in Jewish thinking and practice. I feel that I, and many other women still fairly young, have witnessed a revolution. I had my own small part to play in this revolution. I was the first woman undergraduate at the Jewish Theological Seminary permitted to be a Talmud major and take part in the Talmud major seminar. It seems incredible to believe that there was a time when a woman's registering for a class in Talmud was a major achievement. As with most other barriers, once breached, it was almost as if it had never existed. There were soon several women studying Talmud seriously, a woman graduate student was admitted to the seminar of the grand master of Talmud, and there were women Talmud Ph.D.'s. Of course, we say now: the study of Talmud, like any study, is not the property of any one gender! How could anyone ever have thought that women could be excluded from *study*? And yet, they were—until our generation.

Change has come very rapidly. In the early 1970s, as the first Reform and Reconstructionist women Rabbis were being ordained, a group of women called "Ezrat Nashim" (Women's Section) presented a list of demands to the Rabbinical Assembly of the Conservative movement. They expressed their extreme discomfiture that they, highly educated and knowledgeable in Jewish texts, liturgy, and practice, should not be able to lead services and even to attend as full members of the prayer community. There could be no prayer community without ten men—no matter how many knowledgeable and devout women were sitting there. They could not be honored with a blessing over the Torah, while a man who set foot in a synagogue once in a decade and had to mumble the blessings from an English transliteration could be so honored. They could not read liturgically from the Torah that they loved, they could not represent in song the prayer community they felt such a part of. Some Conservative Jews laughed at them, not even comprehending the pain out of which they spoke. But the Conservative Rabbis listened, and less than twenty years later, the agenda of Ezrat Nashim has been completely fulfilled. Women are full members of congregations, they receive equal honors with men, and they can be Rabbis and Cantors.

From derision to fulfillment in twenty short years! There was no way of predicting how quickly change could take place. Those of us who were raised before the change sometimes have to play "catch-up" with our own children. I had my religious *Bat Mitzvah* celebration when I was thirty (rather than 12–13), when I learned for the first time how to chant the Haftorah, the reading from the Prophets sung liturgically. I am still learning liturgical skills that my daughter, not yet *Bat Mitzvah,* has already mastered. She knows chants that I am now learning, and assumes that she will master them all. She has been raised to expect to pray and lead prayers, and sometimes finds virtue in doing as little, rather than as much, as she can get away with. Her very nonchalance teaches me how peacefully she can follow the paths carved by revolution.

The task is not yet finished, the sexes are not completely equal; this very rapid revolution has its turmoils. The past is not yet past. Orthodoxy still teaches an extremely gender-segregated lifestyle and religious practice, and declares all change in the other branches of Judaism to be fundamentally non-Jewish. The other branches are evolving, but even in non-Orthodox circles there are many who do not accept and agree to change. Jewish life today is a checkerboard of egalitarian and nonegalitarian practices. In Reform and Reconstructionist Judaism, there is unanimity; in Conservative Judaism, there is division. Officially, the movement, committed to Halakha, has not yet found a Halakhic argument to allow women to serve as witnesses. But the clear majority of the Conservative movement appears headed for complete egalitarianism between the sexes. A small group bands together to encourage each other to resist this change, talks of schism, and establishes its own women-exclusionary seminary. Obstructionist as they are, the dissenting reactionary voices are fighting a rear-guard action. Their objections are vestigial elements of the old separatist system. For the majority of Jews in America, the last two decades have witnessed a major transformation in the thinking and practice of liberal Judaism.

Even the Orthodox may change, but in Orthodox circles change is in its infancy. Officially, many elements of Orthodoxy deny that change is possible. Still others require that change always be dictated from above. Yet there have been major changes. Women are educated in the Orthodox community, though separately from the men and not to the same level of Talmudic knowledge. Women do not lead prayers, but they are not silenced from joining in the singing of Sabbath songs. And there are women actively working and agitating for change. Voices such as Arlene Agus,[3] Blu Greenberg,[4] Rivka Haut,[5] and Norma Josephs[6] express the sentiments of many modern Orthodox women, committed to Orthodoxy but anxious for fuller female participation. The many women's prayer groups and the National Women's Tefillah (prayer) Network attest to the

active desire of women to participate in a community of worshippers. The
developing Orthodox women's religious expression is different from women's
experiences in the other branches of Judaism, for among the Orthodox the newly
developing public ritual life for women is a parallel community, separate from
the male but giving public expression to women's devotion and spirituality.

The Orthodox movement has not yet made peace with the idea that women
want to be part of a public devotional community. There are Rabbis vigorously
opposed to the women's prayer groups in the United States, Rabbinic leaders
who argue vociferously that women need to remain private and individual in
their devotions. This year, the newspapers have been full of reports of the
struggles of progressive women (Reform, Reconstructionist, Conservative, and
Modern Orthodox women together) to achieve the simple right of being allowed
to gather at the Western Wall in Jerusalem and be a congregation of women,
praying together at the site of the ancient Jewish Temple. Their dignity has been
stripped, they have been insulted and physically mauled. Their very presence
as an independent congregation of Jews, proudly praying together without the
mediation of men, has sent shock waves through groups that are used to thinking
of the community of Israel as an assemblage of *men*, each with his mother,
wife, and daughters.

The drama at the Western Wall is the result of a major change. Not because
women came together, but because they continue to do so. Once, I too was
attacked at the Wall. I had gone there to pray as soon as I arrived in the country.
I had worn my most modest outfit: pants with a full dress over them, somewhat
in the Yemenite fashion. The dress was high-necked and long-sleeved, but it
was eyelet, fully lined except for the sleeves. If you stood very close and looked
very hard, you could see pinpoints of arm flesh through the eyes of the fabric.
As I stood praying silently, I suddenly felt blows around my head and shoulders.
Behind me there was a woman, beating me with a pocketbook and yelling at
me that I was shamefully immodest, and insulting to the holy place and its
worshippers. I told her to go away and I think she did—but I never wore that
dress to the Wall again. I conformed to her norms, concerned that I insult her
traditions. Ultimately, I gave up on the Wall, going rarely and reluctantly, having
internalized the sense that my ways were foreign to the Wall, a modern intrusion.
No more. The women at the Wall today have announced by their persistence
that the old strictures against women's public being are simply *wrong*. They are
not more traditional, certainly not in the sense of being authentic. They are
simply wrong, and the women creating new patterns stand more genuinely in
the ongoing tradition of Judaism.

Other legal barriers to women's equality and self-determination have no place
in Judaism. The Orthodox community is agonizing over how to prevent the abuse
of women under a legal system that holds that a woman is not free until her
husband grants her a divorce. *Agunot* (anchored women) are multiplying as
modern mobility enables husbands to move away, as husbands blackmail wives

out of large sums of money before they agree to grant the bill of divorce.[7] Tens of thousands of Orthodox women live shackled by this regulation, unable to marry again. This is an ethical disaster, never intended by the Rabbis. It is a fossil of an age in which Rabbinic authority and community pressure made sure that men properly freed their wives. But the modern abuse of the ancient law shows the inherent danger and ethical error of leaving a woman's future in the hands of her husband. In Reform Jewry, there is no religious bill of divorce; in Reconstructionism, either the husband or the wife can apply to have the divorce issued. Conservative Judaism has solved the problem by reinstituting the ancient system of annulment: if the estranged husband refuses to free his wife, a Rabbinic court can free the woman by annuling the marriage. This action frees women whose husbands simply leave or obtain a civil divorce, and the existence of this possibility eliminates threats and blackmail. Halakhic experts, Conservative and Orthodox, have shown the antiquity and authority of annulment. But the Orthodox community has not adopted it, probably because of the threat it poses to male autonomy.

Orthodoxy attempts to assert the dominance and centrality of males. But it has nothing to do with me. The Orthodox voice is not the voice of ancient tradition; it is one voice among the many interpreters of Judaism today. There are many paths in Jerusalem. My own is egalitarian and traditional in liturgy and observance. Other people, including Orthodox women, may opt for the Orthodox system, may accept it and support it. Patriarchy offers security, rigid rules offer a conviction of righteousness. Patriarchal Orthodox Judaism, male-centered but not misogynist, offers the women who accept the system a sense of appreciation and purpose. This is not my way, and it has no authority over me. Patriarchy is not my ideology and, moreover, any view of Judaism that freezes tradition at a particular point in the past seems to me misguided and in some cases idolatrous. As a pluralist, I cannot object to Orthodoxy. However, I do not have to justify myself before it. It lays no claims on my attentions or emotions, for Orthodox Judaism is one form of modern Judaism. It does not embody the ancient Jewish tradition any more than any other branch of Judaism does. Orthodoxy, too, has developed in response both to external circumstance and its own internal dynamics. At every point of change, there were choices that were made. I see no reason to demand absolute allegiance to early nineteenth-century versions of Judaism when Judaism continues to evolve, and I feel no need to consider these early nineteenth-century formats as normative in any way.

The barriers to women's participation are coming down in the rest of Jewry. But anti-woman feelings find other expression. Threatened by the advances and achievements of women in the world, and denied the bastion of the synagogue as a "men's club," anti-woman sentiment finds its expression in cruel humor, in the proliferation of "JAP" (Jewish American Princess) jokes, crudely misogynist and anti-Semitic. This development is sad, and needs to be combatted. It erodes women's self-esteem and heightens divisions between women. It reinforces sexual and ethnic stereotypes and can cause estrangement between Jewish men and women. But in the long run, it is a rear-guard reaction and cannot stop the tides of change.

In the long history of Judaism, on practically any point at issue, there were many voices eager to speak and be heard, many opinions, equally learned, based on antiquity, faith, and love of God. That is what makes Judaism so exciting. There are many voices today, an array of opinions both bewildering and inspiring. That too is exciting. And now, many of these voices are female. A whole new dimension of experience is being brought to the ancient tradition. Women's lives, women's needs, are heard. Women have always had their own *aggadah* (philosophy, interpretation, folklore, customs), but it was separate, women's own, superceded by the high tradition of Jewish learning with which it never interacted. Now the dialogue has been opened. Now that women speak the language of learning and have access to ritual and ministry, they are offering their insights to everyone: feminist interpretation of the Bible, new liturgy without hierarchical dualism, changing images of God, new liturgy for life cycles, inclusive theology and liturgy, theology of birth and nurture. Some new developments:

Rosh Hodesh—there was an ancient tradition that on Rosh Hodesh (the beginning of each month), women refrained from certain work (particularly washing and sewing) and gathered together for a celebration. This custom has been revived as a woman's occasion, when women come together for fellowship, devising their own creative rituals to mark the year.

Ministry—as more women enter the clergy, trends already present have been intensified. The Rabbinate is becoming ever less authoritarian and more pastoral, ministering to the needs and addressing the spiritual desires of the people.

Blessings—in traditional Judaism, the events of the day—eating, drinking, washing, seeing nature, studying—have all been sanctified by the saying of a blessing, recalling the presence of God, and focusing attention on the transhuman in the midst of the mundane. New forms of these blessings are being written by Marcia Falk and others, forms that stress the activity of humanity and the immanence of God.

Theology—the central ideas and institutions are being reexamined in the light of what they mean to an inclusive community. A feminist Jewish theology is emerging, particularly in the works of Judith Plaskow.[8]

Scholarship—the presence of women in Judaic studies is opening up new areas of research and providing new perspectives on ancient traditions. There are now so many women in Jewish Studies that it would be unfair to try to enumerate them all. Ancient Near Eastern scholars, Biblical scholars, ancient and modern historians, anthropologists, and sociologists are both studying Jewish women and providing women's perspectives on all scholarly issues.

Life Cycle—Jewish women have expressed the need to sanctify the biological events of life, and there has been a profusion of prayers, rituals, and poems for the naming of a daughter, for puberty, menstruation, marriage, birth, and menopause. My own work on

"Motherprayer"[9] seeks to expand traditional insight and vocabulary to encompass a theology of pregnancy and birth.

Song—spirituality is joined to creativity. Women's voices, long silent from the religious arena by law and custom, are now being heard. The songbook of Geela Reezel Raphael,[10] the liturgical music of Shefa Pelicrow (both students at the Reconstructionist Rabbinical College), and the liturgical music of Debbie Freedman are creating a new form of spiritual music, centered in liturgy and expressing modern spirituality.

There are many more contributions of women to Midrash, to scholarship, liturgy, and thought. The list has grown too great to enumerate, and only random names come to mind. There have always been women thinkers; now their offerings enter the mainstream of Judaism and enrich the ancient traditions. Indeed, with all the difficulties and turmoil, it is an exciting time to be a Jew.

NOTES

1. For a detailed presentation of the image of women in the Bible, see my *In the Wake of the Goddesses* (New York: Free Press, forthcoming).

2. It has been noted, and deserves to be noted again, that Adam is not called *ish*, "man," until after the woman is created.

3. Arlene Agus, "This Month is for You," in Elizabeth Koltun, ed., *The Jewish Woman: A New Perspective* (New York: Schocken, 1976), 84–93.

4. See Blu Greenberg, *On Women and Judaism: A View from Tradition* (Philadelphia: Jewish Publication Society, 1981).

5. Rivka Haut is head of the Jewish Women's National Tefillah Network.

6. Norma Josephs, who is Professor of Judaism at Concordia University, Montreal, is well known as a lecturer in Orthodox women's circles and currently working on a study of the women-related response of Reb. Moshe Feinstein.

7. There is a difference in the status of men and women who are civilly, but not religiously, divorced. A man can apply for permission to take a second wife; and even if he does not do so, any children born of his subsequent unions will be fully legitimate. A woman may not, and future children of a woman who has not received a proper religious divorce are considered *mamzerim*, bastards, and are not permitted to marry Jews. Because of this difference, men have leverage over women and can subject them to blackmail.

8. See most recently Judith Plaskow, *Standing at Sinai* (New York: Harper & Row, 1989).

9. Tikvah Frymer-Kensky, *Motherprayer: Readings toward a Theology of Birth.* Forthcoming 1992.

10. Sponsored by the Melton Foundation.

4

A Christian Feminist's Struggle with the Bible as Authority

CONSTANCE F. PARVEY

Though cultural attitudes and the force of tradition have had great power over our lives as Christian women, nothing has been more influential in shaping the roles, behavior, and limitations of Christian women's lives than the Bible. In 1895, Josephine K. Henry wrote in the appendix to *The Woman's Bible*:

Ever since Eve was cursed for seeking knowledge, the priest with the Bible in his hands has pronounced her the most unnatural, untrustworthy and dangerous creation of God. She has been given away as a sheep at the marriage altar, classed with the ox and ass, cursed in maternity, required to receive purification at the hands of the priest for the crime of child-bearing, her body enslaved, and robbed of her name and her property.[1]

Because the Bible is a book that is subject to the interpretation of its teachers, and because men have long held authority over that interpretive power through a patriarchal system wherein succession moves through the male line, the Bible has been captive to men's experience, more specifically to ecclesiastical patriarchy—its principles of reality and organization, and its needs. As a result, women have found themselves not as subjects in scripture, but rather as objects of scripture, their nature and destiny defined, circumscribed, and regulated by patriarchal authority. Thus, claims of "Biblical authority" have been a means by which patriarchal power has undergirded itself relative to women's lives in the church, family, and society. This process has not yet come to an end. Key examples of present church teachings where women's nature, status, and choices are controlled by patriarchal power over sacred texts are seen in the ecumenical debate over the ordination of women, in the controversy over women's reproductive rights, and even in the most up-to-date Biblical translations. Consequently, though there are variances within the different churches (Protestant,

Roman Catholic, Orthodox, or Evangelical), Christian women find that they must continue to struggle with issues of the meaning of sacred texts for their lives; and this challenge initiated by women is shared with growing numbers of men who view women/men relationships as partnerships of equals.

This chapter sketches my own experience as a Christian feminist who has been dealing with the issues of authoritative texts for over four decades, starting as a student, then pastor, seminary lecturer, and former director of the World Council of Churches program, "The Community of Women and Men in the Church." In the past twenty years there has been a burst of publications related to women and the authority of the Bible. Positions range from the impossibility of the Bible, given its inherent patriarchy, to be authoritative for women, to those that accept past Biblical teachings of the church wherein the subordination of women was assumed, to those women who are taking on the task of authoritative interpretation and teaching themselves, breaking significant new ground both in methodology and theology with regard to women and authoritative teaching. Rather than reviewing that rich history and critiquing it, I have chosen for this book, dedicated to interfaith dialogue, to trace my own struggle with the Bible as authority for women, in the hope that others in reading this chapter will use it as a starting point for dialogue and for recollecting their own experiences.

In this span of four decades, though I have critiqued concepts of Biblical authority, I have been unwilling to let go of a faith that is based on the Bible as authority. As Jacob wrestled with the angel and would not let go until he was blessed, so I too have wrestled with the Bible as the authoritative text for my life, and I have been unwilling to let it go until I also receive a blessing. For us as women this means being equal partners, compatriots in faith and life (Rom. 16:7); it means not being circumscribed on the basis of gender to the status of subordinate, dependent, second-class persons with sex-limited personal and vocational choices. Though almost everywhere in the churches women outnumber men in attendance, women are a minority when it comes to the task of interpreting sacred texts. What is changing today is that women are claiming their own experience as authoritative. In the process they are equipping themselves with interpretive skills; they are gradually moving into areas of seminary education, church decision making, priestly roles, and publications and communications to make their own voices heard. Thus, the number of women reshaping issues of Biblical authority is steadily on the increase.

OVERLOOKING WHAT I COULDN'T AGREE WITH

My first encounter with the issue of Biblical authority and women goes back to my days as a seminary student in the late 1950s. I took a course on the letters of St. Paul, the chief missionary of the primitive church and primary interpreter of its message to the Gentiles. Paul's letters are often occupied with practical problems facing a particular church. First Corinthians is a letter of Paul's that has had a major impact on the status of women in the church and in the Western world as it adopted Christianity. Written to the church in Corinth to assist that fledgling community with its many problems, it became, for Christians, one of the authoritative texts that make up the canon of the New Testament. In my first studies of this text, I simply overlooked the negative references about women, considering them out of date and of no relevance to the contemporary situation of women in the church. Because I was interested in gleaning the overall theology of Paul, I just dismissed his anti-woman passages as context-bound, reflecting a particular problem in Corinth at that time, as well as Paul's own attitudes. My reasoning was based on the premise that all cultures and time periods have blinders and boundaries, but faith lives across cultures and is not time-bound; in addition, scripture, inspired by the Holy Spirit, gives us the creativity of new words to express the theological meaning of new realities as we encounter them. This was and still is my position. However, my way of handling these texts and others like them has changed.

At that time, my method was simply to ignore and pass over these texts that appeared to consider women as second best, or second-class relative to men. I was raised to believe that women and men were equal. I could grant that in another time it may not have been that way, but I could not grant that for eternity God intended the inequality between the sexes. My method was a simple one: to overlook those passages that did not resonate with my faith experience of God's love and justice and God's gift of integrity to every human person. The issue for me was not lack of respect for the text; rather it was respect for the text as a whole and how it addressed the question of respect for my life as a woman that enabled me to overlook passages that seemed no longer useful, helpful, or supportive of women. The Bible for me was not and is not a book of law, or of codes of behavior, but a book that enables the transmission and sharing of a living faith, the power of which stretches us to respond with ethical and moral actions. It is thus essential that Biblical contexts of today be examined as closely as students of the Bible are trained to examine the Biblical contexts of the ancient world.

THE NECESSITY OF CONFRONTING TEXTS I HAD IGNORED

It was after seminary, in the late 1960s, when I was reflecting on whether or not women should be ordained in my denomination that I discovered to my dismay that the texts I had simply ignored in seminary were now being used to argue against the ordination of women. For example, opponents to women's ordination argued that women should not be ordained because St. Paul writes in First Corinthians that women should be silent in the church and that women should also keep their heads covered as a sign of their weakness (the ancient argument being that women's heads are weak and defenseless against the penetration of bad angels). These opponents used the same scriptural texts I had decided to ignore to buttress their argument. Additionally, opponents argued that St. Paul had a theology of patriarchy with a hierarchical order of creation in which men came first and women second. Starting with a pyramid theology of the Fatherhood of God at the beginning of creation, the orders moved progressively downward from God the Father, to man (his image), and then to woman, animals, plants, and the earth. They argued that this theology was divinely sanctioned and that it should be mirrored in the practice of the church. Further, they argued that their position was theologically justified by what they considered to be a well-established Christian interpretation of Genesis 2, the second of three creation accounts found in Genesis. The scenario of Genesis 2 is that God created Adam first and later created Eve out of Adam's rib; thus, these interpreters contended that although woman may be equal, because she comes second, she is second. To strengthen their subordinationist argument, they pointed out that Eve was created as a *helpmate* to Adam, and and they interpreted "helpmate" not as an equal, which is the more likely possibility within the text, but as a servant of subordinate status to Adam. This position is based on the patriarchal perception of a helper as a support role, not as someone who can be "in charge" and an equal compatriot in ministry.

It was when these anti-women interpretations were used to argue against the ordination of women that my interest in these texts peaked. I realized then that they could not be ignored. I had to deal with them head on and at many levels. In order to do this I developed a threefold approach:

1. To examine these passages in more detail, contextually;
2. to look at them more wholistically in terms of the overall theology of St. Paul and of the New Testament, and not leave them as isolated texts from which generalizations about women's status and behavior could be made for eternity;
3. to ask what these texts may have meant in their own time and what they might mean today, given our late twentieth-century understanding of gender relationships.

For example, in the case of Paul, he argued that wives must be obedient to their husbands, but he also argued that slaves should be obedient to their masters. We accept today that texts once used to justify and condone slavery no longer hold. Civilized life in our times finds slavery a violation of basic human rights and Christians today argue that it is a violation of a person's God-given rights in creation and redemption. This means that these texts, based on Roman practices of enslaving Greeks and also used to justify slavery of Africans in the Western world until a century ago, are no longer held up as authoritative. They are void. The words in the text remain the same, but they carry no power to make objects of others. Given this perspective, I therefore concluded that similar methods could be used for reinterpreting texts that are used to teach the subordination of wives to their husbands.

In approaching these Pauline passages, some women interpreters have simply said that Paul was a product of his time, and that if he lived today, he wouldn't continue to hold such positions. My methodology was to try to use the tools of Biblical research to get behind and underneath the societal contexts of the era in which these words were first used and written down, unearth what their original intention might have been, and then make the determination of their relevance to contemporary contexts of marriage and women/men relationships.

In other words, I started by looking for clues to help me find text-specific information, to help me work with textual criticism, first among the various writings attributed to Paul, and then within the New Testament as a whole. Further, along with this method of cross-textual analysis, I used cross-cultural analysis, because the writings that make up the New Testament canon come from different cultural, geographical, and class settings of the ancient Mediterranean world. By combining these methods I could point to the apparent contradictions within the writings of Paul himself and also compare these with other New Testament evidence regarding the leadership roles of women and partnerships of women and men in the early church.

This process led to many questions: What were women's roles in the early Christian community? How might they have been different from women's roles in Greco-Roman societies? In Asia Minor? In the seaport town of Corinth? In Alexandria, or Rome itself? When Christianity shifted to becoming primarily a religion of Gentiles, were the roles of Christian women different from those of Jewish women? How different were the role expectations in the institutions of the Christian church from those of other institutions of the societies in which it lived? What do Paul's other letters say about women? Do they all carry the same message? Do Paul's teachings coincide with those of Jesus, or do the parables and stories about the life of Jesus present a different message? What evidence do we have of what might have been happening in the Corinthian church at that time that might provide clues to Paul's admonitions about women's conduct?

What I was able to conclude is that St. Paul's statements in First Corinthians that women in the church should keep silent and keep their heads covered were not statements that he made in other places. This led to the question of what was happening in the Corinthian church. There are various theses on this subject that I will not enter into here, but the important common point for most of them is that these Corinthian passages are not normative for women in the church at all times, and they contradict what Paul has said in other places about the apostolic role of women. As for the passages about wives being subordinate to their husbands, these underlined cultural family practice at the time. What is significant is that they do not say that all women, at all times, are subordinate to all men, which has been the patriarchal extrapolation of these husband/wife references and had led to authoritative teaching of the subordination of women in family and society and has contributed to arguments against the ordination of women. In summary, though the passages I had previously passed over could no longer be ignored, I did discover in the process of confronting them that they lacked the authority to stand in the way of the equal partnerships of women and men in the varied ministries of the early church.

THE TASK OF UNCOVERING THE LOST WOMEN

Grappling with the issues of women and the Bible did not end with St. Paul. The issue of women's marginality in the New Testament itself needed to be addressed. Consequently, in addition to addressing the well-known texts that have been used to argue for the subordination of women, I also had the task of finding the women who, over time, have been lost in the Bible. In order to approach this in a fresh way, I bought two new items for my work: a red pencil, and a new copy of the New Testament in a translation that was unfamiliar to me (The New English Bible). Then I sat down and read the New Testament from cover to cover, underlining in red every reference to women, and any reference that might contain women, such as "the crowds" or "the brethren." When I had completed this task I was amazed at how frequently women were either mentioned or alluded to. This new learning was the starting point for my research. Prior to this exploration, I too had thought of women as rather marginal, or incidental, in the New Testament; I thought women were, at most, hidden behind the text. Though this assumption was not entirely wrong, I did discover many more women leaders and references to women than I expected to find. For instance, even in Paul's letter to the church in Rome, I discovered about a dozen references to women leaders. Listed among the greetings to apostles, ministers, and co-workers in that congregation were women's names, both Jewish and Greek, as well as references to women as the mother or sister of one of the men.

Another discovery I made had to do with gender pairings and their significance. In the parables of Jesus, thought to be the oldest New Testament texts, the closest to the life of Jesus himself, I investigated accounts where the same message is illustrated with two examples: one of a woman, another of a man. Scholarly research at the time, if these pairings were mentioned at all, described these couplings merely as rhetorical devices used to give emphasis through repetition to an important message. For instance, one such gender pairing occurs in Luke's gospel when Jesus rebukes the Pharisees for their teaching about the Sabbath. Jesus accuses the Pharisees of being willing to rescue a work animal that has fallen into a well on the Sabbath, but unwilling to heal a sick man from dropsy, or cure a crippled woman. Another such gender pairing is in Jesus' teaching about the immediate coming of the kingdom and its surprise nature. Jesus, in describing what it will be like, says: "I tell you, in that night there will be two *men* in one bed; one will be taken and other left, there will be two *women* grinding together; one will be taken and the other left" (Luke 17: 34–36).

In reflecting on these gender pairings in the New Testament, I asked myself what other importance they might have. Since the parables of Jesus have from the beginning been oriented toward teaching and helping church members to grow in their Christian discipline, in looking for clues I turned to my own experience as a preacher and teacher. I surmised that the need for these gender pairings could have emerged from a need to appeal to influential constituencies of women as well as to men in the nascent congregations. Of further importance is the fact that these teachings directed to women were unmediated; they did not go first through the men.

Similar rhetorical methods are used today in teaching, preaching, and writing; good communication depends on knowing and speaking forthrightly to the experiences of identified groups and interests. Further, because there continues to be growing evidence from both Biblical and extra-Biblical sources that both women and men were leaders of the primitive church and members of the adult catechumenate, I was able to piece together that these rhetorical examples were important insights into the gender-inclusive nature of the nascent church. Partners in watchfulness, women and men were equally counted on; neither was exempt. In addition, in these gender pairings there is no weighing of men's experience as more important than women's. There is no hint of partiality. The implication in each case is that when the events of the Kingdom come issuing forth, women and men will be equally summoned and equally affected. In light of the demands of the Kingdom, there is no discrimination on the basis of gender, and implicit in the preparation for that time is the demand for practicing that discipline and quality of shared life right now.

Other findings not commented on in this chapter include the prominent roles of women in the Book of Acts, the significance of the women followers of Jesus, and distinct new communities of women such as the widows. On the basis of this research, I was able to give evidence to the following: (1) women were an essential part of the earliest Christian communities and were present in significant enough numbers not to be overlooked in the preaching and teaching; (2) women and men worked side by side as partners in all known aspects of the earliest ministries; and (3) the often quoted passages used by patriarchal authority to justify women's subordination are text-specific and do not accurately reflect the levels of equality of women and men already recognized in the founding and missionary work of the nascent church.

The obvious question posed by the uncovering of these texts, as well as others not mentioned here, is that: If women and men had such partnership roles at the end of the first century, what then is required of women and men in ministerial roles at the end of the twentieth century, including the ordained officers that, as known today, were not even mentioned in the New Testament? The task of uncovering the lost women in the Bible goes hand in hand with not allowing our stories, our present experience in the church, to be passed over and lost to future generations.

WOMEN'S EXPERIENCE TODAY AND AUTHORITATIVE TEXTS

The women's movement in the 1970s extended the question of women's relationships to and interpretations of authoritative texts by adding the question of women's experience. Since women have been left out of the history of interpretation, and since interpretation has reflected men's experience throughout Christian history, what are the implications of introducing women's experience as a key component in the interpretive role? I remember our group Bible Study at the 1974 World Council of Churches Berlin Conference on "Sexism in the 70's." After having shared deeply our experiences as women in the church, we had an explosive conflict over the story of Jesus with Mary and Martha. On the one side, some women in our group were eager to identify with Mary, who sat at the feet of the rabbi Jesus, and under his tutelege; Mary was learning the meaning of scripture, and in fact, through her mentor, was also learning to be an authoritative interpreter. The women in our group who felt supported by this new view of Mary tended to have advanced theological training; some of them were teaching theology and preaching regularly. They found in this model of Mary a liberating Biblical model for the challenge of their new callings. Others, those women whose roles at the moment were mainly that of homemakers, were anxious that Martha's role was being diminished. They felt that Martha, who had taken care of Jesus' meal and provided for his comfort, was being overlooked and in so doing, they felt that they, too, were being overlooked; their roles and contributions were being devalued.

What was happening in our group was that, in bringing our own experiences to the texts, we were finding that both the authoritative new roles of women as interpreters and the older traditional roles of women's lives, as interpreted by patriarchy, were being claimed. Women found ways to be authentic in both situations. The bottom line was that both groups of women brought to the text their experiences and their own well-formed and/or changing identities. What became clear is that there was an unresolved conflict, first among the women, and, second, within the text itself between women's emerging new roles of headship and women's long-standing roles of subordinated, ascribed status.

In the text it is Jesus who resolves the conflict with the words that Mary has "chosen the good portion which shall not be taken away from her" (Luke 10:42), yet in the development of the patriarchal church over the centuries, these words did not resonate a new role for women until women themselves brought their experience to the text and discovered therein their predecessor. Prior to this the assigned roles for women were generally those of silence and servitude to patriarchy. Male authority in the church has claimed itself as the authoritative teacher, yet here, right within the text, women discovered a clear case where a woman was taught authoritatively by Jesus himself. As women today decide to move out of patriarchy, many choose the option to follow in Mary's tradition. If this tradition were unimportant, it would have been dropped from the Gospel in its winnowing process, but it has endured. Long buried, its meaning has emerged to bear a new message, as women's experience today finds validity in Mary's choice.

The conflicts between women over authoritative texts did not end in Berlin. By the time we organized the 1980 Amsterdam consultation on the Community of Women and Men in the Church on the very subject of "Women's Experience and the Authority of Scriptures,'' there was another level of disagreement based on women's experience. This time the tension was global, between women from the North and women from the South. Western European and North American delegates argued that the primary authority is not the Bible, but women's experience: the authority of ourselves as subjects, as major actors in scripture, not just as passive objects with assigned roles. Women from the South, however, from Latin America, Asia, and Africa, saw this position as a threat to the authority of scripture. They argued that, although the Bible creates problems for them as women, they would not let go of the authority of scripture because scripture also serves them as a significant transcultural critique of sexism. They argued that scripture, with reinterpretation, offers more potential for renewal, for the liberation of women's identity and self-esteem, than they can find in many of their existing cultures. At the same time, others argued that though the missionary movement was in a way a step back for women, it was also, through educating women, a step forward toward women's emancipation. They acknowledged that the Bible carried for them a double message: on the one hand that women were subordinate, and on the other, that in Christ barriers of gender, class, race, and religion were overcome. They felt they could handle the first message as long as the second one was there for them as well, offering tension and critique.

This being the case, women who were from cultures that had received Christianity through the nineteenth-century missionary movement were arguing for maintaining the authority of the texts. The importance of this was poignantly underlined for us at our meeting by the fact that on our opening day we received the tragic news of the murder of El Salvador of the three Maryknoll Sisters and one lay woman worker. Their discipleship and martyrdom while struggling with the church of the poor, a movement of transformation through the use of the power of authoritative texts, underlined for all of us both the importance of authoritative texts as well as the vulnerability in living them out under the hostile shadow of ruthless, patriarchal military systems wherein nothing is sacred.

There was yet another conflict in Amsterdam between those women who thought that the canon of scripture should be open to change and those who opposed it. Those arguing for it felt that new texts that are more positive expressions of women's experience needed to be added, and those texts negative to women ought to be omitted. They argued that as the tradition of the church is changing, due to the new experiences of women, so the authoritative texts should also be reconsidered. This same argument has been made for the treatment of anti-Semitic texts, yet even with their misuse as justification for the Holocaust of the Jewish people, they still remain, as does their potential for misuse. The meeting was sympathetic to the intention of this proposal, to delete some texts and add others, but to open up the issue of the reconsideration of the canon was further than the majority was ready to go at that moment.

The 1970s brought about a shift in the consciousness of women from women being seen as objects of history, our reality defined by patriarchy, to women being subjects of history, defining our reality, energized from our own centers.

With this shift, we are now encountering authoritative texts against the backdrop of our own experiences and claims.

MAKING INVISIBLE WOMEN VISIBLE

A further development for women who wanted to hold the Bible as authoritative was to uncover the women's story, the "herstory" (women's history) in texts that had for centuries been written, edited, translated, interpreted, and transmitted by patriarchy. Since so little about women's lives and work is actually documented, to do this requires a leap of the imagination; it requires a knowledge of and sense for social history; it requires an archaeologist's curiosity for unearthing how people might have behaved and what they might have said if given a voice. For instance, a sermon I preached in the early 1970s was about the parable of the Prodigal Son (Luke 15:11ff.). The story, as written, revolves around three men. It is about a father with two sons, an older son who stays at home and is faithful to his father, and a younger son who goes out to seek his fortune in the world. Many years later, the younger son finds himself destitute and homeless, eating the food given to pigs. Assessing his situation, he decides to swallow his pride and return home, thinking that life as the lowest laborer working for his father would be better than pig's food. The news of his return is a source of overwhelming joy for the old father and upon hearing it, he orders a great feast to welcome him back. However, the celebration is marred by the older son, who is not at all pleased, but is envious of the special attention given to his wayward brother. There is no mention in this text of a mother.

Assuming that there was a mother, I preached my sermon about her. I made her visible; I brought her out of the silence into the center of the text, and I asked some questions about her and what her role might have been in this conflict and how it might have come out differently if the mother had been included. Some people, men and women in the congregation, were offended that I had "added to the scripture" something that wasn't there. I agreed with them that she was not written into the text, but I argued that her omission was to be expected because women were not normally included in authoritative texts. The mother is more likely to have been alluded to if she had been dead; then the old father might have been called a widower, which he is not. It is a good guess that she was there, for on the basis of biological evidence alone there were two sons who must have had a mother who birthed them into life. It's true that she might have died, but since the text is silent about this, we can as well infer that she is still living at the time the story takes place.

Since the story of the Prodigal Son appears only in one of the four canonical Gospels, there is no cross-textual reference. However, there is another story where the mother is mentioned in one version of it and not in another. It is a story about James and John, the sons of Zebedee; two accounts exist, one in Matthew, the other in Mark. In Matthew's telling of the story the mother plays a major role, while in Mark's rendering of the same event the mother is not even mentioned. In one story the mother is the major actor; in the other she is invisible. This cross-textual comparison, at the very least, leaves open the question of the presence of the mother in the Prodigal Son story. Over time, in the oral telling of the story, she may well have been edited out, as is the mother of the sons of Zebedee in Mark.

Yet another step has been taken with this text by setting it within a cross-cultural context. Some cultures could not imagine this story without a mother in it. In many cultures of Asia and Africa, she would be present as a figure of authority, probably playing a reconciling role between the two brothers and acting as a bridge between the father and the two sons; a sister, mother-in-law, and some aunts might be in the story as well. I saw a cross-cultural dramatization of this text at the World Council of Churches Assembly in Nairobi in 1975. The story of the Prodigal Son was portrayed in an African and in an Asian setting. In each drama the mother was present, and in the African story, where the context is a matrilineal family system, the wife's brother was also added. In our own Western patriarchal societies, we are inexperienced at looking for the anthropological infrastructure of Biblical stories; for us, the patriarchal story joins with our cultural experience. Because the Prodigal Son story is told in sparse telegraphic style, we tend to fill in the blanks, mirroring our own family structure.

In the case of my sermon, some parishioners argued that there could not have been a woman present; at the most, they said, a mother might have been present, in the background preparing the feast or a room for her son to make him feel more comfortable. To talk about her, they claimed, was to add to the text, not just to enhance, enrich, and expand its meaning. It's hard for those of us who have grown up in the West, where Christianity and our culture have developed conjointly, to have the cultural imagination to make the leap of difference that exists between our own Christian past and present practice. This is not the case, however, for those Africans and Asians who have not grown up in cultures where Christianity has been such a dominant influence for two millennia. For them, other patterns of family and gender relationships come into play; their cultural backdrop for the story of the Prodigal Son contributes many ways for mothers, daughters, and other women relatives to enter the picture.

When as women interpreters we go on the journey to unearth the invisible women behind patriarchy, we put our women's selves in the center of the text. In so doing we let these silent voices speak, and they give words to our herstory. Thus, we learn that we are not in a strange place; women before us have been there as apostles, teachers, interpreters, mothers, sisters, partners. To make invisible women visible, it is important to find and claim our own voice and then place ourselves as subjects (actors) in the text. It is a process of knowing who we are and where we have been. The text is about us, and the authority is ours to resurrect the women buried in it, to give them the visibility and vocation that was theirs and can be there for others. By using the tools of our own Biblical, cultural, and social imagination, our foremothers and foresisters in faith can be called into presence.

THE MOTHER-NESS OF GOD

Since the 1970s some writers have continued to insist that a patriarchal religion requires a patriarchal God. On the one hand, some feminist writers have argued this and consequently left Christianity as an untenable faith for them. And on the other hand, some male New Testament scholars have argued that for Christians, it is essential to refer to God as father because Jesus himself referred to God as father.

This is a difficult problem when encountering authoritative texts. In the gospel of John alone, there are over fifty references to God as father; it is the most frequently used metaphor for God in the New Testament. In trying to confront this issue the most important point to establish at the outset is that all language for God is human metaphor. Jesus used the language that best described God for him; we search for the language that best describes God for us. How much, or how little God changes we do not know, but we do know that language changes constantly. For Jesus, to use the word father was a reference to the most intimate and loving relationship he, or his followers, could imagine. For example, in the Lord's Prayer, the address Jesus chose was *abba*, closer to our word for "Daddy," one of the first words infants learn as they are coming into speech. A father, as Jesus used the word, was ever present, wise, loving, forgiving, taken for granted as a presence there for them. Today, we might use the term father for such a special relationship, but we might also use the word mother, or we might speak of a mothering father. Contrarily, however, in today's materialistic and technocratic society, the word father can also connote absence and distance from the family. Regardless of the women's movement, it is still generally, though not always, the mothers who maintain the connectedness in families and who hold together the parenting responsibilities no matter what the circumstances.

Mothers are hardly perfect, but in the 1980s I learned a lot a about God as mother while working with poor black women in Philadelphia. Among the women I worked with, most were heads of households of three or four generations. They were the chief providers, the ones who related, the ones who made the connections, the ones who forgave and forgave again. The ones who in the midst of violence and chaos, drugs and alcohol, tried to maintain peace, support, and some kind of orderliness. Because of knowing them, now, when I read the words God the Father in the text, I read these women; I see them and hear their stories; I remember their love and recall their struggles and their pain to the point of brokenness on behalf of their families. Patriarchy as a religious system has overlooked the mother-ness of God; in life and in sacred text, this is now being redressed. Women and men are recovering God's authority as Her and claiming Her, as did Jesus himself when he described God like a mother hen whose life is for the sake of her young (Matt. 23:37, Luke 13:34).

CHRISTIAN AUTHORITATIVE TEXTS AND ANTI-JUDAISM

In early Christian feminist writings, there was a tendency to argue that Jesus was a liberator of women by negatively contrasting Jesus' relationships with women to Jewish texts (probably not of the same time period, or context) that illustrated women's subordination, or silence. This is the kind of tactic that politicians sometimes use; they try to make themselves look better by running down, bad-mouthing, their opponents. In the 1970s and 1980s Jewish feminists began pointing this out to Christian feminists, but still today books are published that use this line of argument. In my own teaching of religious feminism, cross-culturally and across the religions, I have seen how some religious writers have argued that in the beginning their religious tradition argued for equality, but then it was corrupted by the patriarchal influence of another religious tradition. This old trick of affirming what is "good" in one's own tradition by blaming what is "bad" in another can sometimes allow us to escape responsibility for both the good and the bad within our own faith communities and sacred texts.

As a Christian feminist struggling with the authoritative texts of my own tradition, I know that I need to take responsibility for the whole text, good and bad, liberating and oppressive. The liberating texts give spirit and motivation for transformation in the present; the oppressive texts are part of the challenging, sobering, unfinished agenda. We cannot "blame the Jews" for what is clearly part of what we have inherited. What we do have is the freedom within our inheritance to select what is important, to hold on to what is helpful to our neighbor, and to let go of what is not.

RITUAL: WOMEN AS SUBJECTS EMBRACING
AUTHORITATIVE TEXTS

One more point about women and authoritative texts. Texts are treated ritually with different sorts of reverence and sacredness in various religions and cultures. Sometimes sacred texts are perfumed, or dipped in precious oil, as signs of love and respect. I have long been fascinated by a Hasidic Jewish practice of embracing the sacred Torah and dancing with her. Traditionally, the dancers are Rabbis (male); the Torah is the inspired *Shekinah* (female spirit). I have a feeling that as women become more deeply the subjects of sacred texts and as we take on the roles of authoritative interpreters (the work of the female muse *hermeneutikos*) we will grow more in touch with the She-ness of God in our midst, claiming her in the text and dancing with her as in a lover's embrace. What I have said about sacred texts and ritual is important for our understanding of authoritative texts, for they are much more than the focus of our intellectual and rational functions; they are about our whole selves, our connectedness with God, with our own experience, and with each other. This implies that what I have written here in prose must ultimately be heard and understood in the language of poetry, art, and dance. These are God-given gestures that transcend rational arguments, and in doing so they can lead us into the intimacies of God's mysterious ways with us, on our behalf and for others.

DIALOGUE UNDERWAY

My hope in writing this chapter is that it can, in a personal way, contribute to an ongoing interfaith dialogue that begins and ends as a personal relationship. This case study of my own experience, yet set within a larger movement, shows how women are struggling with authoritative texts today in a faith tradition shaped by centuries of patriarchy. Slowly, and piece by piece, we are critiquing the tradition and claiming our own, recovering and discovering the voices of our own experience speaking through the ancient texts of faith. Among Christians, a worldwide dialogue is underway between the patriarchal tradition that surrounds sacred texts that is disempowering for women, and the beginning of a tradition of herstory that informs and empowers women as women and opens the way for new partnerships of women and men who will soon be entering a new century of Christian experience.

NOTE

1. Elizabeth Cady Stanton and the Revising Committee, *The Woman's Bible* (New York: European Publishing Company, 1895; Seattle: Coalition Task Force on Women and Religion, 1974), 196.

5

The Issue of Woman-Man Equality in the Islamic Tradition

RIFFAT HASSAN

BACKGROUND OF MY WORK IN THE AREA OF THEOLOGY OF WOMAN IN ISLAM

Experientially I have always known what it means to be a Muslim woman since I was born female in a Saiyyad[1] Muslim family living in Lahore, a historic Muslim city in Pakistan, a country created in the name of Islam. However, it was not until the fall of 1974 that I began my career as a "feminist" theologian—almost by accident and rather reluctantly. I was, at that time, faculty adviser to the Muslim Students' Association (MSA) chapter at Oklahoma State University in Stillwater, Oklahoma. This "honor" had been conferred upon me solely by virtue of the fact that each student association was required to have a faculty adviser, and I happened to be the only Muslim faculty member on campus that year. The office bearers of the MSA chapter at Stillwater had established the tradition of having an annual seminar at which one of the principal addresses was given by the faculty adviser. In keeping with tradition I was asked—albeit not with overwhelming enthusiasm—if I would read a paper on women in Islam at the seminar that was to be held later that year. I was aware of the fact that, in general, faculty advisers were not assigned specific subjects. I was asked to speak about women in Islam at the seminar—in which, incidentally, Muslim women were not going to participate—because in the opinion of most of the chapter members it would have been totally inappropriate to expect a Muslim woman, even one who taught them Islamic Studies, to be competent to speak on any other subject pertaining to Islam. I resented what the assigning of a subject meant. Furthermore, I was not much interested in the subject of women in Islam until that time. Nevertheless, I accepted the invitation for two reasons. First, I knew that being invited to address an all-male, largely Arab Muslim group that prided itself on its patriarchalism, was itself a breakthrough. Second, I was so tired of hearing Muslim men pontificate upon the position, status, or role of women in Islam, while it was totally inconceivable that any woman could presume to speak about the position, status, or role of men in Islam. I thought that it might be worthwhile for a Muslim woman to present her viewpoint on a subject whose immense popularity with Muslim men, scholars and non-scholars alike, could easily be gauged by the ever-increasing number of books, booklets, brochures, and articles they published on it. Having accepted the invitation I began my research more out of a sense of duty (knowing that willing the end involves willing the means to the end) than out of any deep awareness that I had set out on perhaps the most important journey of my life.

I do not know exactly at what time my "academic" study of women in Islam became a passionate quest for truth and justice on behalf of Muslim women— perhaps it was when I realized the impact on my own life of the so-called Islamic ideas and attitudes regarding women. What began as a scholarly exercise became simultaneously an Odyssean venture in self-understanding. But "enlightenment" does not always lead to "endless bliss." The more I saw the justice and compassion of God reflected in the Qur'anic teachings regarding women, the more anguished and angry I became, seeing the injustice and inhumanity to which Muslim women, in general, are subjected in actual life. I began to feel strongly that it was my duty—as a part of the microscopic minority of educated Muslim women—to do as much consciousness-raising regarding the situation of Muslim women as I could. The journey that began in Stillwater has been an arduous one. It has taken me far and wide in pursuit of my quest. When I remember the stormy seas and rocky roads I have traversed, it seems like the journey has been a long one. But when I think of my sisters who, despite being the largest "minority" in the world—more than half of the one-billion-strong Muslim *ummah*[2]—remain for the most part nameless, faceless, and voiceless, I know that there is no end to the journey in sight.

Despite the fact that women such as Khadijah and 'A'ishah (wives of the Prophet Muhammad) and Rabi'a al-Basri (the outstanding woman Sufi) figure significantly in early Islam, the Islamic tradition has, by and large, remained rigidly patriarchal until the present time, prohibiting the growth of scholarship among women particularly in the realm of religious thought. This means that the sources on which the Islamic tradition is mainly based, namely, the Qur'an, the Sunnah,[3] the Hadith[4] literature, and Fiqh,[5] have been interpreted only by Muslim men who have arrogated to themselves the task of defining the onto-logical, theological, sociological, and eschatological status of Muslim women. It is hardly surprising that until now the majority of Muslim women have accepted this situation passively, almost unaware of the extent to which their human (also Islamic, in an ideal sense) rights have been violated by their male-dominated and male-centered societies, which have continued to assert, glibly and tirelessly, that Islam has given women more rights than any other religious tradition. Kept for centuries in physical, mental, and emotional bondage, and deprived of the opportunity to actualize their human potential, even the exercise of analyzing their personal experiences as Muslim women is, perhaps, overwhelming for these women. (Here it needs to be mentioned that while the rate of literacy is low in many Muslim countries, the rate of literacy of Muslim women, especially those who live in rural areas, where most of the population lives, is among the lowest in the world.)

In recent times, largely due to the pressure of anti-women laws that are being promulgated under the cover of "Islamization" in some parts of the Muslim world, women with some degree of education and awareness are beginning to realize that religion is being used as an instrument of oppression rather than as a means of liberation. To understand the strong impetus to "Islamize" Muslim societies, especially with regard to women-related norms and values, it is necessary to know that of all the challenges confronting the Muslim world, perhaps the greatest is that of modernity. The caretakers of Muslim traditionalism are aware of the fact that viability in the modern technological age requires the adoption of the scientific or rational outlook that inevitably brings about major changes in modes of thinking and behavior. Women, both educated and uneducated, who are participating in the national work force and contributing toward national development, think and behave differently from women who have no sense of their individual identity or autonomy as active agents in a history-making process and regard themselves merely as instruments designed to minister to and reinforce a patriarchal system that they believe to be divinely instituted. Not too long ago, many women in Pakistan were jolted out of their "dogmatic slumber" by the enactment of laws (such as those pertaining to women's rape or women's testimony in financial and other matters) and by "threatened" legislation (such as proposals pertaining to "blood-money" for women's murder) that aimed to reduce them systematically, virtually mathematically, to less than men. It was not long before they realized that forces of religious conservatism were determined to cut women down to one-half or less of men and that this attitude stemmed from a deep-rooted desire to keep women "in their place," which means secondary, subordinate, and inferior to men.

In the face of both military dictatorship and religious autocracy, valiant efforts have been made by women's groups in Pakistan to protest against the instituting of manifestly anti-women laws and to highlight cases of gross injustice and brutality toward women. However, it is still not clearly and fully understood, even by many women activists in Pakistan and other Muslim countries, that the negative ideas and attitudes pertaining to women that prevail in Muslim societies, are in general rooted in theology—and that unless, or until, the theological foundations of the misogynistic and androcentric tendencies in the Islamic tradition are demolished, Muslim women will continue to be brutalized and discriminated against, despite improvements in statistics such as those on female education, employment, and social and political rights. No matter how many sociopolitical rights are granted to women, as long as they are conditioned to accept the myths used by theologians or religious hierarchs to shackle their bodies, hearts, minds, and souls, they will never become fully developed or whole human beings, free of fear and guilt, able to stand equal to men in the sight of God. In my judgment, the importance of developing what the West calls "feminist theology" in the context of Islam is paramount today with a view to liberating not only Muslim women but also Muslim men from unjust structures and laws that make a peer relationship between men and women impossible. It is good to know that in the last hundred years there have been at least two significant Muslim men scholars and activists—Qasim Amin from Egypt and Mumtaz 'Ali from India—who have been staunch advocates of women's rights, though knowing this hardly lessens the pain of also knowing that even in this age that is characterized by the explosion of knowledge, all but a handful of Muslim women lack any knowledge of Islamic theology. It is profoundly discouraging to contemplate how few Muslim women there are in the world today who possess the competence, even if they have the courage and commitment, to engage in a scholarly study of Islam's primary sources in order to participate in the theological discussions on women-related issues that are taking place in much of the contemporary Muslim world.

Returning to the time when I began my career as a "feminist" theologian, I remember how stricken I felt when I first began to see the glaring discrepancy between Islamic ideals and Muslim practice insofar as women are concerned. Convinced of the importance of underscoring this discrepancy and believing that most Muslim women (even those who were all too well aware of the reality of their own life-situation) were largely unaware of it, I set out to articulate what I considered to be the normative Islamic view of women. This view is rooted largely in what all Muslims accept as *the* primary source, or highest authority, in Islam—the Qur'an, which Muslims believe to be the Word of Allah conveyed through the agency of the angel Gabriel to the Prophet Muhammad, who transmitted it without change or error to those who heard him.

In 1979, while I participated in an ongoing "trialogue" of Jewish, Christian, and Muslim scholars (under the sponsorship of the Kennedy Institute of Ethics in Washington, D.C.) who were exploring women-related issues in the three "Abrahamic" faith-traditions, I wrote the draft of a monograph entitled *Women in the Qur'an*. In this study I gave a detailed exposition of those passages of the Qur'an that related to women in various contexts (e.g., women vis-à-vis God; women in the context of human creation and the story of the "Fall"; women as daughters, wives, and mothers; women in the context of marriage, divorce, inheritance, segregation, veiling, witnessing to contracts, economic rights, afterlife, etc.). In particular, I focused attention upon those passages that were regarded as definitive in the context of woman-man relationships and upon which the alleged superiority of men to women largely rested. It was this study that I hoped to finalize when in the spring of 1983 I went to Pakistan and spent almost two years there, doing research but also watching, with increasing anxiety, the enactment of anti-women laws in the name of Islam and the deluge of anti-women actions and literature that swept across the country in the wake of the "Islamization" of Pakistani society and its legal system.

As I reflected upon the scene I witnessed, and asked myself how it was possible for laws that were archaic if not absurd to be implemented in a society that professed a passionate commitment to modernity, the importance of something that I had always known dawned on me with stunning clarity. Pakistani society (or any other Muslim society for that matter) could enact or accept laws that specified that women were less than men in fundamental ways because Muslims, in general, consider it a self-evident truth that women are not equal to men. Anyone who states that in the present-day world it is accepted in many religious as well as secular communities that men and women are equal, or that evidence can be found in the Qur'an and the Islamic tradition for affirming man-woman equality, is likely to be confronted, immediately and with force, by a mass of what is described as "irrefutable evidence" taken from the Qur'an, Hadith, and Sunnah to "prove" that men are "above" women. Among the arguments used to overwhelm any proponent of man-woman equality, the following are perhaps the most popular: according to the Qur'an, men are *qawwamun* (generally trans- lated as "rulers," or "managers") in relation to women;[6] according to the Qur'an, a man's share in inheritance is twice that of a woman;[7] according to the Qur'an, the witness of one man is equal to that of two women;[8] according to the Prophet, women are deficient both in prayer (due to menstruation) and in intellect (due to their witness counting for less than a man's).[9]

Since I was (in all probability) the only Muslim woman in the country who was attempting to interpret the Qur'an systematically from a nonpatriarchal perspective, I was approached numerous times by women leaders (including the members of the Pakistan Commission on the Status of Women, before whom I gave my testimony in May 1984) to state what my findings were and if they could be used to improve the situation of women in Pakistani society. I was urged by those spirited women who were mobilizing and leading women's pro- tests in the streets to help them refute the arguments that were being used to make them less than fully human on a case-by-case or point-by-point basis. I must admit that I was tempted to join the foray in support of my beleaguered sisters who were being deprived of their human rights in the name of Islam. But I knew through my long and continuing struggle with the forces of Muslim traditionalism (which were now being gravely threatened by what they described as "the onslaught of Westernization under the guise of modernization") that the arguments that were being broadcast to "keep women in their place" of sub- ordination and submissiveness were only the front line of attack. Behind and below these arguments were others, and no sooner would one line of attack be eliminated than another one would be set up in its place. What had to be done, first and foremost, in my opinion, was to examine the theological ground in which all the anti-women arguments were rooted to see if, indeed, a case could be made for asserting that from the point of view of normative Islam, men and women were *essentially* equal, despite biological and other differences.

My inquiry into the theological roots of the problem of man-woman inequality in the Islamic tradition led to the expansion of my field of study in at least two significant areas. First, realizing the profound impact upon Muslim consciousness of Hadith literature, particularly the two collections *Sahih al-Bukhari* and *Sahih Muslim* (collectively known as the *Sahihan,* which the Sunni Muslims regard as the most authoritative books in Islam next to the Qur'an), I examined with care the women-related ahadith in these collections. Second, I studied several important writings by Jewish and Christian feminist theologians who were attempting to trace the theological origins of the antifeminist ideas and attitudes found in their respective traditions.

As a result of my study and deliberation I came to perceive that not only in the Islamic, but also in the Jewish and Christian traditions, there are three theological assumptions on which the superstructure of men's alleged superiority to women (which implies the inequality of women and man) has been erected. These three assumptions are: (1) that God's primary creation is man, not woman, since woman is believed to have been created from man's rib, hence is derivative and secondary ontologically; (2) that woman, not man, was the primary agent of what is customarily described as the "Fall," or man's expulsion from the Garden of Eden, hence all "daughters of Eve" are to be regarded with hatred, suspicion, and contempt; and (3) that woman was created not only *from* man but also *for* man, which makes her existence merely instrumental and not of fundamental importance. The three theological questions to which the above assumptions may appropriately be regarded as answers, are: How was woman created? Was woman responsible for the "Fall" of man? Why was woman created?

Given the profound significance—both theoretical and practical—of these three questions in the history of ideas and attitudes pertaining to women in the Islamic (as well as the Jewish and Christian) tradition, I hope to write a full-scale book in response to each. However, at this time I would like to focus on the first question, which deals with the issue of woman's creation. I consider this issue to be more basic and important, philosophically and theologically, than any other in the context of woman-man equality, because if man and woman have been created equal by Allah who is the ultimate arbiter of value, then they cannot become unequal, essentially, at a subsequent time. On the other hand, if man and woman have been created unequal by Allah, then they cannot become equal, essentially, at a subsequent time.

MADE FROM ADAM'S RIB? THE ISSUE OF WOMAN'S CREATION

The ordinary Muslim believes, as seriously as the ordinary Jew or Christian, that Adam was God's primary creation and that Eve was made from Adam's rib. If confronted with the fact that this firmly entrenched belief is derived mainly from the Bible and is not only extra-Qur'anic but also in contradiction to the Qur'an, this Muslim is almost certain to be shocked. The rather curious and tragic truth is that even Western-educated Muslims seldom have any notion of the extent to which the Muslim psyche bears the imprint of the collective body of Jewish and Christian ideas and attitudes pertaining to women.

The Biblical account of the creation of the first human pair consists of two different sources, the Yahwist and the Priestly, from which arise two different traditions, subject of much Jewish and Christian scholarly controversy. There are four references to woman's creation in Genesis: (1) Gen. 1:26–27, 5th century B.C.E., Priestly tradition; (2) Gen. 2:7, 10th century B.C.E., Yahwist tradition; (3) Gen. 2:18–24, 10th century B.C.E., Yahwist tradition; (4) Gen. 5:1–2, 5th century B.C.E., Priestly tradition. A study of these texts shows that the Hebrew term "Adam" (literally, "of the soil," from *adamah:* "the soil") functions mostly as a generic term for humanity. Pointing out that the correct translation of this term is "the human," Leonard Swidler observes: "It is a mistake to translate it ["ha Adam"] in Genesis 1 to 2:22 either as man in the male sense or as a proper name, Adam (until Genesis 4:25 the definite article "ha" is almost always used with "Adam," precluding the possibility of its being a proper name: in 4:25 it becomes a proper name, "Adam" without the "ha"). Moreover, it is clearly a collective noun in Genesis 1 to 2:22, as can be seen in the plural 'let *them* be masters' (Genesis 1:26)."[10] Of the four texts referring to creation, undoubtedly the most influential has been Genesis 2:18–24, which states that woman (*ishshah*) was taken from man (*ish*). From this text it has generally been inferred that: (1) Adam was God's primary creation from whom Eve, a secondary creation, was derived, hence Eve is inferior and subordinate to Adam; and (2) Eve was created simply and solely to be the helpmate of Adam.

While in Genesis specific reference is made to the creation of Adam and Eve, there is no corresponding reference in the Qur'an. In fact, there is no mention of Eve (*Hawwa'*) at all in the Qur'an. The term *Adam* occurs twenty-five times in the Qur'an, but there is only one verse (Surah 3: *Al-'Imran*:59) that refers to the creation of Adam: "Certainly with Allah the likeness of 'Isa [Jesus] is as the likeness of Adam. Allah created him from the earth, then said to him, "Be," and he was." Here it needs to be mentioned that the term "Adam" is not an Arabic term but a Hebrew term, and the description of Adam as a creature of earth in the verse cited above is no more than an explication of the meaning of the term. There are three other verses (Surah 3: *Al-'Imran*:35; Surah 19: *Maryam*:58; Surah 5: *Al-Ma'idah*:30) in which the term "Adam" is used as a proper name for an individual who was probably a prophet. Since Arabic has no capital letters, it is often not possible to tell whether a term is used as a proper name or as a common noun without looking at the context in which it occurs. However, there is no categorical statement in the Qur'an to the effect that Adam was the first human being created by Allah. The term is used most frequently in reference to more than one or two human beings. That the term "Adam" functions as a collective noun and stands for humankind is substantiated by an analysis of several verses in which this term occurs. It is also corroborated by the fact that all human beings are assimilatively addressed as "Children of Adam" (*Bani*

Adam) in Surah 7: *Al-'Araf*:26, 27, 31, 35, 172, Surah 17: *Bani Isra'il*:70, and Surah 36: *Ya-Sin*:60, and also by the fact that the Qur'an sometimes replaces the term "Adam" by *al-insan* or *bashar,* which are both generic terms for humanity. Here it is important to note that though the term "Adam" mostly does not refer to a particular human being, it does refer to human beings in a particular way. As pointed out by Muhammad Iqbal:

Indeed, in the verses which deal with the origin of man as a living being, the Qur'an uses the word "Bashar" or "Insan," not "Adam," which it reserves for man in his capacity of God's vicegerent on earth. The purpose of the Qur'an is further secured by the omission of proper names mentioned in the Biblical narration—Adam and Eve. The word "Adam" is retained and used more as a concept than as the name of a concrete human individual. This use of the word is not without authority in the Qur'an itself.[11]

It is noteworthy that the Qur'an uses the terms *bashar, al-insan,* and *an-nas* while describing the process of the physical creation of human beings. It uses the term "Adam" more selectively to refer to human beings only when they become representative of a self-conscious, knowledgeable, and morally autonomous humanity.

Instead of "Adam and *Hawwa',*" the Qur'an speaks of "Adam and *zauj*" in Surah 2: *Al-Baqarah*:35, Surah 7: *Al-'Araf*:19, and Surah 20: *Ta-Ha*:117. Muslims, almost without exception, assume that "Adam" was the first human being created by Allah and that he was a man. If "Adam" was a man, it follows that "Adam's *zauj*" would be a woman. Hence the *zauj* mentioned in the Qur'an becomes equated with *Hawwa'.* Neither the initial assumption nor the inferences drawn from it are, however, supported in a clear or conclusive way by the Qur'anic text. The Qur'an states neither that Adam was the first human being nor that he was a man. The term "Adam" is a masculine noun, but linguistic gender is not sex. If "Adam" is not necessarily a man, then "Adam's *zauj*" is not necessarily a woman. In fact, the term *zauj* is also a masculine noun and, unlike the term "Adam," has a feminine counterpart, *zaujatun.* (Here, it may be noted that the most accurate English equivalent of *zauj* is not "wife" or "husband," or even "spouse," but the term "mate." The Qur'an uses the term *zauj* with reference not only to human beings but to every kind of creation, including animals, plants, and fruits.) However, neither the term *zaujatun* nor the plural form *zaujātun* is used anywhere in the Qur'an, which consistently uses the masculine forms *zauj* and *azwaj.* It has been pointed out by the authoritative Arabic lexicon *Taj al-'Arus* that only the people of Al-Hijaz (Hejaz) used the term *zauj* in reference to women, and elsewhere the usage was *zaujatun.* Also, Arabic legal terminology always uses the term *zaujātun* in reference to women. Why, then, does the Qur'an, which surely was not addressed only to the people of Al-Hijaz, use the term *zauj* and not *zaujatun* if the reference is indeed to woman? In my opinion, the reason why the Qur'an leaves the terms "Adam" and *zauj* deliberately unclear, not only as regards sex but also as regards number, is because its purpose is not to narrate certain events in the life of a man and a woman (i.e., the Adam and Eve of popular imagination), but to refer to some life experiences of all human beings, men and women together.

The Qur'an describes human creation in thirty or so passages that are found in various chapters. Generally speaking, it refers to the creation of humanity (and nature) in two ways: as an evolutionary process whose diverse stages or phases are mentioned sometimes together and sometimes separately, and as an accomplished fact or in its totality. In the passages in which human creation is described "concretely" or "analytically," we find that no mention is made of the separate or distinct creation of either man or woman, as may be seen, for instance, from the following: Surah 15: *Al-Hijr*:26, 28, 29; Surah 16: *An-Nahl*:4; Surah 22: *Al-Hajj*: 5; Surah 23: *Al-Mo'minun*:12–14; Surah 25: *Al-Furqan*:54; Surah 32: *As-Sajdah*:7–9; Surah 36: *Ya-Sin*:77; Surah 38: *Sad*:71–72; Surah 39: *Az-Zumar*:6; Surah 40: *Al-Mo'min*:67; Surah 55: *Ar-Rahman*:3, 4, 14; Surah 71: *Nuh*:14, 17; Surah 76: *Ad-Dahr*:2; Surah 77: *Al-Mursalat*:20–22; Surah 82: *Al-Infitar*:6–8; Surah 86: *At-Tariq*:5–7; Surah 95: *At-Tin*:4; and Surah 96: *Al-'Alaq*:1–2. In some passages (e.g., Surah 49: *Al-Hujurat*:13; Surah 53: *An-Najm*:45; Surah 78: *An-Naba*:8), though reference is made to Allah's creation of human beings as sexually differentiated "mates," no priority or superiority is accorded to either man or woman.

There are, however, some verses in the Qur'an that are understood in such a way that they appear to endorse a version of the *Genesis* 2 story of woman's creation from man. These verses can be grouped into two categories. The most important verses in the first group are: Surah 16: *An-Nahl*:72; Surah 30: *Ar-Rum*:20–21; and Surah 35: *Al-Fatir*:11. Muslim arguments that women were created from and for men are supported as follows: (1) Surah 30: *Ar-Rum*:21 uses the term *ilaihā* to refer to "mates" created from, and for, the original creation. Since *hā* is a feminine attached pronoun, the "mates" it refers to must be female (thus making the original creation male); (2) all three verses cited use *kum* as a form of address. Hence these verses are addressed not to humanity collectively, but only to men, since the term used is a masculine attached pronoun (second person plural). Men are, therefore, the primary creation from and for whom the "mates" were created. Regarding (1), *ilaihā* literally means "in her" and not "in them" and refers not to women (who are not mentioned here) but to *azwaj* (masculine plural used in the Qur'an for both men and women). If the "mates" were clearly designated as women, the term used would be *hunna*, not *hā*. The use of *hā* here is consistent with the Arabic grammatical rule that permits the use of feminine singular terms for a class or collectivity. The fact that the creatures to whom the passage is addressed are referred to as *bashar* further supports the argument that the "mates" created by Allah are not only women (for men), since *bashar* obviously has a bisexual reference. Regarding (2), Arabic usage permits the use of *kum* in reference to men and women together. When women alone are concerned, *kunna* is used. Here it is of interest to note that in his book *Haquq-e-Niswan* (The Rights of Women, 1898), Mumtaz 'Ali pointed out that the Qur'an uses the masculine form of address to prescribe fundamental duties (e.g., salat, zakat, fasting) to Muslim men and women. If masculine terms of address are understood by the entire Muslim *ummah* to apply to both men and women in highly significant contexts, such as the prescription of basic religious duties, then it cannot consistently be argued that these terms apply to men invariably and exclusively.

Regarding the second group of verses that are cited to prove man's ontological priority and superiority to woman, the following are of exceptional importance: Surah 4: *An-Nisa'*:1; Surah 7: *Al-'Araf*:189; and Surah 39: *Az-Zumar*:6. In these verses (as also in Surah 6: *Al-An'am*:98 and Surah 31: *Luqman*:28) reference is made to the creation from one source or being (*nafsin wahidatin*) of all human beings. Muslims, with hardly any exceptions, believe that the one original source or being referred to in these verses is a man named Adam. This belief has led many translators of the Qur'an to obviously incorrect translations of simple Qur'anic passages. For instance, Surah 4: *An-Nisa'*:1, if correctly translated, reads as follows: "O *an-nas* be circumspect in keeping your duty to your Sustainer who created you [plural] from one being [*nafsin wahidatin*] and spread from *her* [*minhā*] *her* mate [*zaujahā*] and spread from these two beings many men and women." However, most translators (e.g., Hashim Amir-'Ali, Muhammad Ali, A. J. Arberry, A. K. Azad, A. M. Daryabadi, N. J. Dawood, S. A. Latif, A. A. Maududi, M. M. Pickthall, George Sale, and M. Y. Zayid) translate the feminine attached pronoun *hā* in *minhā* and *zaujahā* as "his" instead of "her". How is such a mistake possible? Could it be the case that given their preconceptions and psychological orientation, these interpreters of the Qur'an (who all happen to be men) are totally unable to imagine that the first creation could have been other than male? Or are they afraid that a correct translation of *hā* might suggest the idea—even for an instant—that woman, not man, was the prior creation (and therefore superior if priority connotes superiority) and that man was created from woman and not the other way around (which, in a reversal of the Eve from Adam's rib story would give Eve the primacy traditionally accorded to Adam)? Certainly no Qur'anic exegete to date has suggested the possibility that *nafsin wahidatin* might refer to woman rather than man.

Summing up the Qur'anic descriptions of human creation, it needs to be emphasized that the Qur'an evenhandedly used both feminine and masculine terms and imagery to describe the creation of humanity from a single source. That Allah's original creation was undifferentiated humanity and not either man or woman (who appeared simultaneously at a subsequent time) is implicit in a number of Qur'anic passages, in particular Surah 75: *Al-Qiyamah*:36–39, which reads:

Does *al-insān* think that he will be left aimless? Was he not a drop of semen emitted then he became something which clings; Then He [Allah] created and shaped and made of him [*minhū*] two mates [*zaujain*] the male and the female.

If the Qur'an makes no distinction between the creation of man and woman, as it clearly does not, why do Muslims believe that Hawwa' was created from the rib of Adam? Although the Genesis 2 account of woman's creation is accepted by virtually all Muslims, it is difficult to believe that it entered the Islamic tradition directly, for very few Muslims ever read the Bible. It is much more likely that it became a part of Muslim heritage through its assimilation in Hadith literature, which has been, in many ways, the lens through which the Qur'an has been seen since the early centuries of Islam.

Hadith literature, which modernist Muslims tend to regard with a certain skepticism, is surrounded by controversies, centering particularly around the question of the authenticity of individual ahadith as well as the body of the literature as a whole. These controversies have occupied the attention of many Muslim scholars since the time of Ash-Shafi'i (d. A.H. 204/A.D. 809). Fazlur Rahman has pointed out that "a very large portion of the Hadiths were judged to be spurious and forged by classical Muslim scholars themselves," but goes on to add that "if the Hadith as a whole is cast away, the basis for the whole historicity of the Qur'an is removed with one stroke."[12] Noted Islamicists such as Alfred Guillaume,[13] H. A. R. Gibb,[14] and M. G. S. Hodgson[15] have underscored the importance of the Hadith literature, which not only has its own autonomous character in point of law and even of doctrine, but also has an emotive aspect, hard to overstate, relating to the conscious and subconscious thought and feeling of Muslims, both individually and as a group. That the story of Eve's creation from Adam's rib had become part of the Hadith literature is evident from the following Hadith related from Ibn 'Abbās and Ibn Mas'ūd, which is referred to by authoritative commentators on the Qur'an, including Fakhr ud-Din ar-Razi, Isma'il ibn 'Umar Ibn Kathir, and al-Fadl ibn al-Hasan al-Tabarsi:

When God sent Iblis out of the Garden and placed Adam in it, he dwelt in it alone and had no one to socialize with. God sent sleep on him and then He took a rib from his left side and placed flesh in its place and created Hawwa' from it. When he awoke he found a woman seated near his head. He asked her, "Who are you?" She answered, "Woman." He said, "Why were you created?" She said, "That you might find rest in me." The angels said, "What is her name?" and he said, "Hawwa' " They said, "Why was she called Hawwa'?" He said, "Because she was created from a living thing."[16]

Another Hadith, related from Ibn 'Abbas and cited by Ibn Kathir in his *Tafsir*, which also refers to the creation of Hawwa' from Adam's rib, reads as follows:

After Iblis had been chastised and Adam's knowledge had been exhibited, Adam was put to sleep and Hawwa' was created from his left rib. When Adam awoke he saw her and felt affection and love for her since she was made from his flesh and blood. Then Allah gave Hawwa' in wedlock to Adam and told them to live in al-jannah.[17]

Both of the above ahadith clash sharply with the Qur'anic accounts of human creation, while they have an obvious correspondence to Genesis 2:18–33 and

Genesis 3:20. Some changes, however, are to be noted in the story of woman's creation as it is retold in the above ahadith. Both mention "the left rib" as the source of woman. In Arab culture great significance is attached to "right" and "left," the former being associated with everything auspicious and the latter with the opposite. In Genesis, woman is named "Eve" after the Fall, but in the above ahadith she is called Hawwa' from the time of her creation. In Genesis, woman is named Eve because "she is the mother of all who live" (thus a primary source of life), but in the first of the aforementioned ahadith, she is named Hawwa' because "she was created from a living thing" (hence a derivative creature). These variations are not to be ignored. Biblical and other materials are seldom incorporated without alteration into ahadith. The above examples illustrate how in respect of woman, Arab biases were added to the adopted text.

The citing of the above ahadith by significant Muslim exegetes and historians shows the extent to which authoritative works both of Qur'anic exegesis and Islamic history had become colored by the Hadith literature. In course of time, many ahadith became "invisible," the later commentators referring not to them but to the authority of earlier commentators who had cited them, to support their views. This made it very hard to curtail their influence since they became diffused throughout the body of Muslim culture. A typical example of how the Qur'anic account of human creation is distorted by means of inauthentic ahadith (which identify *nafsin wahidatin* from which all human beings, including Hawwa', originated, with Adam the man), even when these ahadith are not mentioned or affirmed directly, is provided by A. A. Maududi, author of a well-known modern commentary on the Qur'an[18] and one of contemporary Islam's most influential scholars. In commenting on Surah *An-Nisa'* 1, Maududi observes:

"He created you of a single soul." At first one human being was created and then from him the human race spread over the earth. . . . We learn from another part of the Qur'an that Adam was that "single soul." *He was the first man from whom the whole of mankind sprang up* and spread over the earth. "And of the same created his mate": we have no definite detailed knowledge of how his mate was created of him. *The Commentators generally say that Eve was created from the rib of Adam and the Bible also contains the same story. The Talmud adds to it that she was created from the thirteenth rib of Adam. But the Qur'an is silent about it, and the Tradition of the Holy Prophet that is cited in support of this has a different meaning from what has been understood.* The best thing, therefore, is to leave it undefined as it has been left in the Qur'an, and not to waste time in determining its details.[19]

In the above passage, Maududi has no difficulty in affirming what has traditionally been made the basis of asserting woman's inferiority and subordination to man, namely that woman was created from man. Having made the deadly affirmation, however, he is reluctant to explicate it further, nor does he reveal what he considers to be the "true" meaning of the Hadith pertaining to Eve's creation from Adam's rib. His justification for not discussing the issue of woman's creation is that the Qur'an has deliberately left it undefined. But this is simply not the case. The creation of woman is as clearly defined in the Qur'an as the creation of man, and the Qur'anic statements about human creation, diverse as they are, leave no doubt as to one point: both man and woman were made in the same manner, of the same substance, at the same time. Maududi (like the majority of Muslim exegetes, who happen to be all men) does not want to face this fact, so he declares that the discussion of the issue of woman's creation is a waste of time. If the issue in question was not worthy of serious theological reflection, or one that had no significant effect on the lives of human beings, particularly of women, one would, perhaps, be less critical of a scholar who has had massive impact on the minds of the Muslim masses, for dereliction of scholarly duty. But theologically the issue of creation of woman is of such import that it cannot be allowed to be dismissed in the manner in which Maududi has done.

Perhaps no better proof can be given of how totally ahadith such as the ones cited above have penetrated Muslim culture than the fact that the myth of the creation of Hawwa' from Adam's rib was accepted uncritically even by Qasim Amin (1863–1906), the Egyptian judge and feminist whose books *Tahrir al-Mara'* (The Emancipation of Women, 1899) and *Al-Mara' al-Jadida* (The Modern Woman, 1900) were epoch-making in the history of Muslim feminism. Amin's romantic interpretation of the myth, reminiscent of Milton's, shows that he did not realize how fundamentally the issue that concerned him most deeply, namely, woman's social equality with man in a strongly male-centered and male-dominated Muslim society, hinged upon the acceptance or rejection of a creation story that asserted woman's derivative status and had been interpreted traditionally to affirm her inferiority and subordination to man. It is unfortunate that many present-day Muslim advocates of women's rights also do not realize the profound implications of this myth that undergirds the anti-women attitudes and structures they seek to change.

Anti-women ahadith are found not only in the significant secondary sources of Islam but also in *Sahih al-Bukhari* (compiled by Muhammad ibn Isma'il al-Bukhari, A. H. 194–256/A.D. 810–870) and *Sahih Muslim* (compiled by Muslim bin al-Hajjaj, A. H. 202 or 206–261/A.D. 817 or 821–875), the two most influential Hadith collections in Sunni Islam. Cited below are six ahadith, the first three from *Sahih al-Bukhari* and the last three from *Sahih Muslim*, that have had a formative influence upon the Muslim mind:

1. Abu Karaith and Musa bin Hazam related to us: Husain bin 'Ali told us that he was reporting on the authority of Zai'dah who was reporting on the authority of Maisarah al-Ashja'i who was reporting on the authority of Abu Hazim who was reporting on the authority Abu Hurairah (with whom may Allah be pleased) who said: Allah's Rasul[20] (may peace be upon him) said:

    Treat women nicely, for a woman is created from a rib, and the most curved portion of the rib is its upper portion, so if you should try to

straighten it, it will break, but if you leave it as it is, it will remain
crooked. So treat woman nicely.[21]

2. 'Abd al-'Aziz related to us that he was reporting on the authority of 'Abd Allah who
said: Malik had told us that he was reporting on the authority of Abu Zinad who was
reporting on the authority of al-A'raj who was reporting on the authority of Abu
Hurairah (with whom may Allah be pleased) who said: Allah's Rasul (may peace be
upon him) said:[22]

> The woman is like a rib, if you try to straighten her, she will break.
> So if you want to get benefit from her, do so while she still has some
> crookedness.[23]

3. Ishaq bin Nasr related to us: Husain al-Jo'fi related to us that he was reporting on the
authority of Za'idah who was reporting on the authority of Maisarah who was reporting
on the authority of Abu Hazim who was reporting on the authority of Abu Hurairah
(with whom may Allah be pleased) who said: The Holy Prophet (may peace be upon
him) said:[24]

> Whoever believes in Allah and the Last Day should not hurt (trouble)
> his neighbor. And I advise you to take care of the women, for they
> are created from a rib and the most crooked part of the rib is its upper
> part; if you try to straighten it, it will break, and if you leave it, it
> will remain crooked, so I urge you to take care of woman.[25]

4. Harmalah bin Yahya related to me: Ibn Wahb informed us: Yunus informed me that
he was reporting on the authority of Ibn Shihab who said: Ibn al-Musayyab told me
that he was reporting on the authority of Abu Hurairah (with whom may Allah be
pleased) who said: Allah's Rasul (may peace be upon him) said:[26]

> Woman is like a rib. When you attempt to straighten it, you would
> break it. And if you leave her alone you would benefit by her, and
> crookedness will remain in her.[27]

5. 'Amr an-Naqid and Ibn 'Umar related to us saying: Sufyan related to us that he was
reporting on the authority of Abu Zinad who was reporting on the authority of al-
A'raj who was reporting on the authority of Abu Hurairah (with whom may Allah be
pleased) who said: Allah's Rasul (may peace by upon him) said:[28]

> Woman has been created from a rib and will in no way be straightened
> for you; so if you wish to benefit by her, benefit by her while crook-
> edness remains in her. And if you attempt to straighten her, you will
> break her, and breaking her is divorcing her.[29]

6. Abu Bakr bin Abu Shaibah told us: Husain bin 'Ali told us that he was reporting on
the authority of Za'idah who was reporting on the authority of Maisarah who was
reporting on the authority of Abu Hazim who was reporting on the authority of Abu
Hurairah (with whom may Allah be pleased) who said: The Holy Prophet (may peace
be upon him) said:[30]

He who believes in Allah and the Hereafter, if he witnesses any matter
he should talk in good terms about it or keep quiet. Act kindly towards
women, for woman is created from a rib, and the most crooked part
of the rib is its top. If you attempt to straighten it, you will break it,
and if you leave it, its crookedness will remain there so act kindly
towards women.[31]

While it is not possible, within the scope of this chapter, to give a detailed
critical analysis of either the *isnad* (list of transmitters) or *matn* (content) of the
above ahadith, a few comments on both may be useful. With regards to the
isnad the following points may be noted: (1) All these ahadith are cited on
the authority of Abu Hurairah, a Companion who was regarded as controversial
by many early Muslim scholars, including Imam Abu Hanifah (A.D. 700–767),[32]
founder of the largest Sunni school of law. Here it is pertinent to point out that
though a more critical attitude toward Hadith and Hadith-transmitters prevailed
during the earliest phase of Islam, later, as stated by Goldziher,[33] it became "a
capital crime" to be critical of any Companion; (2) All six of the above ahadith
are *gharib* (the lowest grade of Hadith classification) because they contain a
number of transmitters who were single reporters. (Al-Hakim Abu 'Abd Allah
al-Naysaburi and Ibn Hajar al-'Asqalani, who were eminent scholars of Hadith,
defined a *sahih* or sound Hadith as one that is related in the first place by a well-
known Companion, in the second place by at least two Followers, and thereafter
by many narrators.);[34] (3) All of the above ahadith are *da'if* (weak) because they
have a number of unreliable transmitters (e.g., Maisarah al-Ashja'i, Harmalah
bin Yahya, Zaidah, and Abu Zinad).[35]
  Analysis of the *matn* of the above ahadith leads to the following statements:
(1) Woman is created from a rib or is like a rib; (2) The most curved and crooked
part of the rib is its top; (3) The crookedness of the rib (and of the woman) is
irremediable—any effort to remove it will result in breakage; and (4) In view
of the above, an attitude of kindness is recommended and those who wish to
benefit from women are advised to do so "while crookedness remains in her."
Concerning these statements the following observations are made: (a) The rib
story obviously originates in Genesis 2, but no mention is made in any of these
ahadith of Adam. This eliminates the Yahwist's androcentrism but also deper-
sonalizes the source of woman's creation (i.e., the "rib" could, theoretically,
be nonhuman); (b) The misogynist elements of the ahadith, absent from Genesis,
clash with the teachings of the Qur'an which describes all human beings as
having been created *fi ahsan-i taqwim* (most justly proportioned and with the
highest capabilities); (c) I cannot understand the relevance of making the statement that the most crooked part of the rib is at the top; (d) The exhortation to
be kind to women would make sense if women were, in fact, born with a natural
handicap and needed compassion. Is "irremediable crookedness" such a handicap? (e) The advice to benefit from women without making any effort to help
women deal with their "crookedness" (in case it is a natural handicap) smacks

of hedonism or opportunism and is hard to appreciate even if women were indeed "irremediably crooked."

The theology of woman implicit in the above ahadith is based upon generalizations about her ontology, biology, and psychology that are contrary to the letter and spirit of the Qur'an. These ahadith ought to be rejected on the basis of their content alone. However, "*matn*-analysis" (which was strongly urged by Ibn Khaldun, A.D. 1332–1406)[36] has received scant attention in the work of many Muslim scholars, who insist that a Hadith is to be judged primarily on the basis of its *isnad*. It is not difficult to see why *isnad*-criticism—particularly if it excludes a scholarly scrutiny of initial reports of a Hadith—is not a sufficient methodological tool for establishing the reliability of a Hadith. Not all initial reporters of ahadith were the Prophet's close Companions whose word would be difficult to question. (The word "Companion" has come to be applied rather loosely to a variety of persons, some of whom spent only a limited amount of time with the Prophet and cannot necessarily be presumed to have known him well.) Furthermore, it is not always possible to say in the case of a Hadith whether its *isnad* (including the name of the Companion initially narrating the Hadith) is authentic and not fabricated. In such cases references to the *matn* of other ahadith ascribed to the same initial narrator, or to other ahadith with similar content, become critically important in determining the degree of reliability of both the narrator and the Hadith in question.

CONCLUSION

To sum up the foregoing discussion on the issue of woman's creation, I would like to reiterate that according to the Qur'an, Allah created woman and man equal. They were created simultaneously, of like substance, and in like manner. The fact that almost all Muslims believe that the first woman (Hawwa') was created from Adam's rib shows that, in practice, the Hadith literature has displaced the teaching of the Qur'an at least insofar as the issue of woman's creation is concerned.

While all Muslims agree that whenever a Hadith attributed to the Prophet conflicts with the Qur'an it must be rejected, the ahadith discussed in this chapter have not only not been rejected, they have in fact remained overwhelmingly popular with Muslims through the ages, in spite of being clearly contradictory to the Qur'anic statements pertaining to human creation. While being included in the *Sahihan* gives the ahadith in question much weight among Muslims who know about the science of Hadith, their continuing popularity among Muslims in general indicates that they articulate something deeply embedded in Muslim culture—namely, the belief that women are derivative creatures who can never be considered equal to men.

Even the courageous Muslim women presently leading women's movements in oppressively conservative Muslim societies, which in the name of "Islamization" are systematically legitimizing the reduction of women to a less than fully human status, are not aware of the far-reaching implications of the ahadith that make them derivative or devious creatures. It is imperative for the Muslim daughters of Hawwa' to realize that the history of their subjection and humiliation at the hands of sons of Adam began with the story of Hawwa's creation, and that their future will be no different from their past unless they return to the point of origin and challenge the authenticity of ahadith that make them onto-logically inferior, subordinate, and crooked. While it is not a little discouraging to know that these ahadith (like many other anti-woman ones) represent not only the ideas and attitudes regarding woman of the early generations of Muslims (whose views were reflected in the Hadith literature), but also of successive generations of Muslims until today, it is gratifying to know that they cannot be the words of the Prophet of Islam, who upheld the rights of women (as of other disadvantaged persons) throughout his life. Furthermore, regardless of how many Muslim men project their own androcentrism and misogyny upon the Prophet of Islam, it is valid to question how, being the recipient of the Qur'an, which states that all human beings were made from a single source (i.e., *al-insan, bashar,* or *nafsin wahidatin*), the Prophet of Allah could say that woman was created from a crooked rib or from Adam's rib.

NOTES

1. Saiyyad: a descendant of the Prophet Muhammad.
2. *Ummah* (from *umm:* mother): community of Muslims.
3. Sunnah: practical traditions attributed to the Prophet Muhammad.
4. Hadith (plural: ahadith): oral traditions attributed to the Prophet Muhammad.
5. Fiqh: jurisprudence.
6. Surah 4: *An-Nisa'*:34.
7. Surah 4: *An-Nisa'*:11.
8. Surah 2: *Al-Baqarah*:282.
9. Reference here is to ahadith from *Sahih al-Bukhari.*
10. Leonard Swidler, *Biblical Affirmations of Woman.* (Philadelphia: Westminster Press, 1979), 76.
11. Muhammad Iqbal, *The Reconstruction of Religious Thought in Islam* (Lahore: Shaikh Muhammad Ashraf, 1962), 83.
12. Fazlur Rahman, *Islam* (Garden City, NY: Doubleday and Company, 1968), 73.
13. Alfred Guillaume, *The Traditions of Islam* (Beirut: Khayats, 1966), 15.
14. Hamilton A. R. Gibb, *Studies on the Civilization of Islam,* ed. Stanford J. Shaw and William R. Polk (Boston: Beacon Press, 1966) 194.
15. Marshall G. S. Hodgson, *The Venture of Islam: Conscience and History in a World Civilization.* Vol. 1, *The Classical Age of Islam* (Chicago: University of Chicago Press, 1974), 332.
16. Hadith quoted in Jane I. Smith and Yvonne Y. Haddad, "Eve: Islamic Image of Woman," *Women's Studies International Forum* 5 no. 2 (1982): 136–37.
17. I.B.U. Ibn Kathir, *Tafsir Ibn Kathir* (Karachi: Nur Muhammad Karkhana Tijarat-e-Kutub, n.d.) 1:101.

18. A. A. Maududi, *The Meaning of the Qur'an* and *Tafhim ul-Qur'an*, 6 vols. (Lahore: Maktaba-e-Ta'mir-e-Insaniyyat, 1974).

19. Maududi, *Meaning of the Qur'an*, 2: 298, footnote 1 (emphasis is mine).

20. Rasul: a Prophet sent by God with a message. Reference here is to the Prophet Muhammad.

21. M. M. Khan, translation with notes of *Sahih al-Bukhari* (Lahore: Kazi Publications, 1971), vol. 4 "Book of Prophets," chap. 1, Hadith 548, p. 346.

22. *Sahih al-Bukhari* 7: 33.

23. *Sahih al-Bukhari* (translation), vol. 7, "Book of Wedlock," chap. 80, Hadith 113, p. 80.

24. *Sahih al-Bukhari* 7: 33.

25. *Sahih al-Bukhari* (translation), vol. 7, "Book of Wedlock," chap. 81, Hadith 114, p. 81.

26. Muslim bin al-Hajjaj, *Sahih Muslim*, 2 vols. (Cairo: 'Isa al-Babi al-Halbi, n.d.), 1:625.

27. A. H. Siddiqui, translation with notes of *Sahih Muslim* (Lahore: Shaikh Muhammad Ashraf) vol. 2, "Book of Wedlock," chap. 576, Hadith 3466, p. 752.

28. *Sahih Muslim*, 1:625.

29. *Sahih Muslim* (translation), vol. 2, "Book of Wedlock," chap. 576, Hadith 3467, p. 752.

30. *Sahih Muslim*, 1: 625.

31. *Sahih Muslim* (translation), vol. 2, "Book of Wedlock," chap. 576, Hadith 3468, pp. 752–53.

32. 'Abdul Wahab Ash-Shairani, *Al-Mizan al-Kubra* (Cairo), 1:59.

33. Ignaz Goldziher, *Muslim Studies* trans. C. R. Barber and S. M. Stern, ed. S. M. Stern (Chicago: Aldine Publishing Company, 1971), 2:163.

34. See Muhammad bin 'Abd Allah al-Hakim, *Ma'rifat 'Ulum al-Hadith*, ed. Mu'azzam Hussain (Cairo: 1937), 62; and Ibn Hajar al-'Asqalani, *Sharh Nukhbat ul-Fikr fi Mustaleh Ahl al-Athar* (Cairo: 1934), 5.

35. See, for example, Shams ad-Din Adh-Dhahabi, *Mizan I'tidal fi Naqd ar-Rijal*, 4 vols. (Cairo: 'Isa al-Babi al-Halbi, n.d.). This is a highly authoritative work investigating the credentials of Hadith-transmitters by a renowned Hadith critic (A.D. 1274–1348).

36. Hodgson, *Venture of Islam*, 2:480.

6

Women and the Hindu Tradition

KANA MITRA

Several factors in my life account for my interest in religion in general, and in interreligious dialogue and feminist theology in particular. I was born to a Vaisnavite[1] mother who was a believer and a Smarta[2] father who, like many late nineteenth and early twentieth-century Hindus, was an agnostic of sorts. Early in my life, I was led by my "karma," life situation, or providence to my acquaintance with Christianity. The first school that I went to at age seven (which happened to be the only school for girls in the small town of West Bengel where my father, a government employee, was posted) had been established and was being run by a woman Protestant missionary. I do not know to which denomination she belonged, but I remember that during the morning prayer meetings we used to listen to excerpts from the Bible. The teachings of the Bible did not lead to any conflict or questioning regarding the Hindu teachings that I had learned from my mother.

The questions "What is life?" "What is death?" had become important to me at a very early stage of life, perhaps due to the death of one brother when I was about two and of another when I was fourteen. Initially I studied philosophy for answers; later I was led—once again by providence—to the study of religion and the social sciences. My interest in feminist studies is largely due to the circumstance of my being in the United States. Both here and earlier in my life in India, I have been led to assume roles that are not typical for Hindu women. My struggle has been, and still is, to free myself from my cultural conditioning.

In the course of this struggle, I have come to confront the oft-repeated charge that the Hindu tradition has contributed to the oppression of women at the hands of the dominant male sex. In this chapter I wish to call this charge into question by examining the role of women in Indian culture in general and in the Hindu tradition in particular. As a "Hindu witness" I will pay special attention to the

distinction between those ideological teachings within Hinduism that support the
equality of male and female, and the very imperfect ways in which such teachings
have been actualized in real life.

HINDUISM: PRELIMINARY REMARKS

Some preliminary statements regarding the history of Hinduism may be useful
at the outset. In its approximately four thousand years of history there has not
been one uniform scripture, creed, or way of being religious among the Hindus.
Hinduism has various forms and has passed through a number of quite different
periods in its development. Each form and period contains many and diverse
currents and influences. This makes it very difficult to give a simple account of
the Hindu tradition. However, it is customary to divide the Hindu texts into *śruti*
and *smṛti*. The *Vedas* (2000–1000 B.C.) and the *Upaniṣads* (1000 B.C.) are the
śruti ("revealed texts" or texts based on direct hearing of truth). They deal
primarily with the transcendent or perennial aspect of Truth or Reality. Ultimate
Reality is seen as asexual, although it is concretely expressed in pluriform. For
example, the *Śvetāśvatara Upaniṣad* states: "Thou art woman, thou art man;
Thou art youth, maiden too. Thou art a tottering old man walking with a staff;
it is you alone who, when born, assume diverse forms."[3] The emphasis of these
texts is on ultimate spiritual realization, as the following extract shows:

It is not for the sake of husband that the husband is loved, he is loved for the sake of
the Self [Supreme]. It is not for the sake of wife that the wife is loved, but she is loved
for the sake of the Self. It is not for the sake of sons that sons are loved, but they are
loved for the sake of the Self. It is not for the sake of wealth that wealth is loved, but
it is loved for the sake of Self. . . . It is not for the sake of all that all is loved but for the
sake of Self. Dear Mitreyi, it is the Self that should be realized—should be heard of,
reflected on, and meditated upon. By realization of the Self, my dear—through hearing,
reflection, and mediation—all this is known.[4]

The *smṛti* texts are numerous. Well known among them are the *Dharma Śāstras*
(600–300 B.C.) and the epics of *Rāmāyana* and *Mahābhārata,* of which the
Bhāgavad-Gītā is a part (300 B.C.–300 A.D.). These texts are primarily about
praxis. They point out that since ultimate spiritual realization comes from and
through the concrete diversities of life, the distinctiveness and particularity of
concrete reality need to be recognized. Briefly, then, these texts deal with responsibilities and duties of different sexes, ages, and castes.

Due to the difficulty of dating certain important texts and ideas or practices
pertaining to women, I will not attempt in this work to discuss the question of
the position of women in Hinduism in strictly chronological terms. Rather, I
shall describe what it is to grow up female in present-day Hindu society. The
ideological basis of contemporary Hindu society and the interrelationship between
this society and sacred texts will also be discussed. Finally I will offer some

suggestions regarding new directions to be followed in the quest for the attainment of human liberation.

THE ROLE OF HINDU WOMEN IN DAILY LIFE

The primary role of women in relationship to men in Hindu society—as in many traditional societies—is perceived to be that of wife and mother. In the hierarchical ideology of Hindu society, equality between the sexes is not understood as egalitarian reciprocity but as a form of mutual dependence or relatedness. In the actual translation of this ideal into the day-to-day life of Hindu society, the subordinate position of the wife is compensated for by the elevated position of the mother. This dual attitude toward women is reflected in public affairs also. As mothers, women are respected. Indira Gandhi, in so far as she represented a mother figure, did not have difficulty in holding her position. But a young woman, especially if she is unmarried, may find it very difficult to obtain or maintain a high leadership position. Hence it is not surprising that many Hindu women are not motivated to seek such a position.

Anthropological and sociological studies of Hindu women by and large depict an overall situation of male "dominance" and female "oppression." However, anthropologists often miss the dual attitude of subordination and respect operating simultaneously in Hindu society. For instance, anthropologist David Mandelbaum describes the situation of women in Hindu culture as follows: "A young wife of any *jati,* or region, usually has the lowest status in the family and is given the most onerous chores. Whatever goes awry, she is apt to be called the culprit. Whenever the finger of blame is pointed, it somehow swings to her."[5]

The actual situation of women in Hindu society is much more complex than is depicted in the above description. In other words, there is always more to the situation than meets the eye. The actual condition of a particular woman depends on diverse conditions. For instance, the geographical area of her birth can be critically important in this regard. A case in point is that of the women of South Indian ancestry who, on account of kinship marriage, enjoy better treatment as wives than women of North Indian origin.[6] At present, one state in South India especially to be noted in this regard is Kerala, where a woman plays more of a partnership than a servitude role in relationship to her husband and his family.[7]

The caste of a woman can also be a factor in determining her status. Lower-caste women are freer in this regard than those belonging to upper castes. Working outside the home to perform a menial job that may be performed by low-caste women is considered to be beneath the dignity of an upper-caste woman. Her "cultured" status prohibits her from going outside of her home. Her educational background and professional status, especially in comparison with her husband's, are very important factors in determining her position in the family. In the extended family of the Hindus, the mother-in-law, who has the high status of mother of the husband, presides over domestic affairs. The daughter-in-law, whatever her status may be with regard to all the above-mentioned factors, is subservient to her.

Women in Hindu society even today participate less than men in the public arena. Since the independence of India (1947) many women have worked in government and business offices, but are barely represented in top management positions. Also men and women do not receive equal pay for the same job, even if it is performed better by a woman than by a man. In this context, the experience of the Canadian ambassador's wife in South India is relevant. Noticing women doing hard manual work in a shipping yard, she asked the male officer in charge if women were less hardworking than men. "Oh, no!" he said. "In fact, our women are some of the most skillful workers we have; they are more nimble, they climb up and down more quickly and carry every bit as much." She asked, "Do you pay them the same salary as you pay men?" "Oh, no," he said, "they are only women."[8]

The legal system may provide a means of eliminating discrimination in salaries paid to women, but how does one alter the perception that women are inferior? Not only men but also women regard themselves as inferior. Rabindranath Tagore's short story *Mashi*[9] exemplifies this. A dying man who was raised by his mother's sister (Mashi or aunt) told her that he wished her to be born as as his daughter in the next life so that he could take care of her the way she took care of him in this lifetime. The aunt was horrified at the prospect of being born again as a woman and asked her nephew why he did not wish her to be born as his son instead.

Ved Mehta's autobiographical work *Daddyji*[10] gives another example of how a woman cannot attach value to her own life. She is a father's daughter, a husband's wife, or a son's mother. He describes the agony of his grandmother who, as a young wife, was diagnosed as unable to bear a child. Mehta's grandfather was a doctor and was educated in England. His parents had arranged his marriage. After learning the doctor's diagnosis, the wife clasped her hands and implored her husband not to banish her from his household and send her back to her parents' home. She told him that she wanted him to marry again and offered to take care of the children born to the second wife. When the husband told her that city-educated people do not reject their wives because they are infertile, she said, "But we Hindu women are like breeding cows. Our value lies in our sons."[11]

Monisha Roy gives a very vivid picture of contemporary middle-class Hindu women in Bengal.[12] Although the joint family system is breaking up and is being replaced by single unit families, women—whether in a joint family or a single unit family—are still expected by others to sacrifice their personal aspirations and goals for the sake of their husbands and other members of the family. Such expectations are internalized by the majority of women in India, which is not a place of plenty. The Hindu wife serves every member of the family before she can sit down to her own meal, and by the time her turn comes to eat, nothing much is left anyway. Thus, besides all the psychological deprivations endured by Hindu women, many of them also endure hunger.

THE ROLE OF WOMEN AND HINDU IDEOLOGY

To understand the connection between religious ideology and instances of women's self-abnegation cited above, reference must be made to *Tyāga*, which means sacrifice, unselfishness, and renunciation, and is regarded as a cardinal virtue in Hindu ideology. The importance of this concept may be seen in numerous texts. For instance, *Katopanisada* states that "both good and pleasant are laid before them. The wise choose the good."[13] Further, "the ignorant souls pursue the external pleasures, and fall in the snare of death. The wise do not desire anything in this world as they know the eternal in the midst of the transient."[14] The *Brhadānanyaka Upanisad*,[15] the *Mahābhārata*,[16] including the *Bhāgavad-Gītā*,[17] and the *Purānas*[18] also emphasize the need for renunciation, while Manu's *Dharma Śāstra* states: "Harmlessness, truthfulness, non-stealing, purity of body and mind, control of sense-organs can be considered briefly as the path of virtue for all."[19]

Thus, in Hindu religious thought spiritual growth is seen as dependent on cultivation of renunciation. However, in Hinduism generally, and with reference to Hindu women in particular, renunciation is often confused with asceticism. While renunciation implies a conscious choice of a goal and action, asceticism is mortification of flesh and embodies what Freud referred to as repression. There is an element of unconscious coercion is such repression. Hindu women often become ascetic in their acts of self-sacrifice. They do not give up their own interests as a result of conscious choice, but due to unconscious motives or from fear of social stigma. The results of this repression often become visible in the form of self-deception or the attempt to deceive others. Hindu women often maintain their self-interest through trickery and manipulation of others. Thus the role perception of women, instead of leading to the Hindu goal of unselfishness, has become counterproductive for spiritual fulfillment.

M. N. Srinivasa, the anthropologist, describes the Hindu mother's training of her daughter. She teaches her to adjust and to be accommodative, but suggests—by words as well as example—how to manipulate or get one's own way.[20] The typical "I have a headache" is used as a ploy against men. Even regarding food, a woman sometimes will use trickery to get her way. In our joint family, I recall my mother and aunts sitting down for their meals and having some inexpensive but good food just by themselves. They used to do this essentially out of a trickster spirit. But what needs to be emphasized is that women feel guilt and shame doing something for their own pleasure, such as having an enjoyable meal, and regard this as being contrary to the Hindu ideal of self-sacrifice. Here it may also be noted that in Hindu society women's deprivations are enforced not only by male members of the family but by the mother-in-law as well. Thus women are not "victims" only of male predominance, but also of the dominance of other women.

Why is renunciation commonly interpreted as self-abnegation by Hindu women? One important reason seems to be the way women and men learn about their gender roles and the value that their religious tradition attaches to these separate and distinct values. Hindus do not receive any formal education concerning their religious values. There is no Sunday School to impart any systematic education about matters such as right and wrong or the specific duties of mother, father, son, or daughter; ideas regarding these are mostly derived from observation.

Peter Berger pointed out that the relationship between the individual and society is dialectical. The dialectic involves three steps—externalization, objectivation, and internalization.[21] In Hindu society all these steps take place without much deliberate reflection, for this society is tradition-bound. People do what their ancestors did even if they incur material loss by doing so. For instance, in the 1960s many local farmers resisted the efforts of Peace Corps volunteers who wanted to teach them more productive ways of farming. The resistance was due to the farmers' unwillingness to give up the way of their forebears.

Reliance on tradition has had the effect of preserving ancient Hindu values to the present time. Here it may be noted that in Hindu society the freedom of the individual to do what he or she pleases is very limited and cannot be obtained simply by asserting that what one wants to do is not hurtful to anyone else. Thus, in this society the absoluteness of inherited moral values is seldom questioned.

Due to lack of critique of ancient ways and customs, many outmoded traditions continue and have a detrimental effect upon future generations. Acceptance of traditional values is also upheld by Hindu scriptures that state or suggest that one gains knowledge of right and wrong by following the customs, watching the cultured (*sanskṛta*), and seeking the advice of the holy people, though practice of some form of spiritual discipline is also indicated as necessary for spiritual development. In any event, discarding customary ways is not encouraged, lest expediency alone becomes the guidepost for a person's behavior.

Yoga (i.e., the common name for Hindu scriptural practice systematized in the *Yogasūtra* of Patañjali) and various Hindu scriptures indicate that all aspects of a person's life are involved in the process of spiritual development. This process begins with a commitment that one will refrain from the moral "don'ts" (*yama*)[22] and observe the moral "do's" (*niyama*).[23] After gaining spiritual maturity one can understand the meaning of *yama* and *niyama*, but in the meantime it is advisable to abide by convention. The discipline of yoga not only involves the body and the mind but also what is referred to as the unconscious mind.

While following convention is useful at the beginning stage of pursuing a path of spiritual development, it is to be remembered that unquestioning adherence to societal norms could lead to the following of imperfect precedents. Here it may also be mentioned that the majority of Hindus, especially those who are secular and Western-educated, do not study any scripture today. Once "cultured" meant *refined* or *pure* in a religious sense. Now it means *powerful* or *potent* in a secular sense. Many contemporary Hindus think that being cultured means adopting a Western lifestyle, speaking English with a British accent, and not speaking in one's mother tongue.[24] Tagore once said to such a "cultured" person that disrespect of one's own tradition leads not to the learning of a new language but to forgetting one's own. Westernization, in its "meism" aspect, permeates modern Hindu society and there is little conscious reflection on religious ideology, although many Western-educated Hindus still practice some Hindu rituals.

WOMEN AS ROLE MODELS IN EPICS AND TALES: SITA, SAVITRI, AND SATI

Besides learning from role models within the family, Hindus imbibe religious ideology from the two great Hindu epics, the *Rāmāyana* and the *Mahābhārata*. In pre-television India, stories from these epics presented in the form of open-air theaters, films, and recitals were the chief form of entertainment for many Hindus. Now in the television era these stories are presented in the privacy of people's homes. The characters in these epics provide guidance to Hindus with regard to values. In particular, the women portrayed in these epics as wives, mothers, and daughters initiate a process of teaching Hindu girls about the value that is attached to various roles performed by women in Hindu society. It is hardly surprising to note that, as wives, Hindu women learn to emulate Sita (the ideal wife of the epic *Rāmāyana*),[25] Savitri (the supreme example of the power of a chaste wife from the epic *Mahābhārata*),[26] and Sati (a character from the *Purāṇas*),[27] since these female figures are highly regarded in Hindu ideology.

Of all the figures mentioned above, Sita is probably the most important for women. Princess Sita gives up her royal lifestyle and, like a hermit, accompanies her husband Rama to the forest when he abdicates his throne for his stepbrother. When Rama's father, the old king, was ill, one of his wives, Kaikeyi, had performed the wifely duty of taking very good care of him. The king wanted to reward her, but she took a "rain check." When Rama, the heir apparent, was about to be crowned, Kaikeyi asked the king to fulfil his promise to her and make her son the king, banishing Rama to fourteen years of exile in the forest. The king was reluctant to oblige Kaikeyi, but Rama honors his father's word to his stepmother and goes into exile voluntarily. Rama tries to dissuade Sita from accompanying him because of the harsh living conditions of the forest, but she insists upon going with him. In the forest they live simply and quite happily. However, Sita is abducted by the demon King Ravana. In Ravana's kingdom Sita does not succumb to the temptations of wealth or pleasures but remains faithful to Rama. Rescued by Rama, with the help of the monkey troops, she proves her chastity by entering into fire—which does not burn a chaste wife. However, on his return to his kingdom Rama sends Sita back to the forest because his subjects spread rumors about her lack of chastity during her captivity. Here I am reminded of the fact that King Edward VIII of England abdicated his throne to marry the woman he loved, while Rama sent his beloved wife away to honor the wishes of his subjects.

In the story related above, Hindu values are presented in the context of societal living rather than an individual's life. Rama is Sita's husband, but he is also a son, brother, and king. The duties of individuals at any particular time are determined in the context of the totality of their relationships. Here it may be observed that in Western society there is much awareness of "rights" but not of "duties"; in Indian society there is much discussion about "duties" but not about "rights." In the context of the Hindu value system, priorities in moral behavior are in part dependent on the number of people to be affected by one's action. Thus, the action of a king affects all the people of the kingdom, but the action of a husband affects his wife only. From the perspective of such a value system, it would be considered an act of selfishness and escapism, not chivalry or honesty, to abdicate one's throne for the sake of one's wife.

In the *Bhāgavad-Gītā* (the Hindu scripture best known in the West) we note that Krishna warns Arjuna that if he wants to escape an unpleasant war in order to avoid the grief involved in killing one's relatives, he would be acting selfishly and, therefore, not morally. Thus, considerations of personal gain or loss—material or emotional—cannot be used as criteria of right and wrong in Hindu society.

Most Hindus regard Sita as an embodiment of obedience and loyalty to her husband, and these virtues are the most highly regarded in a wife. Sita, the ideal wife, never acts selfishly. Despite all the severe humiliation she undergoes, she never complains against or blames Rama. However, in the end, when Sita returns to the capital and Rama asks her to enter the fire again in order to assuage the suspicions of his subjects, she begs her mother earth to take her back and enters the earth's bosom. Even today many Hindu women commit suicide rather than seek divorce because they empathize with their husband's position as part of a complex network of relationships.[28] Other factors influencing a woman's behavior include economic dependence of a wife on her husband or her inability to support herself independently due to lack of education, as well as the social stigma attached to being an abandoned wife.

Another example of the ideal wife is to be found in the person of Savitri in the epic *Mahābhārata*. She "falls in love" with the prince Satyavana and wants to marry him, even when Satyavana's horoscope indicates that he will die in a year, and she also knows about the privations of the life of a Hindu widow. After her marriage Savitri takes vows of austerity and observes them. On the final day of the year Satyavana falls ill, and Savitri takes his head on her lap. Yama, the king of death himself, arrives to take away the chaste woman's husband. Savitri starts to follow Yama and asks him many profound questions. Yama, pleased with Savitri's wisdom, wants to give her some reward. She requests the return of the sight of her father-in-law. Then she continues to follow Yama and engages in discourse with him. Yama again wishes to reward her. She requests her father-in-law's kingdom back. Next she wants to have one hundred children. In order to fulfill the wish of the chaste wife who can have children only with her husband, Yama gives Satyavana back to Savitri.

This story may be read in such a way as to suggest that Savitri is using trickery to get her way. However, a better interpretation is that a life lived religiously leads to fulfillment in all respects.[29]

Here again, we get a picture of a value system that is not bilateral but multilateral. Savitri does not merely seek the restoration of her husband's life, but also looks after the well-being of the entire family. Like Sita, Savitri is perceived as an embodiment of the loyal and chaste wife whose virtues can overcome even death.

Yet another example of an ideal wife is Sati, a Purāṇic character. She is the wife of the ascetic-erotic god Śiva. Sati performs many austerities to become the wife of Śiva, who comes in many disguises to dissuade Sati. Finally the marriage takes place. Sati is so loyal to Śiva that she dies of heartbreak when her father makes slanderous remarks about Śiva. Śiva is still a model of the ideal husband for many Hindu women. Even college-educated, Westernized girls observe a twenty-four hour fast and vigil to be married to a man of Śiva-like qualities. Śiva is indifferent to worldly affairs, such as how his wife runs the family, but he is very loyal to her. When he hears about Sati's death, he does not want to let go of her body and starts his famous dance. Failure to cremate a chaste woman's body puts all creation in danger. Viṣṇu (Preserver God) intervenes and by his disc (*Cakra*) cuts and scatters Sati's body. The fifty-two places where parts of Sati's body fall have become places of pilgrimage for those who follow the Sati tradition in Hinduism.

Such Purāṇic stories, when read by people not born and raised in this tradition, or even by those who do not grow up listening to these stories from early childhood, are unlikely to be empathetically understood. However, these stories do exercise some kind of influence on the role perceptions of listeners. In the story of Sati and Śiva, we see a picture of conjugal love where reciprocity is supreme. Śiva does not let go even of a dead wife, whereas Rama sends his living wife away. Like Sita and Savitri, Sati is also perceived in the Hindu tradition as a shining example of wifely loyalty and chastity, whose virtues are rewarded richly.

The physical and spiritual expectations of woman as wife can lead to the situations described by Mandelbaum. If anything goes wrong, it is perceived to be the wife's fault. I remember, at fourteen as I prayed fervently for my brother who had suffered a stroke, I thought that if my brother had a wife like Savitri, he could be saved from death.

In Hindu society the single woman is an anomaly. For a Hindu woman marriage is the most important event of her life. The premarital life of a woman is mostly a preparation for the roles of wife and mother, which are considered to be the two most important roles for women in Hindu society. In the marriage ceremonies she is adorned like a queen and showered with gifts. It is interesting to note here that mantras that are uttered during the marriage ceremony do not indicate dominance of the husband over the wife but a relationship of interdependence. In the wedding hymns the groom says to the bride: ''I am the word you are the melody, I am the melody you are the word; let us be the joint upholders of the household.'' When the bride comes to join the husband's family she is received by blessings such as: ''Be the master of the household, rule over your in-laws.''[30]

In the epics and Purāṇas that we have examined, the role models of wives are clearly described. Women tend to emulate them and men expect women to live by them. In concluding this part of my chapter, however, I wish to point out that, contrary to what one might have expected, the mother characters in these stories are not inspiring and not usually seen as ideal mothers. For instance, Kunti, a mother character in *Mahābhārata,* abandons her illegitimate first-born to protect her other five children. The mother is supposed to be naturally caring and protective of her children. This is implied by the common Bengali saying: *Skuputra yadiva haya kumata kakhona nayal* (even if it is possible that there are bad sons, there can never be a bad mother). The epic stories highlight the son's loyalty to his mother, but not the mother's love of her children. The five Pandavas of *Mahābhārata* marry one woman, Draupadi, to honor their mother's desire for them to share everything equally. Isvara Chandra Vidyasagara, the nineteenth-century reformer, crosses the huge river Damodara on a stormy night to be with his mother when she needs him. An even more extreme example of filial loyalty is to be found in the story of Ghatothkacha, who kills a brahmin to pacify his mother's craving for the flesh of a brahmin. Thus it would be true to say that in Hindu society it is as difficult to be a son as it is to be a wife.

MAN-WOMAN EQUALITY AND HINDU SOCIETY

Educated women today, especially those trained in the secular model of the social sciences and/or those who are acquainted with the ideology of individualism, find it very difficult to identify the religious reasons for Hindu women's oppression. For instance, Monisha Roy's study, though accurate descriptively, fails to diagnose the roots of the problem in terms of religious ideology. Those who consciously try to figure out the theology of women in Hinduism tend to idealize the early phase of Hinduism (the golden past syndrome). They seem to believe that during the historical period of the Vedas and the Upaniṣads the condition of women was ideal, and only corruptions of later times changed the situation.

The connection between religious ideology and concrete societal structures— such as relations between men and women—is often not easy to perceive, even for those who have been exposed to Hindu ideology since an early age. It is obviously much more difficult to comprehend for those who have grown up exposed to other ideologies. To facilitate understanding of this linkage, I will explore the interrelationship between the core teachings of Hinduism regarding men-women equality and its societal expressions.

Conscious reflection upon Hindu ideology indicates that all of human life is sacramental. Marriage is a very important sacrament of human life because the life of the "householder" is not only the backbone of society, but also, for the majority of human beings, the essential path toward spiritual transformation. Thus, in all the *Dharmaśastras* the "householder" stage of life is emphasized and glorified. The purgative discipline of worldly love experienced in this stage of life makes one a receptacle and transmitter of divine love. The Indian poet Tagore attempts to capture this in one of his songs: "You are nurturing me in your house, you kept me in the bosom of my father, gave me birth in the lap of my mother, bonded me with love of friendship."[31] In each of these relationships, our love and concern for the other, rather than for ourselves, becomes the priority. Thus worldly love becomes the instrument for purging us of our selfishness or self-centeredness.

I had believed at an earlier time that to be a wife and mother was the ideal of Hindu womanhood. At that point it had seemed to me that an overemphasis on the virtue of chastity and its discriminatory application to women was the core source of societal problems. I was intrigued by the fact that women marry only once, whereas a man could have many wives. I felt that it was only fair that either both men and women should be monogamous or both should have the right to practice polygamy. However, I see now that such a perspective arises when one views man and woman as being in opposition to each other. It is also the result of looking at life from a secular rather than a religious viewpoint (the latter, unlike the former, does not regard this world as an end in itself).

Looked at from the Hindu perspective of life-as-sacrament, chastity is a virtue for all humans and not only women. Manu's laws, which are often cited in Hindu society as the cause of women's inferior status and the wife's unconditional obedience to her husband, also apply to men, as the following extracts show:

Let mutual fidelity continue until death.

Let men and women, united in marriage, constantly exert themselves, that (they may not be) disunited (and) violate their mutual fidelity.[32]

It is important to note that while Manu regards motherhood as the woman's ideal role, he also regards fatherhood as the man's ideal role:

To be mothers are women created, and to be fathers men; religious rites, therefore, are ordained in the Veda to be performed (by husband) together with the wife.[33]

Chastity for human beings also forms a part of the Hindu concept of *āśramas* or stages of life. The first stage—that of being a student—is the stage of strict discipline that is considered a prerequisite for learning. During the second stage—marriage—fidelity is considered an ideal for both spouses. Manu states:

The husband receives his wife from the gods, (he does not wed her) according to his own will; doing what is agreeable to the gods, he must always support her (while she is) faithful.[34]

Manu does not prescribe that a man should marry many wives, but since offspring are very important in Hindu society, if a woman is infertile it is society's demand that a man should marry again. In case a man is infertile, a woman, too, is allowed to conceive another man's child. In this context Manu observes:

> On failure of an issue (by her husband) a woman who has been authorized, may obtain, (in the) proper (manner prescribed), the desired offspring by (cohabitation with) a brother-in-law or some *sapinda* (of husband).

> He who is appointed to (cohabit with) the widow shall (approach her) at night anointed with clarified butter and silent, (and) beget one son, by no means a second.[35]

Thus the procreation of children, as well as study and marriage, are regarded by the Hindu tradition to be sacramental acts, that is, acts that have the capability of bringing about spiritual transformation. However, if any of these acts is engaged in only for the purpose of physical gratification or pleasure, then they cease to be sacramental. When a Hindu couple reaches the third stage of life—*Vānapryastha*—they are required to hand over the responsibilities of managing their worldly affairs to their eldest son and his wife, and to spend their time in worship or in performing pilgrimages.

The final stage—*sānyasa*—is the time for solitary pursuit of liberation. Here it is interesting to note that, judging by the pronouns in the rules for the ascetics, it appears that Manu is writing for men only. For instance, he says: "Let him patiently bear hard words, let him not insult anybody, and let him not become anybody's enemy for the sake of this (perishable) body."[36]

However, Manu's words can also include women by implication. The virtues of patience and self-sacrifice are required of women even during the "householder" stage, though these are generally associated with a later stage of life when a person has attained greater spiritual maturity. Before such spiritual maturity is achieved, self-surrender is unlikely to come from within. While women sages (e.g., *Gargeyi*) and *sanyāsis* (renouncers-monastics) are mentioned in the Upaniṣads, as also in later Hinduism, Manu's well-known injunction, "In childhood a female must be subject to her father, in youth to her husband, when her lord is dead to her sons,"[37] suggests that the *sanyāsi* stage is not meant for women.

In general, it can be stated, then, that chastity is central to a life led sacramentally whether by men or women. However, in the case of women, this virtue is overemphasized in many cases. It is involved, for instance, in anti-women rules prescribing suttee and child-marriage and prohibiting widow remarriage.

HINDU IMAGES OF GOD

Katherine K. Young, in the introduction of *Women in World Religions*,[38] argues that there is a correlation between patriarchy and predominance of male deities in a religion. The apparently contrary cases are explained by the hypothesis that while during the formative periods of these religions male deities were dominant, later—due to other factors—this situation changed. However, this thesis is not supported by Hindu images of God and Hindu theological thinking regarding the ultimate. It is not easy to assert the dominance of male deities in the history of Hinduism. Though the Vedas have more names of male than female deities, the suprasexual nature of the ultimate is nonetheless recognized. *Sat*—reality, truth—which is what matters ultimately, is not gender specific. In the Upaniṣads, the pronouns used interchangeably for Brahman, the Ultimate Principle, are: That (*tat*), He (*sa*), and This (*idam*).[39] Hindus, in general, do not think of Brahman as male or female. In fact, the concept of Brahman is so abstract for most Hindus that only a few can comprehend it or relate to it. The majority of Hindus have a personal deity (*Iṣṭa Devatā*) that each individual worships in his or her own special way.

This personal deity may be envisaged as a male (e.g., Viṣṇu or Śiva) or female (e.g., Kālī). However, sometimes physical representations of a deity may be neither male nor female. For example, Śiva is often worshipped in the form of the bisexual symbol of *liṇga*, which combines male-female organs, and *Viṣṇu* in the form of *sālagrāmaśila*, a small, round, black stone. Sometimes Śiva, a male deity, is sculpted in half-male, half-female form. Conceptually, most Hindu deities, whether male or female, have a counterpart, and it is difficult to substantiate the thesis that the Hindu tradition conceptualizes deity only in male terms or form.

It may also be noted here that the various creation stories do not suggest the primacy of males. One story, known as the *Puruṣa śukta* or cosmic person, portrays the picture of a thousand-headed, thousand-eyed Being as the transcendent ground of all creation.[40] Another one[41] is gender-free:

> Then was not non-existence nor existence: there was no
>   realm of air, no sky beyond it.
> What covered it, and where? and what gave shelter?
>   Was water there, unfathomed depth of water?
> Death was not then, nor was there aught immortal:
>   no sign was there, the day's and night's divider.
> That one thing, breathless, breathed by its own nature:
>   apart from it was nothing whatsoever. . . .
> Who verily knows and who can here declare it, whence
>   it was born and whence came this creation?
> The gods are later than this world's production.
> Who knows, then, whence it first came into being? He,
>   the first origin of this creation, whether he formed
>   it all or did not form it. Whose eye controls this
>   world in highest heaven, he verily knows it, or perhaps he
>   knows not.[42]

Nothing in the above hymn suggests male dominance.

From the preceding analysis it can be argued that the Hindu concepts or images of God do not imply patriarchy. It is true that as a wife the status of a Hindu woman is inferior to that of her husband, but this is balanced by the fact that a mother's status is very high. Adoration of God as mother is common in Hindu society, and even a so-called monist, Śamkara, who lived in the 8th century A.D., composed poems in adoration of mother:

> O Mother, in this world in the midst of Thy numerous
> worthy sons, I happen to be the specimen of wantonness.
> Yet, Thou Beneficent One, it is not proper for Thee to
> abandon me, Thy child. For, a bad son may sometimes be
> born but never has there been a bad mother.[43]

Ramaprasad's songs for Mother are commonly sung in Bengal by both men and women. Women are spiritual teachers, having both men and women disciples who usually call them "Mother." Because of the nurturing qualities associated with motherhood, many Hindus feel that it is easier to surrender to a Mother God than to a male God traditionally associated with a disciplinarian father.

REINTERPRETATION OF SITA, SAVITRI, AND SATI

Reference has been made to the way in which Sita, Savitri, and Sati have served as role models for women in the Hindu tradition. Feminist theologians in various traditions have demonstrated, however, that scriptural texts, in which "normative" images of women are grounded, can generally be interpreted in more than one (patriarchal) way. This is also true in the case of the Hindu tradition.

Sita, Savitri, and Sati, who have been seen traditionally as models of female obedience and subservience to men, can be reinterpreted as women with independent minds. Each chose to do what she wanted to do. Sita accompanied her husband to the wilderness against his wishes. Savitri and Sati defied parental authority to marry spouses of their own choosing. In *Rāmāyana*, Sita appears to be more active in character than Rama. This accords with the perspective of the Sākhya School of thought, which holds that society is divided into *puruṣa* and *prakṛti*—the former signifying male immovability and the latter signifying female activity.

HINDU HIERARCHICAL VALUES AND SPIRITUALITY

Sociological studies of Hinduism shed further light on characteristics of the Hindu value system, which is hierarchial and multidimensional. In this system woman's status as wife is different from her status as mother. In the husband-wife relationship the husband is "superior" and the wife is "inferior." In terms of priority of relationship, the son is to give primacy to the mother, followed by the father: "The teacher [is] ten times more venerable than the subteacher, the father a hundred times more than the teacher, but the mother a thousand times more than the father."[44] Thus, in Hindu society, as in Confucian, relationships are hierarchical in nature.

In *Homo Hierarchicas: The Caste System and Its Implications*,[45] Dumont indicates that the very word hierarchy is unpalatable to Westerners, whose culture is dominated by the ideology of individualism. However, "hierarchy" need not necessarily suggest a ladder-like linear system. It may suggest a multirelational, multidimensional value system. In this system, "superior" does not imply a privileged status, or an easier life. In Hindu society, being a husband is not considered an easier role than being a wife. Ideally, the husband is responsible for taking care of all of his wife's needs, and "reprehensible is the husband who approaches not (his wife in due season)."[46] Because the wife is confined to the home, the husband has to shoulder all the financial responsibilities of maintaining the family. Many Hindu women inflict guilt on their husbands by accusing them of not being good providers. Likewise, though a mother's role is "superior," it is not, therefore, an easy one. As pointed out by Gilligan,[47] a serious psychological aptitude for caring makes her an ideal caregiver for children. Here I am reminded of how during my early childhood, whenever I was ill, my mother would not eat any of the dainty dishes she prepared for the family because I could not eat them. Appreciation of this attitude of caring can emancipate a man, as its practice can emancipate a woman. But if caregiving is merely the result of convention or coercion, it can lead to self-abnegation, with various negative results. For instance, cases of hysteria and similar illnesses are often found among Hindu women who become martyrs to an unhealthy cult of self-sacrifice that is externally, rather than internally, motivated.

The notion of hierarchy functions in Hindu society as it does in Confucian society. Confucius speaks of hierarchy in terms of reciprocity and says: "Act in the same way as you would expect others to act towards you."[48] Alluding to the example of a father-son relationship, Confucius points out that the father has to treat his son in the same way as he would expect his father to treat him. Here reciprocity refers not only to the fact of father and son treating each other with dignity and respect, but also to each being a role model for fathers and sons respectively.

While similar notions are found in India and China, the former, generally speaking, has been more inclined to critique its religious tradition than the latter, which has continued to be tradition-bound in rather uncritical fashion.

HUMAN LIBERATION IN HINDUISM: CONCLUDING REMARKS

In summation regarding the position of women in Hinduism, it may be stated that the roles of wife and mother are considered to be the ideal ones for women in Hindu society.

The way women are perceived in any society tends, in general, to influence not only their self-perception but also their spirituality. In an essay entitled "The Effects of Women's Experience on Their Spirituality,"[49] Sandra M. Schneider explores both positive and negative impacts of women's given/perceived roles on their spirituality. In the context of Hindu society one can see that when women live up to the idealized roles of wife and mother, they are respected by men and also have self-esteem. However, these roles also imply that women's one arena of activity is the home. Thus the very roles that ensure the respectable status of the majority of Hindu women also ensure their exclusion from public affairs. While economists such as Galbraith and Mishan[50] have pointed out what housewives contribute to national economy, such contributions remain largely unacknowledged in Hindu society because women remain largely behind the scenes. Since women's primary role is seen as being located within the domestic sphere, their education becomes a matter of secondary importance. It is not surprising, therefore, that Hindu women have seldom acquired the skills to write philosophical or theological works, though some did become known as poets. Here it is of interest to note that in the early authoritative texts of the Hindus (*śrūtis*), there are references to women sages or wise ones. Perhaps these women contributed to the creation of scriptures. However, there is no record of women's participation in the production of texts containing Hindu traditions (*smṛtis*). Hindu laws seem to embody only a male perspective. For instance, in the context of chastity, men (who felt tempted by women) found it natural and easy to depict women as temptresses!

Though biographical works about Hindu women sages are scant, it would appear that a number of Hindu women did achieve spiritual maturity. For instance, we see from the biography of Sarada Devi,[51] who is much less known than her husband, Ramakrishna Paramahamsa, that she reached a high level of spiritual development. Also of interest is the autobiographical writing of Srimata Gayatri Devi,[52] a twentieth-century woman spiritual leader. A Hindu widow, she came to the United States in the early 1930s with a monk of the Ramakrishna order. After the death of this monk, she became the religious leader of the monastic order in Boston. However, lacking the ability to reach a wider public, the influence of these women remained confined to a small circle.

Hindu women, in general, have not participated in public spheres of legislative activity, either religious or secular. Thus women's experience in these arenas is not noteworthy. Even when conscious attempts were made to figure out the paths of spiritual growth for different human beings, models were constructed and understood solely in terms of men's experience. Thus assertiveness (which is traditionally seen as a "masculine" quality), or what Diekman named as "active mode of consciousness," became the accepted model for spiritual maturity. The "receptive mode of consciousness" (which is traditionally seen as "feminine") became devalued. This harmed not only women but also men, who became part of an oppressive hierarchy.

Some nineteenth and twentieth-century Hindu reformers have been conscious of the need to educate women so that they can articulate their needs. For example, the spiritual teacher Vivekananda suggested that instead of men trying to change the situations of women, it would be better for women to become educated and change their own situation.[53] His British disciple, Sister Nivedita (Margaret Noble), therefore established schools for women in Calcutta.

That education is the most important priority for Hindu women is self-evident. However, it must be borne in mind that education does not refer only to the acquisition of formal knowledge or information but to the unfolding and development of the full human potential. As pointed out by Jung, in order to attain an integrated personality a balance of feminine and masculine characteristics is needed. Thus, a mature person is a self that is in relationship with others. As Jung observes in *Modern Man in Search of a Soul*: "the ego is ill for the very reason that it is cut off from the whole and has lost its connection with mankind as well as with the spirit."[54]

The ultimate goal of life according to Hinduism is *moksa,* or total freedom. A liberated person, according to the *Bhāgavad Gitā,*[55] is the *sthitaprajña* (one who is established in wisdom), or a person who wants to be, rather than to have. That is why such a person is fearless and without anger; is dispassionate and not swayed by the fluctuations of fortunes; is calm and serene and able to penetrate the apparent; is spontaneous but not impulsive, and hence self-restrained; is free and autonomous because of being grounded in the true self and not in the selfish ego. While a literal and "masculine" interpretation of this text could lead a spiritual seeker to lack of involvement with anyone, a different, "feminine" interpretation could lead to togetherness and compassion. I believe that a liberated human being is compassionate. The question is, how can men and women be so transformed that they can be autonomous and related at the same time? Here the ideal of the complementarity of male and female may be helpful. Traditionally, the substantive mode of thought in Hinduism gives the impression that male and female are names of substances that are atomistic or unrelated. Against such substantive thought Buddhism developed the ontological thinking of relationality, which is depicted in the theory of conditional origination (*Pratitya-samutpāda*). From the perspective of relational ontology it may be noted that male and female suggest masculinity and femininity, and such characteristics are not exclusive to any one gender, as is noted by Jung. Men may have a predominance of "masculinity" and women of "femininity." The integrated person would have both characteristics simultaneously. Masculinity is generally understood as assertiveness, self-direction, conscious choice, etc., while femininity is receptivity, caring for the other, openness, etc. Thus the *sthitaprajña,* or one established in the transcendental reality (*Sanātana Dharma*), is autonomous and compassionate at the same time.

This way of looking at reality is not alien to classical Indian thought (e.g., the Sāmkhya School of thought, which speaks of *purusa* and *prakrti* in relational terms). The idea of *guna* has the potential of being developed in this context.

A relational methodology of interpretation would enable one to see feminine spirituality as distinctive, yet related to masculine spirituality. It would also enable both kinds of spirituality to overcome the danger of becoming one-sided.

Hindu religious ideology recognizes the distinctiveness of each individual, as the notion of *svadharma* or one's own particular and concrete nature, demonstrates. Thus man and woman, child and adult, each is recognized as a person with a distinctive disposition who needs to develop according to his/her concrete, distinctive nature. However, due to various reasons mentioned in the foregoing account, the model of spiritual development has been fashioned in "masculine" terms. What is needed is the development of an inclusive model that also takes account of the distinctive nature of "feminine" spirituality. We, Hindu women, can learn from social scientists and theologians of other traditions to become aware of critical issues relating to all levels of women's lives and religious experience, and to communicate effectively with others. Today, many are thinking about a female model for spiritual growth. For instance, Marietta Geray in her essay "Expressing the Feminine: In Search of a Model,"[56] refers to H. J. J. Buytendijk, who indicates that femininity is

Adaptive dynamism (which) does not elicit any resistance and leads to the discovery of quality and stature, to encounter with things as they are, and thus to the discovery of value.

And further,

Motherliness, as a respectful, careful togetherness in selfless giving, fostering, nourishing, cherishing and caressing, is always the power that everywhere elicits the unfolding, the realization of hidden potential of what is good, tender, fragile or subtle, whether in human beings or in nature or culture.[57]

There are instances of religious traditions (e.g., Taoism) identifying wisdom with the feminine spirit. In Hinduism, *Stri dharma* or woman-duty does not confine women to the physical roles of wife or mother, but requires them to be nurturing and caring. While there is no need for Hindu women to feel defensive about seeking fulfillment through the roles of wife or mother, there is also no need for them to accept such roles due to societal pressure. Imposition of roles on men or women end up hurting both, and the true liberation of humanity cannot come about until both men and women can exercise freedom of choice in matters both material and spiritual, external and internal.

NOTES

1. A devotee of Visnu, commonly described as preserver God.
2. One who worships the Ultimate in the form of many deities.
3. *Śvetāśvatara Upaniṣad*, 4:3. All quotations from the Upaniṣads are my free renderings of the Sanskrit verses, if not mentioned otherwise. The English translations

consulted are S. Radhakrisnan, *The Principal Upaniṣad* (London: Allen Unwin, 1968), and Swami Nikhilananda, *The Upaniṣads* (New York: Harper Torchbooks, 1963).

4. *Bṛhadaranyaka Upaniṣad*, 11, 4:5.

5. David Mandelbaum, *Society in India: Continuity and Change* (Berkeley: University of California Press, 1970), 1:86.

6. Iravati Karve, *Kinship Organization of India* (Bombay and New York: Asia House, 1965).

7. Trivandrum Journal, *New York Times,* Friday, 29 Jan. 1988.

8. Jayasree, *India and Indian Women as Seen by Women of the World* (Aligarh, India: Granthyan, 1980), 35.

9. Rabindranath Tagore, *Mashi and Other Stories* (New York: Macmillan, 1918). Bengali version was published in *Prabashi* (Calcutta), Asvin, 1332 (1925).

10. Ved Mehta, *Daddyji* (New York: Farrar, Straus, and Giroux, 1972).

11. Ibid., 142–43.

12. Monisha Roy, *Bengali Women* (Chicago: University of Chicago Press, 1971).

13. *Kaṭa Upaniṣad*, 2, 1–2.

14. Ibid., 4, 1–2.

15. *Bṛhadaranyaka Upaniṣad*, 2, 4:3.

16. One of the central values taught in the various episodes of the *Mahābharata* is renunciation. One famous story is that of King Yajati who, when he lost his ability of sense gratification due to aging, exchanged his body with his youngest son to enjoy sensual pleasures again. Eventually he came to the realization that humans cannot be satisfied by indulgences, and he then practiced austerity.

17. *Bhāgavad-Gitā, 3*, 34–43.

18. An example from one of the well-known *Purāṇas*, the *Bhagavāt*, Chapter 2, describes a perfect yogi as someone in total control of their mind, a person of total desirelessness.

19. Manu, *The Laws of Manu*, trans. G. Buhler, with extracts from seven commentaries (Oxford University Press, 1886; Delhi: Motilal Benerassidas, 1964), 10:63.

20. M. N. Srinivasa, *Social Change in Modern India* (Berkeley: University of California Press, 1966).

21. Peter L. Berger, *The Sacred Canopy* (New York: Doubleday Anchor, 1969), 4: "Externalization is the ongoing outpouring of human being into the world both in the physical and the mental activity of men. Objectivation is the attainment by the products of this activity (again both physical and mental) of a reality that confronts its original producers as a facticity external to and other than themselves. Internalization is the reappropriation by men of this same reality, transforming it once again from structures of the objective world into structures of the subjective consciousness. It is through externalization that society is a human product. It is through objectivation that society becomes a reality *sui generis*. It is through internalization that man is a product of society."

22. *Yama* literally means restrictions. It refers to: *ahimsā* (nonviolence), *asteya* (nonstealing), *satya* (truth), *brahmachrya* (continence), and *aparigraha* (nonacceptance of charity).

23. *Niyama* literally means rule. It refers to: *saucha* (purity of body and mind), *santosa* (contentment), *tapas* (austerity), *svādhyāya* (self-study), and *iśvarapranidhana* (self-surrender).

24. Srinivasa, in *Social Change in Modern India*, discusses how Westernization is a way of upward mobility in Indian society and is considered to bring "culture" to India.

25. Sita is the central woman figure of *Rāmāyana,* written by Valmiki in Sanskrit, likely from some stories that used to be sung as ballads. The current versions of three different recensions have seven books. The story perhaps originated in 500 B.C. Later, many versions in different vernaculars of India were composed by various authors. Tulsidas's *Rāmacaritamānasa* is popular in North India. Most Hindus know *Rāmāyana* stories in the different vernacular versions. Sita's story is present in the *Purāṇas* also, for example *Devi Bhāgavata.*

26. Savitri's story is in the Vānaparva of *Mahābhārata,* popularly attributed to the authorship of Vedavyāsa; it is not the work of one author. In its present form, it is considered to be later than the *Rāmāyana.* Its main story is interwoven with so many moral teachings that some scholars consider it an encyclopedia of moral teachings. Most Hindus read and know the different vernacular versions of the story. In Bengal the *Mahābhārat* of Kashidasa is popular.

27. Sati is the wife of Siva and is presented under many names and worshipped in many forms as Umā, Kālī, Durgā, etc. Her story can be found in many *Purāṇas* and in *Mahabhābhārata. Devi Bhāgavata* describes the incarnation of Sati. The oral stories are conglomerates of these various sources, and most Hindus know about the story from oral sources.

28. The nineteenth-century reformer Isvarachandra Vidyasagara supported widow marriage, the stopping of suttee (immolation of the widow), and having a minimum age for the marriage of a girl (derived from the Hindu scriptures). The government passed laws regarding these matters. However, even to this day there are occurrences of widow-burning.

29. An analogue is the Protestant idea of being in grace.

30. Wedding hymns of the Hindus.

31. My free translation of Tagore's Bengali song "Tumy dhanya dhanya he."

32. Manu, 9:101–2.

33. Ibid., 9:96.

34. Ibid., 9:95.

35. Ibid., 9:59–60.

36. Ibid., 6:47; also, 33–36, 41–43, 45–49, and 60–65.

37. Ibid., 5:148.

38. Arvind Sharma, ed., *Women in World Religions* (Albany: State University of New York Press, 1987).

39. The famous advaitic statement *tat tvam asi* (that thou are) of *Chāndogya Upaniṣad,* 6.8, 6–7, is a good example.

40. *Ṛg Veda,* 10:90.

41. Ibid., 10:129.

42. Translation of *nāṣadiya sukta* in Louis Renou, ed., *Hinduism,* reprint (New York: Washington Square Press, 1969), 47–48.

43. Sri Sankara, *Deyyāparādhakṣāmapaṇa Stotram,* vol. 3, trans. and quoted in Swami Yatiswarananda, *Meditation and Spiritual Life,* (Bengalore: Sri Ramakrishna Asrama, 1979), 367.

44. Manu, 2:145.

45. Louis Dumont, *Homo Hierarchicas: The Caste System and Its Implications,* trans. M. Sainsbury (Chicago: University of Chicago Press, 1970).

46. Manu, 9:4.

47. Carol Gilligan, *In a Different Voice* (Cambridge: Harvard University Press, 1982).

48. Charles J. Adams, ed., *A Reader's Guide to the Great Religions of the World* (London: Free Press, Collier-Macmillan, 1965), 39. Quoted by J. B. Noss, *Man's Religions*, 6th ed. (London and New York: Macmillan, 1980), 273. On the same page Noss quotes from the *Doctrine of the Mean*: "There are four things in the moral life of a man, not one of which I have been able to carry out in my life. To serve my father as I would expect my son to serve me: that I have not been able to do. To serve my sovereign as I would expect a minister under me to serve me: that I have not been able to do. To act towards my elder brother as I would expect my younger brother to act towards me: that I have not been able to do. To be the first to behave towards friends as I would expect them to behave towards me: that I have not been able to do."

49. Sandra M. Schneider, "The Effects of Women's Experience on Their Spirituality," in Joann Wolski, ed., *Women's Spirituality* (New York: Paulist Press, 1986), 31–38.

50. Galbraith, John, *Economics and Public Purpose* (Boston: Houghton Mifflin, 1973). Mishan, *The Cost of Economic Growth* (London: Staples Press, 1967).

51. For a biography of Sarada Devi, see Swami Gambhirananda, *Holy Mother Sri Sarada Devi*, 2d ed. (Madras: Sri Ramakrishna Math, 1969).

52. Srimata Gayatri Devi, *One Life's Pilgrimage* (Cohasset, MA: Advaita Asrama, 1977).

53. Swami Vivekananda, "On Indian Women—Their Past, Present, and Future," in *Complete Works of Swami Vivekananda*, 10th ed. (Delhi: Advaita Asrama, 1971–73), 5:228–32.

54. Carl G. Jung, *Modern Man in Search of a Soul* (London: Routledge and Kegan Paul, 1952), 141.

55. *Bhāgavad-Gītā*, 2, 55–72.

56. Marietta Geray, O. S. B., "Expressing the Feminine: In Search of a Model," *Review for Religions* 47 no. 1 (1988).

57. Ibid., 44–45.

7

"The Dharma...Is Neither Male Nor Female"*: Buddhism on Gender and Liberation

RITA M. GROSS

I am a Western woman who became a Buddhist in my adulthood. By then, feminism and concern that my human dignity be fostered were already well developed in me. Previously, in my experiences with Christianity and later with Judaism, I had encountered serious frustration regarding negative images of women and had felt blocked by institutionalized sexism in those traditions. I did not want a third such experience. I was also very attracted to *dharma,* the basic teachings of Buddhism, and especially to its meditation practices because dharma and meditation are so profoundly liberating. Nevertheless, I knew that potential for the same kind of blockage and frustration existed in Buddhism because Buddhism's record on gender issues is not especially clean. Since Judaism and Christianity also contain a normative liberating set of core teachings beyond their institutionalized sexism, why become Buddhist rather than working within the institutions of Judaism or Christianity?

My choice had little to do with gender issues. Problems regarding gender equality exist in all religions, though they are deeper in some religions than others. My answer is enigmatic; karmically,[1] it seems that I am Buddhist. That is the simplest explanation for my strong sense of affinity and familiarity with Buddhism. I needed only to determine for myself that my gender would not be made into a major obstacle. In the context of contemporary North American Buddhism, one can avoid that obstacle. At the same time, because Buddhism's record on gender issues is flawed, sometimes quite seriously, it is critical to bring a feminist perspective into Buddhism.[2]

This chapter will survey both the inherently liberating, gender-free Buddhist

*From the *Sutra of Sagara, the Naga King,* quoted by Diana Y. Paul, *Women in Buddhism: Images of the Feminine in Mahyana Tradition* (Berkeley: Asian Humanities Press, 1979), 276.

dharma and the ways in which this *dharma* has been contaminated throughout the centuries by male supremacist statements and institutions. On the one hand, core Buddhist teachings are remarkably free of gender bias. On the other hand, Buddhist institutions have failed women. In all periods and in all sects, women have not done as well as men in achieving the goals of Buddhism, at least according to public record and communal memory.

Though all versions of Buddhism recognize some women as completely accomplished, no version of Buddhism expects women to achieve these goals in roughly equal numbers with men, and no version of Buddhism expects or experiences women to be as influential in the development of Buddhism as are men.

This discrepancy between view and achievement can only be the result of massive institutional failure. Buddhists have not noticed the contradiction between their inherently gender-free core teachings and the male supremacist social and cultural forms, the popular attitudes and practices that have also characterized Buddhism as a sociological reality throughout its history. However, Buddhism does not include, as a religious norm or sacred ideal, the two beliefs that build male supremacy into the ideological foundations of a religion. First, because Buddhism is nontheistic, it avoids the main problem in monotheistic religions— the existence of a Supreme Being who is popularly imagined as a male and always referred to in male terms, thereby promoting the feeling that somehow men are closer to that supreme being than are women. Second, unlike Hinduism, Judaism, or Islam, Buddhism does not have a divinely given sacred social code or set of religious laws governing social and cultural life, including the interactions of men and women. Therefore it also lacks the sacred ideal of separate but complementary spheres for women and men that is part of the law code of these religions. For Buddhism, all phenomenal, worldly, social customs and ideals are merely customary and cultural; they are *not* part of *dharma*, the eternal truths of existence. Therefore, there is no normative or religious basis (as opposed to basis in convention) for gender roles in Buddhism. Why then does the debate about women continue for centuries in the Buddhist texts? Why is there a need for Buddhist feminism?

In trying to untie this knot, to present both the promise and the problems of Buddhism, I will draw upon both my academic and Buddhist training and concerns. As an academic, I am trained in the comparative study of world religions. I am by no means a professional Buddhalogist, though my major area of interest has always been Indian religion. As a Buddhist, I belong to a Tibetan Vajrayana lineage and my root *guru* is Chogyam Trungpa.[3] This affiliation inclines me to emphasize Mahayana teachings, which are generally considered by scholars to be more "pro-women" than the teachings of earlier Buddhism. My training in Vajrayana Buddhism, which has teachings unique in the Buddhist world regarding women and the "feminine principle," also profoundly influences my understanding of gender and Buddhism.[4] Both my academic and my Buddhist training are far more extensive in Indo-Tibetan Buddhism than in Far Eastern forms of Buddhism. As a result, unfortunately, this chapter will not give Far Eastern forms of Buddhism the attention they deserve.

HISTORICAL OVERVIEW OF WOMEN IN BUDDHISM

Buddhism began roughly 2,500 years ago in North India. It was founded by Siddartha Gautama, an upper-caste male of royal status who had abandoned his family, social position, and wealth. Such actions were not unusual in India of that day; liberation was thought to be difficult or impossible to attain while one was involved in domestic and social activities, and many young (and older) men did as Siddartha Gautama had done. Almost immediately after his enlightenment experience and his first sermon, several other male world-renouncers became his followers. The monastic community grew rapidly.

After some years, his aunt, Mahaprajapati, who had raised him from birth, approached the Buddha and asked that she and her women companions also be allowed to shave their heads, put on monastic robes, and join the renunciant community. At first the request was refused, but eventually the institution of a nuns' order was permitted. However, the nuns were required to accept eight special rules as a precondition for their admission to the order; these rules subordinated the nuns' order to the monks' order. Additionally, the comment was made that, since women had been permitted to join the order, the *dharma* would last only 500 years instead of 1,000 years. In modern scholarship, it has often been suggested that this narrative is a later interpolation, since it seems quite contradictory with the actual achievements of women in very early Buddhism and is not found in the oldest stratum of Buddhist literature. However, as Nancy Falk points out, because this statement was widely circulated, it has had a great impact on Buddhism.[5]

Such restrictions and proclamations did little to deter women from entering the renunciant *Sangha* (Buddhist community) and had even less effect on their ability to gain the insights required for liberation from *samsara* (cyclic existence). Many women became nuns and many women attained *nirvana*, the extinction of craving, which brought cessation of rebirths, the goal and ideal of early Buddhism. These women's moving stories, often in the form of eloquent poems in which the women express their realization and their penetrating insight, were collected as the *Therigatha*, the Songs of the Women Elders. The literature was preserved by Theravadin Buddhism, found today in Southeast Asia.[6]

However, historians of Buddhism generally conclude that some centuries after the death of the Buddha, attitudes hardened. The monastic *Sangha* reserved more and more power and respect for itself. Lay people were thought of *merely* as patrons and, despite the *Therigatha*, belief that women could not attain enlightenment grew more popular. However, at the same time, new tendencies were developing. Within 500 years of the Buddha's death, full-blown Mahayana (literally, Great Vehicle) Buddhism emerged. In addition to significant philosophical differences with earlier Buddhism, nascent Mahayana Buddhism understood the *Sangha,* or Buddhist community, differently. As the monastic *Sangha* grew more self-aggrandizing, Mahayanists deliberately emphasized the larger *Sangha,* including lay people and women. Therefore, many scholars include greater (or renewed) openness to women among the general characteristics of the Mahayana.

Indeed, many of the most famous and influential Mahayana texts explicitly take up the question of how much a woman can attain, concluding that women's abilities are unlimited and equal to men's. Often the Mahayana Sutras present a debate between a highly developed female and a male representative of the older viewpoint. He is always astounded and disgruntled by the woman's intelligence. She always confounds him. He always asks why, if she is so realized, she is not a man. At this point two motifs end the story. In one variant, the female magically transforms her body into a male body. In the other she retains her female body, demonstrating by magic or by logic the utter relativity and unimportance of sexual differentiation.[7]

However, these narratives do not answer another important question: can a woman attain complete perfect enlightenment, or Buddhahood? One of the critical developments in Mahayana thinking was the Bodhisattva path, recommended now for all serious practitioners. Instead of striving for individual *nirvana* bringing release from cyclic existence, Buddhists were encouraged to take the Bodhisattva vow to attain enlightenment for the sake of all sentient beings. No one doubted that women could achieve the inspiration to take the Bodhisattva vow, but some contended that at some point in the progression toward complete perfect enlightenment and Buddhahood, the future Buddha would stop being reborn as a female. Thus, the Bodhisattva would repeat the pattern of the life-history of the historical Buddha, Siddartha Gautama. In all versions of the stories about his previous lives, he stopped being reborn as female quite early, before he stopped being reborn as an animal.[8] Many Mahayana texts simply saw womanhood and Buddhahood as antithetical to each other. A few texts draw this conclusion for misogynist reasons. Much more common, however, is the reasoning that to become a Buddha, a being must first experience five other conditions that are simply unavailable to women.[9] Other texts state that Buddhahood is neither male nor female, but beyond gender altogether, while a few texts may possibly portray a Buddha in female form.[10]

Later, Vajrayana or Tantric Buddhism, which is based on the Mahayana but also goes beyond it, developed in India and subsequently spread to Tibet. Vajrayana Buddhism is often regarded as the form of Buddhism that most radically includes women and the feminine because of an appreciation of women and the feminine principle intrinsic to this form of Buddhism. This form of Buddhism has also been much maligned in Western scholarship and is suspect in some Buddhist circles because of appreciation of women and the feminine principle, which has frequently been misinterpreted as a permission for wholesale and indiscriminate sexuality. Much of this misinterpretation stems from misunderstanding basic Vajrayana imagery, in which all the Buddhas and Bodhisattvas can be portrayed as partners—female and male—in sexual union. The fundamental pair consists of discriminating awareness (*prajna*), which brings insightful liberation, and her partner, compassion. Though she represents the epitome of realization she is not isolated, but is joined in male-female union with compassion (*karuna*)—activity to save all sentient beings. No wonder this version of Buddhism reveres many important female leaders and founders, especially in Tibet. That female Buddhas exist is not a question in Tibetan Vajrayana. Of course Yeshe Tsogyel and other women became Buddhas within a single lifetime.[11]

Nevertheless, women, as a class, did not even remotely experience equality with men, as a class, over time, even in Tibetan Vajrayana. The nuns' full ordination died out after the persecutions of the eighth century. Though male monastic orders became extremely important, especially after the twelfth century, no one thought it important to revive the nuns' order until the twentieth century; even now it remains a questionable issue. Meanwhile, nuns were treated essentially as servants and their education was appallingly limited compared to the monks. Vajrayana and Tibetan Buddhism also recognized a non-monastic path to realization as equally valid and equally conducive to full realization. Many Vajrayanists with consorts are recorded as having achieved high levels of realization and being important to the development of Vajrayana. However, in too many cases, the focus is on *him* and *his* consort; in very few, if any, cases, does the venerated story focus on her and her consort.[12]

Southeast Asia received the older, Theravadin, version of Buddhism. The nuns' ordination was allowed to die out in all forms of Theravadin Buddhism; contemporary attempts to revive it are extremely controversial and often meet with extreme skepticism, or even hostility. Furthermore, in Theravadin countries, a monastic-lay hierarchy seems to have prevailed, limiting the access of laypersons, both female and male, to the most valued dimensions of Buddhist meditation practice and evaluation.

East Asian Buddhism, both in China and Japan, presents a different and somewhat more complex picture. Though Far Eastern forms of Buddhism are institutionally male dominated, Buddhism nevertheless brought new options to women in East Asian societies.[13] Furthermore, in East Asian Buddhism, some aspects of Buddhism favorable to women are highlighted more than in other forms of Buddhism. The full ordination for nuns has been preserved in China. This lineage of ordination, unique in the Buddhist world, is critically important in contemporary Buddhism, since this lineage will be the source for renewing nuns' full ordination in other parts of the Buddhist world. In Japanese forms of Buddhism another kind of ordination is also available to women. Without taking monastic vows, women, like men, can be ordained as "priests" and then fill leadership and liturgical functions in their communities.[14] Furthermore, popular devotional forms of Buddhism, both in China and Japan, do give significant reverence to female mythical and iconographical representations of Buddhas and Bodhisattvas.[15]

Currently, all forms of Buddhism are being transmitted to the West. This event provides the greatest opportunity in Buddhist history for Buddhist institutions to manifest, rather than to contradict, Buddhism's worldview regarding gender relations. In the West, currently, women are active and influential in all forms of Buddhism.[16] It is too soon to tell whether women will continue their strong presence and influence in future generations of Western Buddhism. With neglect, with too much complacency about possible patriarchal backlash, this exemplary situation could be defused in subsequent generations, as has happened previously not only in Buddhism but in other major world religions.[17]

LIBERATION IN BUDDHISM

Many attempts have been made by both Buddhists and Buddhalogists to define the essentially ineffable quality of liberation.[18] All such attempts ultimately fail because liberation is a matter of experience, not theory. Perhaps liberation is best defined as knowing how to untie the knot of existence. To be liberated is to know "things as they are," a classic Buddhist phrase, and to know how to live with those conditions freely and compassionately.

Compacted into the definition is the claim that life, as conventionally lived and felt, presents a puzzle and a problem, a gnawing and pervasive feeling of frustration, alienation, and inadequacy. The knot of existence is classically presented as the First Noble Truth—all conditioned existence involves suffering. Nevertheless, that knot can be untied. The Second Noble Truth states that this knot is kept tight by clinging, attachment, and greed. The Third Noble Truth states that when the causes of such frustration, alienation, and inadequacy are given up, they themselves dissolve. What this means is inexpressible; some versions of Buddhism, especially earlier forms of Buddhism, define this dissolution and liberation in essentially world-denying and negative terms such as freedom from rebirth. Mahayana and Vajrayana forms of Buddhism use different language and stress that liberation involves knowing how truly to live "neither wandering in *samsara* (cyclic existence) nor dwelling in *nirvana* (cessation of cyclic existence)." This definition of liberation avoids the issue of whether liberation is worldly or otherworldly, an important element of an adequate definition of Buddhist liberation. Liberation is simply knowing what is and how to work with what is, as well as knowing how to appreciate what is.

Buddhism prescribes a clear path, a total lifestyle, that facilitates the achievement of such liberation. That lifestyle is defined by the Fourth Noble Truth, the truth of the path. Though the path contains eight elements, it is conveniently condensed into three major disciplines—*Sila, Samadhi,* and *Prajna,* or moral discipline, spiritual cultivation, and the pursuit of wisdom.

GENDER AND LIBERATION IN BUDDHIST TRADITION

Liberated existence and the lifestyle fostering liberation clearly have nothing to do with gender. Nevertheless, as already demonstrated in the historical overview of Buddhist attitudes toward women, Buddhist texts and institutions do not manifest this irrelevance of gender. In all historical periods and in all Buddhist cultures, texts debate how far women can proceed on the path and institutions systematically exclude women or demand their subservience to men. It should be pointed out that whenever gender does become an issue in Buddhism, the debate and the special rules concern themselves *always* with the female gender and *never* with the male gender. Thus, Buddhism demonstrates one of the primary characteristics of patriarchy and androcentrism pointed out by feminist scholars. Men are assumed to be normal human beings, while women are exceptions to that norm, needing to be explained, objectified, and given a place.[19]

Throughout this long Buddhist debate on gender, two basic conclusions are repeated in numerous variations. One conclusion is that there is some basic problem with the female gender. Women are thought to be much less likely to make significant progress on the path and Buddhist men declaim on the preferability of maleness over femaleness. The variants of this conclusion range from hostility toward and fear of women to pity for the misfortune of female rebirth, readily explainable as due to the *karma* of those reborn as women. This "solution" to the problem of gender is perhaps somewhat more frequent and popular than the second, much more normative, conclusion that being female presents no barrier to the achievement of liberation. This position is stated explicitly and clearly in texts of all major variants of Buddhism. Two major variants of this position occur. More frequently, gender is declared to be irrelevant and essentially nonexistent; somewhat rarely, one finds statements that positively link femaleness and spiritual attainments.

It is important to emphasize that this second conclusion is common and long-standing in Buddhism. The claim, made by some feminist critics of religion, that *all* major world religions are *essentially* patriarchal and serve men's interests[20] is defused by this information. The Buddhist record on this issue is ambiguous, not clear-cut. Buddhism is not without patriarchal tendencies, but the more normative statements are those denying any link between gender and liberation.

When femaleness is viewed negatively in Buddhism, does that negativity reflect misogyny? Or is it the result of other concerns? Religious misogyny is so common that one is automatically predisposed to see misogyny in statements such as the famous passage in which the Buddha advises a monk. The monk asks, "How are we to conduct ourselves, Lord, with regard to womenkind?" "As not seeing them, Ananda." "But if we should see them, what are we to do?" "Not talking, Ananda." "But if they should speak to us, Lord, what are we to do?" "Keep wide awake, Ananda."[21] Scholars are divided on whether such passages should be interpreted as evidence of misogyny or more simply as a male expression of the difficulties of asceticism and world renunciation. The more cogent interpretation, in my view, is that such passages reflect feelings not about the evils of women, but about the difficulty of celibacy. Nuns would experience similar difficulties; since so little is recorded by the nuns, we do not hear of them.[22]

Unambiguously misogynist statements do exist in Buddhist texts, but they are relatively rare. Many of them are found in Mahayana debates about whether a woman could become a Buddha. One of the most negative statements I have encountered occurs in an important Mahayana work by an important Mahayana teacher. Asanga writes in his *Bodhisattvabhumi*, "Completely perfected Buddha-s are not women. And why? Precisely because a bodhisattva . . . from the time he has passed beyond the first incalculable age [of his career] has completely abandoned the women's estate. . . . Ascending . . . to the most excellent throne of enlightenment, he is never again reborn as a woman. All women are by nature of defilement and of weak intelligence. And not by one who is by nature full of defilement and of weak intelligence is completely perfected Buddhahood attained."[23] Such statements, even when made by teachers as important as Asanga, are not necessarily normative and are directly contradicted by other statements made by at least equally important teachers.

In my view, this negative assessment of femaleness is not primarily due to either male ascetics' fears of women or to unabashed misogyny. Rather, being female is regarded as an *unfortunate,* not an *evil* or *inferior* condition. In Asian societies, women's lives were difficult and harsh. The ideal human lifestyle is the life of spiritual cultivation leading to enlightenment. Nevertheless, throughout the Buddhist world, that lifestyle was routinely made more difficult for women than for men to pursue. Consider further difficulties of female life under conditions of intensive agriculture: complete lack of birth control, high maternal death rate, high infant mortality rate, heavy domestic responsibilities, and subservience to males. No wonder, with all these difficulties as a woman's lot, we encounter a widespread assumption that male existence is preferable to female existence. This is why it is so often stated that female birth is the result of unfortunate *karma* and why there is such a widespread presumption that women who make significant progress in this life will be reborn as men in future lives. Who would return to a more difficult and less fortunate existence if she had accrued sufficient merit for a less difficult and more fortunate mode of existence?

The promise of future rebirth as a male stems from pity and compassion, not scorn and misogyny. Thus, though it can cause modern readers some shock, one can more readily understand the famous thirty-fourth vow taken by Buddha Amitabha: "if, after I have obtained Bodhi [enlightenment], women in immeasurable, inconceivable, incomparable, immense Buddha countries on all sides, after having heard my name, should allow carelessness to arise, should not turn their thoughts toward Bodhi, should, when they are free from birth, not despise their female nature; and if they, being born again should assume second female nature, then may I not obtain the highest perfect knowledge."[24] In this text, Amitabha, in a previous life, is vowing to create a Pure Land upon achieving Buddhahood. This Pure Land, to be the result of Amitabha's infinite merit and compassion, will offer ideal conditions for the attainment of liberation.[25]

Texts of equal, sometimes superior, authority and popularity portray females who manifest high levels of spiritual attainment. In these texts, their femaleness is viewed as irrelevant or is positively valued. Often this point of view is voiced by women in reply to men who question how a woman could be so highly developed. Thus, such texts reflect not only male bias, in that women's abilities *are* questioned, but also disapproval of that bias—something noteworthy for a tradition that was male-dominated and in which, for the most part, men kept the records.

Gender is irrelevant in Buddhism because liberation involves mental and spiritual composure and insight—traits not particularly linked with male anatomy. This basic point is made most forcefully and eloquently in the story of one of the highly accomplished nuns of early Buddhism. Taunted by the (male) Tempter Mara that she possesses only the limited intelligence of a woman she replies,

> What does the women's nature do to us if the mind
>   is well-composed
> If our knowledge progresses rightly, giving insight
>   in the Teaching?
> Pleasure is completely destroyed for me; dark ignorance
>   has been pierced
> Thus know, Evil Death, you are destroyed!
> If a person still thinks to ask: "Am I a woman in these
>   things? Or am I a man?"
> This is one to whom Mara can talk.[26]

Other texts, especially in the Mahayana literature, go further, asserting not only the irrelevance of gender but also the nonexistence of gender as a category of absolute, rather than relative, significance. Obviously, if gender does not really exist at a profound level of experience, one cannot make distinctions and restrictions based on gender. Though this insight was never put into widespread practical application in the Buddhist world, its prestige, even its very presence in important literature, always served to counter misogynist and patriarchal tendencies.

The most famous version of this evaluation of gender is found in the *Vimilakirtinirdesa-Sutra*. It takes the form of a dialogue between Sariputra, parodied as a representative of the conservative viewpoint, and a "Goddess," a highly developed female who has lived in Vimalakirti's palace for twelve years. Finding the Goddess highly developed spiritually, Sariputra asks her why she doesn't change her female form (remember: some Mahayana texts *do* involve the motif that an accomplished female acquires male anatomy in the present life).[27] She replies, "I have been here for twelve years and have looked for the innate characteristics of the female sex and haven't been able to find them. How can I change them?" After further metaphysical discussion, the Goddess, by supernatural power, changed Sariputra into a likeness of herself and herself into a likeness of Sariputra. Then she asked, "Why don't you change your female sex?'' The befuddled Sariputra has no cogent answer, whereupon the Goddess remarks, ''Sariputra, if you can change into a female form, then all women . . . can also change. Just as you are not really a woman but appear to be female in form, all women also appear to be female in form but are not really women. Therefore, the Buddha said *all are not really men or women*'' (emphasis mine). After the Goddess changes Sariputra back into his own form, she asks him, ''Where are the female form and innate characteristics now?'' The much chagrined and more insightful Sariputra replies, ''The female form and innate characteristics neither exist nor do not exist.''[28]

Denying the relevance or existence of gender undercuts misogyny and patriarchy negatively. Misogyny and partriarchy could also be countered by positive affirmations of femaleness. This option is much less frequent in Buddhist literature, occurring, to my knowledge, only in the literature of Vajrayana Buddhism, which presents two variants of this theme.

On the one hand, human females can be seen as more apt at spiritual practice, a view attributed to Padmasambhava, the first great teacher of Buddhism in Tibet:

> The human body is the basis of the accomplishment of wisdom.
> And the gross bodies of men and women are equally suited,
> But if a woman has strong aspiration, she has the higher potential.[29]

The second possible affirmation of femaleness is more common in Tibetan Vajrayana literature. Whether human females are respected or not, the Feminine Principle is highly regarded. One of the core symbols of Vajrayana Buddhism, omnipresent in both Tibetan art and *sadhana*-s (spiritual practices), is the sexual union of masculine and feminine. All the Buddhas and Bodhisattvas of the Varjrayana mythical universe can be thus portrayed. Virtually every other important phenomenon also embodies either the male or the female principle. Furthermore, these two principles are not viewed hierarchically in any way. Rather, they are essentially complementary and mutually necessary, forming a dyadic unity in which each is distinctive, neither is superior, and they are inseparable. Though the symbolisms are subtle, profound, and vast, they can be summarized as the interplay of (female) wisdom and (male) compassion, of space and activity, both of which are necessary for attaining liberation for both one's self and for others.

Though this form of Buddhism does involve a highly positive assessment of femaleness, at least in the form of the Feminine Principle, such symbolism is inadequate and incomplete by itself. It does not necessarily guarantee equality in life between men and women. Indeed, for Tibetan culture, the long-term historical record on this point is bleak and depressing, despite Tibetan appreciation of the Feminine Principle and Padmasambhava's positive assessment of women's potentials.

Because Buddhist literature contains such contradictory attitudes about gender, easy generalizations about historical materials are unconvincing. The Buddhist record on gender equality is highly mixed. In some ways it is exemplary; in others depressing. A Buddhist feminist can easily compliment or criticize her tradition; in fact, in most cases, any institution or text could be both criticized and complimented. For example, the basic institution of nunship was intensely liberating in the context of ancient India and throughout the Buddhist world. It remains an important and liberating option for contemporary Buddhist women. The eight special rules, though they formally subordinate nuns to monks, do not undermine the essentially liberating potential of the nuns' lifestyle. Do we positively evaluate the existence of the nuns' order or should we criticize the eight special rules because they demean the nuns' order and are, therefore, at odds with basic Buddhist teachings? Probably both assessments are important.

BUDDHIST DOCTRINES RELEVANT TO GENDER

Buddhist doctrines were not usually formulated with any reference to gender in mind. Only some Buddhist institutions, especially the rules of monasticism, involve any specifications regarding gender. Indeed, as would be the case with any major religion, the basic insights of Buddhism are so elemental that they are in no way more relevant for or applicable to either gender. "The dharma . . . neither male nor female."[30] All-pervasive suffering, its origin in clinging, the possibility of its cessation, and the eightfold path outlining the lifestyle conducive to liberation—how could such basics about the human condition be linked with gender?

However, as with the other major world religions, because the historical record and many important texts are so inconsistent and self-contradictory about gender, because in fact gender-biased statements and practices abound despite the genderless dharma, it is necessary to deduce implications about gender from basic doctrines. Given the limited feminist analysis of Buddhism, my selections and interpretations will be somewhat idiosyncratic; they are also grounded in knowledge about, love of, and commitment to Buddhist teachings and practices.

In my view, key Buddhist doctrines provide no basis for gender privilege in Buddhism and in fact mandate gender equality at the same time as they undermine the relevance of gender. Most knowledgeable Buddhists, I believe, would agree with me on that assessment. Their disagreement with my position would probably stem from their reluctance to criticize Buddhism severely and to advocate changes in long-standing institutional practices and social customs prevalent in the Buddhist world. In many cases, they would not share the urgency with which I contend that misogyny, patriarchy, and gender privilege in any form are totally at odds with the *dharma* and therefore completely inappropriate in the Buddhist world.

As has already been discussed, gender inequality and privilege can be *explained* in Buddhist terms by means of teachings about karma and rebirth. Presumably, there are no injustices in the system of karma and rebirth. Everyone's present situation is a result of karma, and their skill in relating to that present situation is the karmic basis for determining future situations. Since, empirically, women's usual lifestyle, as dictated by the norms of all Buddhist cultures, has been harsher than men's and provided less opportunity to engage in formal study and practice, their unfortunate present situation must be due to karma accrued in the past. At the same time, since future rebirths are assumed and assured, coping well with the limitations of a woman's existence would lead to a more fortunate rebirth as a male. Buddhism is relatively optimistic among world religions in that it is generally believed that eventually all sentient beings will be reborn in conditions in which they can achieve liberation. Since a human birth is among the requisite endowments, women are, in fact, very close to such a rebirth. In a situation of strong faith in rebirth, such a set of explanations can work fairly well; in fact I have been assured that Buddhism is totally immune from any accusations that it fosters male privilege in any way because "deserving women will be reborn as men." Those who advocated this position to me were truly mystified when I tried to point out that their very statement was sexist, patriarchal, and male supremacist.

Though there are many problems with the line of argumentation that justifies continuing male privilege by appeal to doctrines of karma and rebirth, this argument is fundamentally flawed in its confusion of *descriptive* and *normative* statements. Karma can *explain* why women have been or are treated badly. It *does not justify continuing* to treat them badly. Though teachings about karma have often been used to justify complaisance and privilege, that is not the thrust of such teachings. If anything, since one's *present* actions create one's *future* situation, no one should be willing to support fundamentally repressive and cruel situations or institutions, such as gender privilege, militarism, or economic exploitation. Additionally, contributing one's efforts to undermining such situations and institutions would seem to produce karma leading to more fortunate future situations. Unfortunately, such socially relevant interpretations of the teachings about karma and rebirth have been relatively rare in Buddhism.

No other key doctrines of Buddhism can be or ever have been used to explain or attempt to justify gender hierarchy and privilege. In fact, all other major Buddhist teachings contradict any form of gender hierarchy. In some cases, these teachings have been used in traditional Buddhist arguments against gender-based privilege, in others not. All of them are highly relevant to a contemporary discussion of Buddhist teachings on gender and liberation.

Crucial among the core teachings of early Buddhism and all subsequent versions of Buddhism are the teachings concerning ego and egolessness. Everyone with elementary knowledge of Buddhism knows that Buddhists believe that ego is impermanent and not ultimately real and that, furthermore, belief in ego is the cause of suffering. It is also common knowledge that Buddhists believe that our true nature is our egolessness, our lack of permanent, immortal selfhood. Recognizing and deeply experiencing this lack of selfhood, this egolessness, is another among the many ways of trying to describe liberation.

Though the implications of teachings about ego and egolessness for gender-related issues have not been noticed in Buddhist literature, they are vast and profound. Gender identity is a dimension of ego identity rather than part of one's realization of egolessness. Even more so, gender privilege and gender hierarchy reinforce rather than undercut ego. Thus, any Buddhist institutions, such as the eight special rules subjugating nuns to monks, or any popular Buddhist stereotypes, such as the preference for male rebirth, that reinforce clinging to male ego are highly questionable and subject to criticism. Clinging to gender identity and basing access to important institutions and practices upon gender is not an aspect of liberation, but of *samsara,* inherently unliberated and painful existence. It has always seemed strange to me that a religion so keenly aware of the pitfalls and perils of ego has not been equally keen in its recognition that gender privilege is one of the more destructive manifestations of ego.

Among key doctrines of Buddhism, the one most frequently used in classical texts to refute the presupposition of male superiority is the doctrine of emptiness. This important Mahayana concept extends the realization that all things are empty of inherent existence, own-being, or ego to the entire phenomenal universe. Not only is ego ephemeral, impermanent, and ultimately nonexistent; likewise all phenomena are not really as solid and enduring as they seem to be. They too are ephemeral and ultimately nonexistent.

Because, as previously mentioned, Mahayana Buddhism deliberately advocated wider horizons socially, as well as doctrinally, Mahayanists more readily stressed the implications of emptiness for gender identity than did earlier Buddhists. Obviously, if nothing possesses inherent existence, then femaleness and maleness cannot, as such, be found; they lack substantiality and definite existence. This insight is, in fact, the basis of the many Mahayana texts in which a female bests a skeptical and condescending male in doctrinal debate, including the previously quoted exchange between the goddess and Sariputra. She always proves, and gets him to concede, that femaleness cannot bar her from high spiritual achievement and deep insight into things as they are. Critical in that demonstration is the argument that since nothing has inherent existence, femaleness does not have inherent existence and, therefore, cannot be used as a basis for discrimination.

As has been noted, the story has two endings. According to some texts, the woman changes her physiological sex into that of a male to demonstrate and prove her capabilities. This resolution of the debate seems inconsistent with her basic argument about the emptiness of gender as a category through which people can be limited and defined. Those texts in which she retains her femaleness, presumably without clinging to it or fixating upon it, are much truer to the insight that gender, like all phenomena, is empty of inherent existence.

Teachings about emptiness undercut gender hierarchy negatively, by denying that phenomena such as gender have any real or inherent existence. An equally important Mahayana teaching undercuts the basis of gender privilege positively, by asserting that all sentient beings share the most basic and important trait.

Everyone, without exception, has *tathagatagarbha* (seed of Buddhahood or the inherent potential for enlightenment) as their most fundamental characteristic. This trait alone accounts for the possibility of liberation. Furthermore, this Buddha-nature is simply Buddha-nature, inherent in one's very existence, unborn, unceasing, and non-dwelling, not subject to causes and conditions, unchanging, and certainly not different in women than in men. Such a statement would be incomprehensible and has never, to my knowledge, been made in any Buddhist text, important or minor. Discussions of inherent Buddha-nature always make the opposite point; even if a sentient being, through evil deeds and negative karma, descends into a subhuman form of existence, inherent and indwelling Buddha-nature nevertheless continues to characterize that being as its essential nature.

That all sentient beings, and all women and men, equally have the inherent potential for enlightenment as their most basic trait has always seemed to me to provide an incredibly strong critique of existing Buddhist institutions. If women and men have the same basic endowment, the same potential for enlightenment, then their vastly different achievements, as recorded throughout Buddhist history, can only be due to inadequate institutions, institutions that promote, encourage, and expect men to achieve higher levels of insight and realization. Someone trying to justify the status quo of gender privilege might try to argue that it simply is a woman's karma to live in a world in which her inherent potential is not fostered and encouraged as much as is a man's. However, that attempted explanation, by way of women's less fortunate karma, is simply an aspect of the inadequate institutions and lowered expectations limiting women.

Together, the concepts of emptiness and *tathagatagarbha* provide a very firm basis from which to argue that gender equality is a normative rather than an optional position in Buddhism. If gender equality is normative, then actively working to undercut gender hierarchy and privilege is a required ethical norm for Buddhists, not merely a marginal position for a few feminists. On the one hand, because all phenomena are empty and lack inherent existence, intrinsic maleness and femaleness cannot be found or defined. Therefore, men and women cannot be limited or defined by gender roles or stereotypes. On the other hand, the intrinsic nature of all beings, without regard to gender, is their potential for Buddhahood. Therefore, it is not appropriate to place institutional obstacles, such as formal subordination, lower expectations, or discouragement from the life of study and practice, in the path of either gender. Unfortunately, Buddhist texts have not emphasized, or even noted, how these key Mahayana concepts, especially in conjunction with each other, undercut the current Buddhist norms and expectations regarding gender.

Mahayana Buddhism includes another, perhaps even more basic key concept whose relevance to a discussion of gender issues has not been sufficiently noted. The concept of the Bodhisattva path may well be the heart of the entire Mahayana enterprise. According to teachings regarding the Bodhisattva path, one should work for the liberation of all sentient beings, rather than merely working for one's own liberation. The implications of such teachings for gender issues are obvious. If one is to help others attain liberation, one method of providing such help is working to alleviate social problems and inequities and also working to construct more humane and helpful alternative social conditions. Clearly, gender inequities are not the only relevant arena for social action motivated by one's Bodhisattva vow and commitments. But I have always been puzzled by the many generations of serious Buddhist practitioners who have taken the Bodhisattva vow with utmost sincerity and yet have retained and even promoted gender hierarchy and privilege in Buddhism. This conservatism may only be part of a general tendency in Asian forms of Buddhism to avoid acting socially and politically on the implications of Buddhist insights and teachings. Nevertheless, as with other important concepts discussed in this paper, it is now timely to engage in such activity. Someone who has taken the Bodhisattva vow should not promote gender inequality, whether by direct action or by merely passively accepting the status quo.

Vajrayana Buddhism also includes teachings that are highly relevant for gender issues. Its core symbolism stresses the co-equality and dyadic unity of the masculine and the feminine principles—concepts that have already been briefly discussed. It is further stated that these principles are not merely theoretical constructs. All people, both women and men, possess both the masculine and the feminine principles in their fundamental being and Vajrayana practices frequently involve developing them both. The implications are clear. If all people have potential to manifest both the feminine and masculine principles in their enlightened activity, then developing the social and religious forms and institutions that encourage and enable them to do so must be a primary agenda.

EXPLAINING BUDDHIST CONSERVATISM

Despite a strong basis for gender equality in core Buddhist teachings, Buddhism's record on gender equality is not significantly better than that of any other religion. The explanations for this discrepancy between Buddhism's vision and its actual sociological form can be explained historically. Throughout its history, Buddhism existed within a social, cultural, and intellectual environment not sympathetic or conducive to gender equality. And Buddhism clearly accommodated itself to that environment rather than standing against it.

By the time Buddhism emerged into history, patriarchy and androcentrism had become firmly established. These interdependent social and intellectual forms are extremely potent in mandating gender inequality. If males hold formal authority and power, as they do in patriarchal societies, then they also tend to be the creators of culture and religion. As such, they "name reality" out of their experience.[31] In that process, they define and limit women as objects in their mental universes. That is why patriarchal societies have an androcentric worldview, and why so often the status of women (but not of men) is a debatable issue. Until recent feminist analysis, no major world religion was aware of its androcentrism; Buddhism was no exception.

Buddhism was further limited in its realization of gender equality by the prevailing Hindu and Confucian ideals of strongly defined gender roles, typically seen as complementary though not of equal importance. These social norms, already entrenched in pre-Buddhist culture, both in India and in East Asia, included a clearly defined "women's place." That "place" was one of formal subordination to males, whether father, husband, or son. Furthermore, that "place" was understood to involve family life, marriage, and reproduction, first and foremost. Though such a lifestyle was not (especially in India) thought to be conducive to liberation, the alternative of world renunciation was always somewhat suspect for women, as we know from the narratives regarding the founding of the nuns' order and their order's relative lack of success.[32] Thus, Buddhism's strong theoretical basis for gender equality was overwhelmed by prevailing cultural mores and prejudices. Patriarchy, androcentrism, and strongly defined gender roles won out, even though they are not normative in Buddhism and are contradictory to its most important teachings.

From our vantage point, as we summarize and evaluate these Buddhist limitations of women, it is most important to recognize that the patriarchy, androcentrism, and strong definitions of gender roles that came to characterize Buddhism are *historical* occurrences, not instances of *eternal* truths or inevitabilities of gender relationship. Such a confusion between historical events and necessary conditions of human existence is probably the greatest problem in most discussions of gender issues. Male dominance and patriarchy are historical occurrences, explainable, but not inevitable. Many pre-patriarchal sources are now available for contemplation.[33] Furthermore, using historical and sociological methods, one can easily demonstrate that gender roles are currently obsolete and dysfunctional. Finally, Buddhism's vision and its sociological form could mesh.

THE DHARMA IS BOTH MALE AND FEMALE: ANDROGYNOUS VISION IN BUDDHISM

According to some Buddhist visions of the Pure Land, in which all rebirths are favorable and conducive to liberation, the problems of gender inequity and the empirical harshness of women's lives are solved by eliminating female rebirth. Perhaps under premodern technological, economic, and medical conditions it was more difficult to imagine eliminating the inequities and harsh *conditions* that women suffered than to imagine eliminating female rebirth. However one tries to explain a text that contains such a vision, it is painful to contemplate the limitations of that vision. Had I the merit to create a Pure Land, I would envision it as a realm in which gender hierarchy and gender privilege, not gender itself, were eliminated. The harshness of female existence under conditions of male domination and patriarchy is the problem to be eliminated, not femaleness.

Under contemporary conditions, especially as Buddhism and feminism mutually interact and transform each other, that vision of eliminating the harshness of female life, rather than altogether eliminating female rebirth, could be actualized. This is most likely to occur in situations in which the wisdom of both Buddhist and feminist visions is available. One could even hypothesize that this meeting and mutual interaction of Buddhism and feminism is a critical element in the long-awaited meeting and mutual transformation of East and West.

Western Buddhism, taking shape in an environment informed by feminist values, may well take the lead in finally grounding Buddhism's gender-free *dharma* in everyday realities that manifest, rather than contradict, its vision. To do so, Western Buddhism may call upon not only the rich teachings already outlined, but also the "prophetic voice" that is more typically found in Western religions and is also one of the major stimuli of the feminist movement in the West. It is physically impossible under current conditions for religions to develop further in isolation from and ignorance of each other. Rather, a process of dialogue and mutual transformation in inevitable. For Buddhism, the most important new ingredient coming out of this process is, in my view, permission to use the "prophetic voice." The permission, the command, and the urgency to voice worldly social criticism and reconstruction will mesh well with the *dharma* that already promotes gender equality. The Pure Land as envisioned by prophetic and androgynous Buddhism will be populated by both women and men.

To think of the Pure Land as peopled by both women and men rather than men only requires a subtle but profound shift in consciousness already well-known in feminist literature. Often thought of as a paradigm shift of the same magnitude as the passage from the geocentric to the heliocentric models of the universe, this shift in consciousness involves substituting one model of humanity for another. The most critical factor is the transition from the androcentric model of humanity to an androgynous model. The fundamental difference between these models is that the androcentric perspective defines women in terms of men, while the androgynous perspective is as interested in the world-construction done by women as in that done by men.[34]

When the androgynous perspective comes to prevail in Buddhism, women's experiences will count for as much as men's experiences (but no more). In such an androgynous perspective, both women's traditionally dictated concerns for motherhood and wifehood and women's nontraditional concerns for independence and self-articulation must be heard. Especially since men have articulated that women should be wives and mothers, and since this voice has been heard so loudly, other voices need to be heard. The voices of educated and consciously articulate women who are not male-identified are especially important, as much for men as for women. These are the voices that speak most clearly for the wholeness of human life beyond the gender roles and gender stereotypes that imprison men as much, though not as painfully, as they imprison women.

The androgynous voice articulates especially that humanity *is* gendered and that both genders are co-equally human, whatever similarities or differences any kind of research may discover. By contrast, androcentrism, which uses a generic masculine voice, sees men as normal and normative; if it sees the problems of gender inequity, it then states that gender does not really exist and is irrelevant. For example, despite their sexism, both Buddhism and Christianity state that the *dharma* is neither male nor female, that in Christ there is neither male nor female, a statement that is often seen as the ultimate truth. However, religions that deny the relevance of gender without affirming the androgynous nature of humanity always also manifest patriarchal social institutions that contradict their egalitarian vision. The sex-neutral model, which sees gender as irrelevant or nonexistent (neither male nor female), needs to be balanced by the androgynous, two-sex model, which sees humanity as *both* male and female. The sex-neutral model of seeing humanity as ultimately not really male or female is certainly accurate at the absolute level. The problem is that at the relative level, one cannot say that humans are neither male or female. At the relative level, we are clearly gendered, clearly both female and male. But the *dharma,* as currently formulated by Buddhism, is weak in its articulation of androgynous, two-sexed understandings of life, since it has relied almost entirely on androcentric or sex-neutral models of humanity.

Among Buddhist resources, one set of teachings is especially relevant to those trying to envision truly androgynous Buddhism. These are the Vajrayana teachings concerning the Feminine Principle and the Masculine Principle outlined previously. These teachings are useful especially for two reasons. The two principles are co-equal and co-necessary; they form a dyadic unity. Furthermore, according to Vajrayana teachings, men do not emulate only the masculine principle, nor women the feminine. Rather, both women and men are encouraged to become whole people manifesting both principles. However, the social implications of this vision need to be drawn out much more clearly and much more prophetically than was the case in Tibetan culture. To create such a truly androgynous Buddhism is the task inherited by Western Buddhists.

A single guideline will suffice. Since the problem in Buddhism is not with theoretical vision but with practical application, the need is to *mandate* and *institutionalize* gender equality, to build it into the fabric of Buddhist life and institutions completely, in a thoroughgoing fashion. This vision would then affect all aspects of Buddhist life and all the institutions that have been significant for Buddhists.

For lay Buddhist life, for householder Buddhists, the implications of androgynous vision are vast and profound. Since most Western Buddhists are householders, these implications are especially important for Western Buddhists. In many ways, the vision of androgynous lay Buddhism parallels the general feminist revisioning of society. Rather than building society on the basis of gender roles that then require women and men to relate out of mutual incompetence, both men and women will be whole human beings. Women will not specialize in reproduction and nurturance nor men in livelihood and defense; rather, human beings will specialize in whatever competencies and endowments their karma brings to them. Additionally, one can envision that certain fundamental human virtues, such as being able to care for one's self and being able to nurture and care for others, will be expected of all human beings.

Monastic Buddhism has traditionally been the major focus of Buddhist life. While it is questionable whether it is or should be the focus of Western Buddhist life, monasticism will remain an important and liberating option for Buddhists, both Western and Asian. The reforms for monastic institutions dictated by the androgynous vision are more obvious and clearcut than those required of householder Buddhists. They may also be more controversial to some Buddhists because direct changes in well-established and old Buddhist institutions are necessary. In forms of Buddhism in which full ordination for nuns has been lost, it needs to be restored immediately. The eight special rules for nuns, which subordinate all nuns to every monk, need to be rescinded despite their venerability as part of the *vinaya*. The horrendous inequities between monks and nuns regarding levels of education, economic support, and prestige that are endemic to all Buddhist cultures need to cease immediately. Finally, Buddhist cultures would no longer prefer women who stay within domestic and reproductive roles to women who seek world renunciation, while men are free to seek liberation beyond the householder lifestyle without suffering ridicule or subordination. In androgynous vision, if monasticism is recommended, then it will be available to all humans for whom it would be beneficial, without gender bias.

Between householder and monastic lifestyles is the Buddhist lifestyle of the *yogi*-s and *yogini*-s—serious practitioners who are not bound by either domestic or monastic rules of conduct. Best known in Vajrayana Buddhism, both Indian and Tibetan, they perhaps offer some of the most creative and open-ended models for contemporary Buddhist life. This model is significant in part because *yogini*-s such as Yeshe Tsogyel do not play second fiddle to their male counterparts.[35] However, the tradition recounts many fewer *yogini*-s than *yogi*-s and they are far less well-known. Androgynous vision would alter that situation.

Perhaps most fundamental, Buddhism informed by androgynous vision would no longer presume that most important Buddhist writers, teachers, and *guru*-s would be men. Well-educated, well-practiced, and articulate Buddhist women will formulate and manifest the unspeakable *dharma* as fully and as well as men. Why should things ever have been different? To an outsider, this issue may seem no more significant than any other. To one whose daily liturgy includes supplication to the *guru*-s of the lineage, no issue could be more central. If Buddhism has a functional equivalent of the male deity of monotheistic religions, it is the expectation and the actuality that the *guru*-s will be males.

If women are *guru*-s, will anything be different? Often, even in feminist circles, the key issue is thought to be that women should have the same chance to do what men have always done. In other feminist circles, it is keenly felt that women may well articulate different concerns that have not been adequately articulated, but concerns that would enrich and benefit the whole human enterprise. Certainly, if women are *guru*-s, at least women will have the kind of role models and heroes that men have always had. In a tradition that values the example of human liberation and perfection in human form as much as does Buddhism, such examples of human perfection in female form will not be irrelevant and without exemplary power.

However, the question remains. Has everything that needs to be said about liberation already been said by male Buddhists? Or when women finally participate fully in Buddhist speech, will they *add* to the sum total of Buddhist wisdom about liberation? The example of Western religions, especially Christianity, in which feminist analysis is far more developed than in Buddhism, suggests that the androgynous voice does not merely amplify what has always been said, but also adds to that message significantly.[36] Among Buddhists, no one has yet written the essays and books articulating a fully androgynous rendition of the wordless *dharma*. We await such proclamations.

NOTES

1. The law of *karma* is a pan-Indian belief about cause and effect. According to the law of karma, all deeds eventually produce an appropriate result to the doer of the deed, whether in this life or in some future life. Thus, at least some of one's current experiences are the result of deeds done in a past life. Strong interests that could not be environmentally induced or the feeling that very new materials are very familiar are frequently explained as due to one's previous involvement with these interests.

2. For an extensive discussion, see Rita M. Gross, "Buddhism and Feminism: Toward Their Mutual Transformation," *Eastern Buddhist*, n.s., 19, no. 1 (1986):44–58; no. 2 (1986): 62–74.

3. Vajrayana Buddhism depends heavily on concepts of lineage and *guru*. "Lineage" refers to the belief that the *dharma* was transmitted from teacher to student from generation to generation from the Buddha to the present day. One's root *guru* is one's major teacher, who stands in that unbroken lineage of transmission. The *guru*-disciple relationship is intense and highly devotional. For more information see Chogyam Trungpa, *Cutting Through Spiritual Materialism* (Berkeley: Shambhala, 1973), 31–47, and Osel Tendzin, *Buddha in the Palm of Your Hand* (Boulder, CO: Shambhala, 1982), 77–93. Trungpa's autobiography provides a fascinating account of a *guru* and of his relationships with his own *gurus*. Chogyam Trungpa, *Born in Tibet*, 3d ed. (Boulder, CO: Shambhala, 1977).

4. Several of my articles deal extensively with this topic. See Rita M. Gross, "The Feminine Principle in Vajrayana Buddhism: Reflections of a Buddhist Feminist," *Journal of Transpersonal Psychology* 16, no. 2 (1984): 179–92, and "I Will Never Forget to Visualize That Vajrayogini Is My Body and Mind," *Journal of Feminist Studies in Religion* 3 no. 1 (1987): 77–89.

5. Nancy Auer Falk, "The Case of the Vanishing Nuns: The Fruits of Ambivalence in Ancient Indian Buddhism," in Nancy Aver Falk and Rita M. Gross, eds., *Unspoken Worlds: Women's Religious Lives in Non-Western Cultures* (San Francisco: Harper and Row, 1980), 219.

6. Carolina A. Davids, trans., *Psalms of the Early Buddhists, vol. 1, Psalms of The Sisters* (London: Pali Text Society, Oxford University Press, 1909). A more recent translation is K. R. Norman, *The Elders' Verses, vol. 2, Therigatha* (London: Pali Text Society, Luzac & Co., 1971). Companion volumes of translations of the *Theragatha*

(Songs of the Male Elders) have been translated and published in the same series by the same translators.

7. Many of these texts have been collected and translated by Diana Y. Paul, *Women in Buddhism: Images of the Feminine in Mahyana Tradition* (Berkeley: Asian Humanities Press, 1979), 166–243. See also Nancy Schuster, "Changing the Female Body: Wise Women and the Bodhisattva Career in Some Maharatnakutasutras," *Journal of the International Association of Buddhist Studies* 4 (1981): 24–69.

8. Edward Conze, trans., *Buddhist Scriptures* (Middlesex, England: Penguin Books, 1959), 31. In this version of the Buddha's previous lives, he stopped being reborn as a woman at the end of the first incalculable eon of his Bodhisattva career, but did not revere Buddha Dipankana and receive confirmation from him of his eventual Buddhahood until the end of his second incalculable eon. From this point onward, he practiced the disciplines of a Bodhisattva leading to complete Buddhahood. In his incarnation as the Wise Hare, he perfected the virtue of generosity—an important stage. For these stories see Henry Clark Warren, *Buddhism in Translation* (New York: Atheneum, 1962), 35, 274–79. Though I know of no primary or secondary source that elaborates or comments on this conclusion, these texts indicate that female rebirth ceases long before animal rebirth in the Bodhisattva's career.

9. The most widely quoted version of this message is found in the *Sadharmapundarika* (The Lotus Sutra). For a citation, see Janice D. Willis, "Nuns and Benefactresses: The Role of Women in the Development of Buddhism," in Yvonne Haddad and Ellison Findly, eds., *Women, Religion and Social Change* (Albany: State University of New York Press, 1985), 68.

10. For a succinct summary of and citations to the literature see Nancy Schuster Barnes, "Buddhism," in Arvind Sharma, ed., *Women in World Religions* (Albany: State University of New York Press, 1987), 121–23.

11. Keith Dowman, *Sky Dancer: The Secret Life and Songs of the Lady Yeshe Tsogyel* (London: Routledge and Kegan Paul, 1984). This biography provides a wonderful example of such a female Buddha.

12. Reginald A. Ray, "Accomplished Women in Tantric Buddhism of Medieval India and Tibet," in Falk and Gross, eds., *Unspoken Worlds*. This article surveys literature on the *Siddha*-s (*yogi*-adepts) of Vajrayana Buddhism. While it focuses on the importance of the women in the narratives, often these women come across as enablers rather than as important for their own achievements and realizations.

13. Nancy Schuster Barnes, "Striking a Balance: Women and Images of Women in Early Chinese Buddhism," in Yvonne Haddad and Ellison Findly, eds., *Women, Religion and Social Change* (Albany: State University of New York Press, 1985), 87–112. This article contains valuable information and citations.

14. See Ruth Tabrah, "Reflections on Being Ordained," *Eastern Buddhist* 16, no. 2 (1983): 124–33, for an informative personal account by one of the few Caucasian women to receive this ordination.

15. Paul, *Women in Buddhism*, 247–302.

16. Sandra Boucher, *Turning the Wheel: American Women Creating the New Buddhism* (San Francisco: Harper and Row, 1988). This wonderful book details the women who are affecting North American Buddhism and the effect they are having.

17. Though not yet, to my knowledge, systematically studied, it is commonly noted that new or "frontier" situations tend to allow women greater equality and freedom than is found later in the same situation. This thesis could easily be documented for the origins

of Buddhism, Christianity, and Islam. But it is also noticeable in many reform movements within religious traditions and even in secular situations. For example, in many Western states women could vote before women's suffrage was achieved throughout the United States.

18. Core teachings in Buddhism are not easy to understand or teach, as anyone who has ever taught a course in Eastern religions can attest. The best way for a novice to begin to grasp these teachings is to combine reading Western academic textbooks on Buddhism with books written by Buddhists. The best introductory academic book on Buddhism is Richard H. Robinson and Willard L. Johnson, *The Buddhist Religion: A Historical Introduction*, 3d ed. (Belmont, CA: Wadsworth, 1982). Several other excellent books by Buddhists give one an understanding of egolessness and nontheism as interpreted by the major schools of meditational Buddhism. For Theravadin Buddhism, see Walpola Rahula, *What the Buddha Taught* (New York: Grove, 1974), and Joseph Goldstein, *The Experience of Insight: A Natural Unfolding* (Santa Cruz: Unity Press, 1976). For Vajrayana Buddhism, see Chogyam Trungpa, *Cutting Through Spiritual Materialism* and *The Myth of Freedom and the Way of Meditation* (Boulder, CO: Shambhala, 1978). Out of the plethora of books of Zen Buddhism, Suzuki Shunryu, *Zen Mind, Beginner's Mind* (New York: Weatherhill, 1974) is my favorite.

19. This analysis has been central to feminist scholarship. Though ignored for many years, an important classic is Simone de Beauvoir, *The Second Sex* (New York: Bantam Books, 1961). This book was first published in 1949. For applications to the comparative study of religions, see Rita M. Gross, "Women's Studies in Religion: The State of the Art, 1980," in Peter Slater and Donald Wiebe, eds., *Traditions in Contact and Change* (Waterloo, Ontario: Wilfrid Laurier University Press, 1983), 579–91.

20. Many radical feminists, both secular and religious, make this claim. The religious feminists go on to suggest that feminist and religious women should create a new spiritual tradition drawing on the ancient, pre-patriarchal religions. For sources on this feminist spirituality movement, as it is often called, see any of the later writings of Carol Christ and Mary Daly. For a useful anthology containing works by other writers who represent this point of view, see Charlene Spretnek, *The Politics of Women's Spirituality* (New York: Doubleday, 1982).

21. From *Mahaparinibbana-suttanta*, trans. T. W. Rhys Davids and C. A. F. Rhys Davids. Cited in Paul, *Women in Buddhism*, 7–8.

22. However, Vajrayana literature, which includes a few accounts of women's inner lives, does include such materials. For an example see Keith Dowman, *Sky Dancer:The Secret Life of the Lady Yeshe Tsogyel* (London: Routledge and Kegan Paul, 1984), 78–80.

23. Willis, "Nuns and Benefactresses," 69.

24. From the Sukhavativyuha (Pure Land) Sutra, quoted in Paul, *Women in Buddhism*, 169–70.

25. Robinson and Johnson, *The Buddhist Religion*, 86–89.

26. Falk, "The Case of the Vanishing Nuns," 218.

27. Many of these texts have been collected and translated in Paul, *Women in Buddhism*, 166–243. See also Schuster, "Changing the Female Body," 24–69.

28. Paul, *Women in Buddhism*, 230.

29. Dowman, *Sky Dancer*, 86.

30. From the *Sutra of Sagara, the Naga King*, quoted in Paul, *Women in Buddhism*, 276.

31. This phrase, patent in feminist analysis of religion, originated with Mary Daly. See her book *Beyond God the Father* (Boston: Beacon Press, 1973), 8–9.

32. Falk, "The Case of the Vanishing Nuns," 220–22.

33. A vast literature on pre-patriarchal cultures and on the emergence of patriarchy is now available. See especially Gerda Lerner, *The Creation of Patriarchy* (Oxford: Oxford University Press, 1986).

34. These concepts are discussed in more detail in Rita M. Gross, "Women's Studies in Religion: The State of the Art, 1980," in Slater and Wiebe, eds., *Traditions in Contact and Change*.

35. Rita M. Gross, "Yeshe Tsogyel: Enlightened Consort, Great Teacher, Female Role Model," *Tibet Journal* 12, no. 4 (1987): 1–18.

36. The best anthology of the literature is C. P. Christ and J. Plaskow, *WomanSpirit Rising: A Feminist Reader in Religion* (San Francisco: Harper and Row, 1979). For an excellent single volume, see Rosemary Ruether, *Sexism and God-Talk: Toward A Feminist Theology* (Boston: Beacon Press, 1983).

Part III

A Spiritual Challenge for Men

8

Male-Female Relations and the Dialogical Imperative

LEONARD GROB

A male writing a chapter in a book that proclaims the need for dialogue between men and women can, with apparent reason, be called upon to examine the nature of his credentials for carrying out the task at hand. In the context of what many feminist theorists have argued is a fundamentally patriarchal society, how is it possible for such a dialogue to be initiated without these same men having to undergo profound and far-reaching change on their own? Is there not "homework" to be done by men before such invitations to dialogue can be meaningfully extended and received? Can it be supposed that men will *ever* reach that point at which it is said that *now* they are ready for dialogue? What, indeed, are the prerequisites to genuine dialogue between men and women who live within the bounds of a patriarchal system?

And, further, it would seem that such a "call to account" of a male declaring the need for dialogue with women might constitute nothing short of a "sound of alarm": what might be the agenda of this man, a member of the privileged sex, in speaking of a dialogical imperative to be heeded by both men and women? Within the confines of a culture of male domination, is not the positing of such an imperative immediately suspect? In his article entitled "Male Feminism," Steven Heath goes so far as to claim that any initiative on the part of a man to enter into dialogue as co-subject with a woman is cause for suspicion: "Men are . . . carriers of the patriarchal mode; and my desire to be a subject there too in feminism—to be a feminist—is then only also the last feint in the long history of *their* colonization."[1]

As a male who wishes to affirm the possibility of and need for dialogue with women, I must, then, address these charges sketched above—charges that are implicit in some radical feminist thought and that were pointedly leveled at me in a recent and deeply disturbing discussion with a feminist colleague. That discussion has prompted me to rethink just what it is that I mean when I (and others) sometimes speak in sanguine (and perhaps facile) terms of "getting the dialogue going" between men and women. In a volume given over to "testimonies of spirit" regarding men's and women's liberation, I will proceed to argue for nothing short of a so-called spiritual politics—a politics that allows for human transcendence—as the sole context in which the struggle for a *genuinely radical* liberation of the sexes can occur. In a book that celebrates the "politics of the spirit" as the truly *radical* politics, I can do nothing other than try my hand at responding to aspects of that thought that also lays claim to the name "radical" in its challenge to the very possibility of authentic dialogue between the sexes.

In carrying out this task I will draw on the initiatives of the contemporary philosopher Martin Buber. Although Buber does not deal directly with the issue of men's and women's liberation, his insights into the nature of dialogue—and most especially, the distinction he draws between authentic dialogue and pretenders to such in an age when this word is overused, misused, and abused— shed significant light on the questions at hand. Buber's prose-poetry celebrates an I-Thou relationship that transcends our ordinary (I-It) goal-oriented modes of relating. It thus provides me with both a point of departure and an abiding inspiration for articulating the possibility of men and women overcoming a heritage of patriarchy in the liberating work of dialogue. The chapter concludes with an autobiographical reflection in which the genesis in the lived world of some of the key ideas I have expressed here will be explored.

PATRIARCHAL OPPRESSION

I will begin by examining the crux of the charges outlined above concerning the possibility of dialogue between men and women. It is argued that in patriarchal culture doubt might well be cast on the meaning of a male initiative to engage in dialogue with women. Nor is it of great import, it might well be added, to determine whether or not the invitation on the part of a male in a given instance is extended with any premeditation to deceive: in light of the overarching nature of the phenomenon of patriarchy-as-system, so well-documented by radical feminist theorists, *any* initiative undertaken by those who dominate might well be seen as part of a network of interlocking forces, all of which serve, willy-nilly, the ends of this very domination. As Marilyn Frye points out in her essay entitled "Oppression," it is just this characteristic of belonging to a fixed and all-embracing network of forces that allows a given element of male, or any other group's, behavior to be labeled oppressive:

The experience of oppressed people is that the living of one's life is confined and shaped by forces and barriers which are not accidental or occasional and hence avoidable, but are systematically related to each other in such a way as to catch one between and among them and restrict or penalize motion in any direction. It is the experience of being caged in: all avenues, in every direction, are blocked or booby trapped.[2]

To be oppressed in a patriarchal system, in other words, is to be confined to a world in which all behaviors of men are, in principle, suspect; none can be accepted at face value as the word or deed of one who means what he says or does.

This system of constraints, moreover, is one that women experience *as women*. As blacks, Hispanics, or Native Americans, for example, women may share the experience of being oppressed with their male counterparts. However—the protestations of some men to the contrary—the status of men under patriarchal rule is *not* the rough equivalent of women's status. Yes, in any oppressive system it is a psychological truth that both oppressor and oppressed suffer; it is said by many men, for example, that the expectation felt by a man to succeed as household provider is a significant limiting force in that male's endeavor to realize his selfhood as a human being. Men are indeed victims of their own victimizing, and many suffer as a result. Yet, as Frye puts it so well:

When the stresses and frustration of being a male are cited as evidence that oppressors are oppressed by their oppressing, the word "oppression" is being stretched to meaninglessness; it is treated as though its scope includes any and all human experience of limitation or suffering. . . . Human beings can be miserable without being oppressed, and it is perfectly consistent to deny that a person or group is oppressed without denying that they have feelings or that they suffer.[3]

Suffering—including suffering that derives from the structures one has initiated in a process wherein others suffer—is not in and of itself the touchstone for one's being labeled oppressed.

It is clear, then, that the sufferings of women differ from those of men not only on a quantitative scale—it can be argued that the former suffer more and more frequently than do the latter—but, more importantly, on a qualitative scale as well. The *quality* of women's enclosedness, their entrapment within a grid of interlocking structures, is distinct from the quality of the male experience of suffering.

It is the *strength* of the radical feminist critique sketched above to have distinguished between an all-encompassing network of male behaviors (patriarchy as an oppressive system) and the appearance of more random acts of harm that befall members of one group at the hands of another. It is its strength, as well, to have distinguished between the suffering of women as women and the "suffering" of *all* human beings from the inevitable constraints and limitations imposed on us by the societies in which we live.[4] This in-depth *structural* critique, furthermore, lays the groundwork for an attack on sexist behaviors at the sole juncture at which any endeavor to redress a wrong can yield fruit: the root (Latin *radix*, from which the word "radical" is derived) of the phenomena observed. Not, for example, until such seemingly disparate acts and attitudes as sexual harassment, denial of abortion, and job discrimination are perceived to fit together into one interlocking grid can truly appropriate countermeasures to combat male sexist behaviors be proposed. It is not until patriarchy as a systematic whole has been distinguished, through such structural critique, both from the play of sociocultural forces that limit us as humans and from the suffering that accrues to men from exposure to the very set of structures they have helped to perpetuate—not until then can the phenomenon of women's oppression be laid bare.

If the strength of such an allegedly radical critique is clear, the dangers inherent in this movement of thought must also be brought to light: in the attempt to bring under its aegis the many and various phenomena observed, such a sweeping critique may fail to continue to heed the humanizing impulse that is its fount and wellspring. In its endeavor to explain, it can easily explain away; in its endeavor to radically analyze that which it observes by uncovering the depth structures of the phenomena in question, such a critique runs the risk of "drying up," becoming ideological in its thrust, and denying on principle the legitimacy of a dialogical initiative that comes to challenge, confront, and ultimately to heal. Any allegedly radical critique that leaves no room for the epiphany of one who means what she or he says, who transcends the terms of a situation in which his or her motives would be "understood" beforehand—in Buber's terms, a Thou—is a critique that is not radical enough! In the next section I attempt to elucidate this claim.

THE RULE OF REDUCTIONISM AND THE CHALLENGE OF DIALOGUE

It is my contention that the same feminist critique that has successfully identified the concept of patriarchy can, with apparent ease, succumb to the temptation of becoming ideological in its essence, of becoming another "ism." Under what I will call the "rule of reductionism," nothing is what it appears to be; the universe of discourse and action is bewitched. (As Heath warned above, under patriarchy, understood as an ultimately reductive concept, male initiatives to become feminists can be nothing other than a "feint.") Indeed, the reified form of feminist critique—dynamic inquiry transformed into stasis, and thus an example of what can be called an "imperialism" of ideas[5]—is but one instance of a prevailing tendency in Western thought to subject the ambiguous, ever-shifting elements of the lifeworld to the totalizing structures of the appropriative mind. If we look to the grand systems of Western philosophy from Aristotle to Hegel and, in our own century, Sartre, we can see that within this tradition, to know is to comprehend (i.e., to take together or unify all that is within a conceptual order that reflects the ideal of the adequacy of the knower to that which is known). Utilizing the mediating force of a concept, such a vision embarks on the task of reducing all that is alien or "other" to the terms of my intellectual grasp in which they become familiar or "the same."[6] This is not to say that the intellectualist bias of Western systematic philosophy has not borne fruit; we have been able, via these same systems of thought, to begin to make sense of our experience! When the making of "sense," however, occurs at the expense of the system maker remaining faithful to lived experience—including moments that may transcend the terms of that very system—such system making can be seen to be nothing short of a totalizing, "totalitarian" activity.[7]

Before turning to an examination of the concept of patriarchy with regard to just such a "totalitarian" potential, it will be helpful to view the "rule of reductionism" at work in one of the most compelling contemporary illustrations of an "imperialism" of ideas barring the door to the possibility of genuine dialogue: Sartre's ontology of interpersonal relations as articulated in his *Being and Nothingness*. For Sartre, an unbridgeable dichotomy exists between object (what he calls *en-soi* or being-in-itself) and subject (*pour-soi* or the for-itself). A subject (or consciousness) is not substantial, not part of "being," but rather an *activity*—that activity that alone can give meaning to objects. As an unsubstantial consciousness, then, I am nothing but the sole and unceasing act of making sense of all that appears before me. As such, I am on principle condemned to give meaning to humans—other meaning-givers also. The other who stands before me, then, cannot appear to me in her or his being-as-subject or as meaning-giver; the other must become my object (*ob-jectum*, one "cast before me"). Unlike all other objects, however, my human other must, again on principle, be attempting to "mean" or objectify me at the very moment that I attempt to objectify him or her! The result is a stalemate in a never-ending contest for power:

Everything which may be said of me in my relations with the Other applies to him as well. While I attempt to free myself from the hold of the Other, the Other is trying to free himself from mine; while I seek to enslave the Other, the Other seeks to enslave me.[8]

In such a struggle it is no surprise that on principle no rupture in the system, no dialogical initiative, can occur. Both the I and the other for Sartre play the role of neutral ciphers caught in a play of power. Within such an all-embracing conceptual system, there can be no authentic dialogue. In Sartre's words, "Thus I am referred from transfiguration [of object to subject] to degradation [of subject to object]"[9] without the possibility of dialogue (of subject with subject) ever being able to be realized.

For Buber, the Sartrean ontology stands as just one example—although, in its unyielding reduction of all individuals to the terms of its schema, a fully representative one—of a system of thought posing as an absolute. The use of the term "absolute," moreover, is no exercise in hyperbole: for Sartre and other system makers in the Western tradition, it is *only* within the boundaries of a conceptual system that meaning can be ascribed. This hegemony of the schema-as-absolute Buber refuses. To face the world according to what might be called a "dialogical absolute" is to take one's stance in the interstices between all systems, on a "narrow rocky ridge between the gulfs"[10]—what Buber calls elsewhere the "realm of the between." This stance alone can merit the designation of a true "absolute."

How is the Buberian absolute to be distinguished from other claimants to such status? The dialogical absolute calls on me "merely"(!) to respond with the whole of my being to whomever I encounter. I thus refuse all fixed points of reference within whose parameters the nature of the other could be determined in advance of that very encounter. I cannot, for example, ascribe, ultimately, to her or him attributes derived from such traditional "absolutes" as orthodox Freudianism, Marx's economic determinism, modern liberalism—or the dogmatics of an allegedly "radical" feminism. Nor can I take permanent refuge in the comforting ascription of roles that is so commonplace in my everyday interactions with others. The other is not merely (or most fundamentally) my husband, teacher, or child; all of these, in Buber's metaphor system, belong to the realm of It. She or he is most essentially a Thou, a unique, unanalyzable being whose ability, in encountering me, to overflow all such role-ascriptions attests to nothing short of the presence of a dimension of transcendence at the core of his or her being. It is precisely this transcendent nature of the other as a Thou that is refused me on principle as long as I remain within the conceptual boundaries of a system-as-absolute. Such a Thou can only be witnessed; it can never be appropriated by any schema established prior to the witnessing itself.

But, finally, if Buber has distinguished his absolute of entering into the "between" from other alleged absolutes in the history of ideas, it still remains to be seen how it can be argued that it is only a dialogical absolute that can lay claim to this status at all: in a competition among alleged absolutes, how am I justified in declaring a (absolute!) winner? How do we know that the absolutes proclaimed by fundamentalist Christians or fundamentalist Marxists, for example, are no more than mere pretenders to the throne reserved by Buber for the call to dialogue?

Here we must recall the special status of the imperative to respond dialogically *as* an *imperative*: The dialogical absolute is more verb than noun, more process than product, an ever-renewed summons to stand in "holy insecurity" before the person who stands over against me. Buber's absolute is no principle among principles. It is a summons rather than a content—which content would itself demand a dialogical initiative to weigh its merits as content against other such contents. In other words, to begin, in good faith, to engage in authentic dialogue with another concerning the claim of such dialogue to constitute an absolute is to bear living witness to the truth of the claim in question. To deny the primacy of dialogue *in the course of dialogical interchange* is to affirm what one appears to deny.

Thus, the dialogical absolute has no fixed content that could be located as one set of ideas among many in a history of philosophy. Rather, it exhausts itself in its ever-renewed will to submit itself to dialogical encounter. I can never get "behind" dialogue in order to evaluate it as one idea among others: to attempt to deny it—in honest engagement, rather than through the use of rhetorical or physical force—is paradoxically to acknowledge that one assumes it! It remains to be seen how an acknowledgement of the primacy of dialogue as the "absolute of absolutes" can help me to respond to the issues concerning dialogue between men and women articulated above.

LIBERATION AND TRANSCENDENCE

The questions raised at the outset of this chapter concerning the legitimacy of male dialogical initiatives are questions that, as we have seen, rest on claims regarding both the vast extent and the depth of the impact of patriarchal politics. It has often been advanced by feminist theorists that patriarchy is *the* core or fundamental oppression and that all true liberation movements must be modeled on feminist responses. In *Sexual Politics,* for example, Kate Millet claims that "sexual caste supersedes all other forms of inegalitarian stratification: racial, political, or economic."[11] Millet goes on to speak with approbation of Jean Genet's thesis in "The Balcony" to the effect that, "in dividing humanity into two groups and appointing one to rule over the other by virtue of birthright, the social order has already established and ratified a system of oppression which will underlie and corrupt all other human relationships as well as every area of thought and experience."[12] The male-female polarization, furthermore, is often taken to be the model for all classical dichotomies: good and evil, soul and body, and reason and emotions, among others. How are we to evaluate these claims and their bearing on the possibility of dialogue between men and women?

It is certainly the case that feminist thinkers have awakened us to the radical implications for us all of what Beauvoir calls "the slavery of half of humanity."[13] It can be argued that at this juncture of history in which women are beginning to be recognized as the "oppressed of (all) oppressed groups," feminist critique, on its many levels, plays a central role in mobilizing both men and women to work for justice and equality whenever and wherever they are denied. It might even be argued that if ever a movement advocating the liberation of a given group could serve as the standard against which the legitimacy of all liberation movements can be measured, feminism, in its implicit critique of all forms of hierarchalism, is that movement. To say the above, however, is not to grant legitimacy to the ultimately reductive claim that all oppression can be understood as a function of "x" or "y" factor. Class, race, gender—all must be dismissed as pretenders, in and of themselves, to the status of an absolute standard according to which we can once and for all comprehend what constitutes the well-being, or lack thereof, of humankind. Much as we yearn for a resting place, a "cause of causes," a home base from which we can move out, with assurance as to the ultimacy of our claim, to fight oppression everywhere—much as we yearn for such bedrock, we must refuse the temptation to indulge in that form of reductive thinking that I have termed "totalitarian" and "imperialist."

Insofar as feminism, or any other liberation "ism," transcends its own (parochial) self in order to embrace a depth or spiritual dimension of its cause, then that movement succeeds in avoiding this charge of reductionism. In Rosemary Reuther's words:

In rejecting androcentrism (males as norms of humanity), women must also criticize all other forms of chauvinism: making white Westerners the norm of humanity, making Christians the norm of humanity, making privileged classes the norm of humanity. Women must also criticize humanocentrism, that is, making humans the norm and crown of creation in a way that diminishes the other beings in the community of creation.[14]

In the name of affirming a call to dialogue with all beings as potential partners, such a self-transcending movement celebrates the Thouness of creation in its myriad forms. It has found no "home" in any set of tenets advocating the absolute primacy of this cause over or against others, an advocacy that often passes for radical politics; rather, it has discovered its home to lie, paradoxically, in the homelessness of living in the "between," in standing in dialogical relationships that endeavor to "wring" as much Thouness as possible from the world. The truly radical politics is the politics of the spirit that attempts to realize a Thou-invested world.

Although a spiritual politics demands that one do justice to one's group, for Buber such justice is not to be directed to the group in and of itself; rather, one must see the group in its agency as performing the sacramental work of "hallowing" existence. One does not have to choose between promoting the interests of one's group and (in Buber's traditional religious imagery) "serving God" by avoiding, in the name of some allegedly universal ethic, all concrete political action rooted in a cause. Rather, the summons is to serve the group's interest "before God"[15] by honoring the spiritual or transcendent dimension of that program *by and through* the realization of particular group aims. That which stands opposed to the particularism involved in an embrace of the parochial interests of one group is not a "fuzzy" ungrounded universalism; such a universalism would ultimately congeal into its own set of ethico-political tenets, which tenets themselves would have to be transcended in the process of overcoming a new particularism. The opposite of universalism, as of particularism, is dialogue, the willingness to affirm different modes of existence in the ongoing mutuality of appeal and response. In Buber's words:

In a genuine dialogue each of the partners, even when he stands in opposition to the other, heeds, affirms, and confirms his opponent as an existing other. Only so can conflict certainly not be eliminated from the world, but be humanly arbitrated and led towards its overcoming.[16]

When this mutuality breaks down we are left with the image of one oppressed group attempting to force upon another the "truth" that "my oppression is greater than yours"—what, in a recent dialogue group I led between blacks and Jews, was expressed in variants of the form "My holocaust is more terrible than yours.'' Failure to transcend the unexamined partisan goals of one's group not only leaves the world unhallowed, without a movement toward solidarity; it also promotes this specter of oppressed groups battling among themselves for the alleged prize of being ''more oppressed than thou.'' To claim that my suffering is totally unique, is certainly true on one level; but to remain fixed at this level allows for that entrapment in reductionism that leads, at best, to acts of exclusivity on my part, and, at worst, to overt conflict in a struggle for power between competing oppressions. Only the presence of a creative tension between particularity and a movement toward solidarity through genuine dialogue can lead one to avoid the excesses of narrow, uncritical partisanship on the one hand, and ungrounded adherence to abstract ideas on the other.

DIALOGUE BETWEEN THE SEXES

Showing Wounds

It is now time to return more pointedly to the questions posed at the beginning of this chapter. It is certainly true, as we have seen, that women's suffering differs substantially from that of men; it is not only the case that her pain is unique, but, like all pain, it has an aspect of infinite depth to it that bars comparison to anyone else's suffering. In the words of Muriel Rukeyser, ''What would happen if one woman told the truth about her life? The world would split open.''[17] In the face of this infinite aspect of women's pain, how are men able to present credentials that would be acceptable to the women with whom they are to engage in dialogue? Will men not have to undergo a radical metamorphosis as men in order for them to become legitimate partners in dialogue?

Indeed, if the question concerning prerequisites to dialogue is posed in this manner, the response must be that men's credentials can never, on principle, be acceptable enough—the metamorphosis to be accomplished can never be one that is sufficiently radical. Given the history of women's suffering within patriarchy, *no* behavior on the part of men could ever be seen as sufficiently reformed, sufficiently enlightened, to allow for the healing work of dialogue to begin. Tainted by facticity, by a history of oppressive behavior, men can never be contrite enough.

The remedy for this situation, we have suggested, is not to be found in some facile denial of the asymmetry of the proposed dialogical encounter; men and women do emerge from dramatically different contexts as creatures of history. Yet it must also be noted that to view men and women solely as the product of history, solely as perpetrators and victims of patriarchal oppression, is to reduce the humanity of each to what Buber terms an It. That such an It-world exists and, in Buber's words, has undergone ''progressive augmentation,''[18] cannot be denied: centuries of women's oppression under patriarchy bear witness to the pervasiveness of the It-dimension of our humanity. What is overlooked here, however, is another dimension of our being, what Buber calls our Thou-being:

each of us is capable, in dialogue with the other, of calling forth an aspect of the divine at the core of our being. "The limits of the possibility of dialogue," Buber exclaims, "are the limits of awareness. . . . Signs happen to us without respite, living means being addressed."[19] Yet our misfortune is that "each of us is encased in an armour whose task is to ward off signs."[20] Realizing the Thou as the core of our being, however, is not to be confused with the predication of some neutral, sexless substratum as the foundation of who we are. Rather, the Thou who is potentially present to the other in dialogue is no-thing at all, no static entity to be posited; it is something encountered, something to be witnessed-to rather than argued-for.

The Thou is thus the most concrete phenomenon to be experienced: I do not face you in dialogue as some abstract personhood, but, rather, as the Thou you are by and through your being this particular man or woman. For Buber, not only is it the case that I do not have to look away from the sex of the person whom I encounter in dialogue—"There is nothing from which I would have to turn my eyes away in order to see";[21] rather, in order to see you as a Thou I *must* see you as male or female, but in a dimension of your maleness or femaleness that gives ultimate meaning to this aspect of human embodiment—as to all others.

For Buber, then, It is not to be denied: patriarchy is indeed our history. History, however, is itself capable of being fundamentally altered or "redeemed" through the progressive awakening of the Thou-being in all creatures. Without this redemptive activity, the activity of dialogue between an I and a Thou, our lives are not fulfilled: to be fully human is to resist the eternal temptation to remain embedded and secure in the world of It.

How are we to realize the Thou in everyday interactions with members of the other sex? The endeavor on the part of those who would demand of men that they atone for their wrongdoing as a prerequisite to dialogue between I and Thou is an endeavor that, as we have seen, is doomed to failure. If, as has often been suggested, dialogue can only take place between full equals, then dialogue cannot take place at all. All dialogue is engaged in by asymmetrical beings: creatures caught up in history can never be "equal" enough, can never achieve an alleged freedom from their temporal natures that allows for symmetry. We are always "in the midst of things." In the midst of imperfection, complicity in misdeeds, errors of omission and commission—through it all, we engage in dialogue, each from her or his lived, and thus impure, experience. There are no innocents with empty slates to replace the guilty as potential partners to dialogue; only sinners engage in dialogue because there are only sinners![22]

Indeed, to demand ultimate equality among partners to dialogue is to risk imposing on them a conceptual system within which the notion of equality would be first formulated and defined; for the It-figures of perpetrator and victim we merely substitute the Its of faceless alter egos, neutral markers in some ontological schema in which equivalence would be determined according to a given, overarching principle. The Sartrean schema examined above is a case in point: for the two consciousnesses facing one another there is "no exit," since each is ultimately subject to the philosopher's schema in which both play shifting but complementary roles. Such a symmetry bars the path, on principle, to the possibility of truly radical change from the given mode of contestation to one of dialogue.

To envision a healing of the relations between the sexes, then, is not to remain content with the demand placed on men that they change as a prerequisite of dialogue. As long as one speaks out solely within the terms of a system of oppressor and oppressed, guilty ones and innocents, such a demand will not allow for the movement in ontological dimension from It to Thou that alone is capable of providing the ultimate healing power—what Buber calls "redemption." This is not to say that demands are not to be made by women of men in the politics of everyday experience. And although full "equality" in some abstract sense is an impossible goal for partners to dialogue, it is certainly the case that moving toward the social, political, and economic equality of those who participate in dialogue will enhance a potential for healing. Ultimately, however, "demand and submission" must be coupled with the "appeal and response" of an I to a Thou in a world where all are responsible (able-to-respond) for dialogue: the It-world of concrete political action—never to be abandoned—must be consecrated by the (spiritual) work of dialogue. Ultimately, "all"(!) we can do is to show our (very different) wounds to one another in the mutual endeavor to heal them.[23]

Separation and Relation

At this juncture a question that has haunted this chapter must be explicitly addressed: how are we to distinguish the form of dialogue spoken of above from any "free for all" in which everyone may jump in at any moment to join in the "relating"? Must we not be careful to set some parameters, some ground rules, that would enable authentic dialogue to get underway? And in our chosen arena, must not something (though different somethings) be required of both men and women before they can legitimately encounter each other face to face? More specifically, must not women draw back and experience their strength as women in a genuine separateness denied them under patriarchy? And must not men draw back from their oppressing modes of being and enter into their own form of separateness in order to examine among themselves just what they have perpetrated, or what has been perpetrated in their name with regard to women?

In response to these questions we might well recast the slogan employed by many peace activists to the effect that there is no way to peace, rather peace is the way: there is, indeed, no way to dialogue; dialogue is the way. In its primordial sense dialogue is not a thesis or theme to be posited as one element among many to be pursued in the course of human experience. More specifically, dialogue is not the mere patching together of separate egos who come together to "work things out." "In the beginning is relation."[24] In making this claim—an alternate creation tale—Buber uses the word "beginning" to signify not only that point that occurs first in time, but also, and more importantly, that which constitutes an ontological point of departure for all of human life: "relation" is the primordial ground within which all of us exist. In opposition to much of the tradition of Western philosophy which posits the solitary ego or consciousness as the fundamental atom or building block of human experience, Buber sees the I-Thou relation as the primary human unit. Only later (in ontological terms, derivatively) do the "component parts" of dialogue, individual persons, emerge. And even in the It-world within which we organize our lives, we are at every instant affected by the universal currents of dialogue that flow all around us, beckoning to us to realize our innate predisposition to relate to others (in Buber's terms, our "innate Thou"), to affirm that which is already there.

Although we may be "born to relate"—Buber speaks of this force of innate relatedness as most clearly manifest both in the life of the infant and in that of the so-called primitive—this fact is no guarantee that the presence of such an "inborn Thou" will eventuate in a never-ending succession of Thou-encounters. To say that dialogue is "already there" is not to say that life is lived continually in the Thou. To claim that dialogue is the prethematic ground of being, in other words, is not to conclude that we succeed in realizing our ontological heritage as humans in any ecstasy of I and Thou. No, our givenness to dialogue is covered over by the pervasiveness of ordinary, instrumental behaviors—not to speak of the evil of such institutions as patriarchy. The It-world congeals, most often obscuring from our sight the primacy of Thou. It remains our task not to eliminate the It in the process of striving for some impossible return to infancy or prim-itiveness, but rather to hallow the ordinary (the so-called "real") by real-izing the truly real that is awaiting us in its midst.

How are these notions advanced by Buber to be brought to bear on the problematic at hand? It is my contention that the "question" of dialogue—its alleged preconditions, the issue of its very possibility—posed by women to men in the terms set forth at the outset of this chapter is at best a pseudo-question that can yield no fruit, and at worst, a call to confession and submission that mirrors the category of dehumanizing acts characteristic of patriarchal oppres-sion. In the former instance, what is forgotten is that, as humans, we are already launched toward dialogue; it is not so much a case of making dialogue happen as it is of ratifying that which is already underway. As I have argued above, to question the possibility of dialogue—in any form of questioning that would be communicated to, rather than forced upon, another—is, paradoxically, to assume the existence of that which is in doubt! Dialogue is not a means drawn up to achieve a humanizing end outside itself; rather, it assumes the humanity, the personhood, of the other to whom I relate. A woman who would deny the possibility of dialogue between men and women and who presents her case to a man is thus implicitly acknowledging that readiness for dialogue on the part of her male interlocutor that is at issue. As I have argued above, we simply cannot get "behind" dialogue in order to thematize it as something that can be called into question or denied.

In the latter instance—confusing a call to surrender with an invitation to examine one's credentials for dialogue—what is at issue is more than a refusal to acknowledge the healing potential of dialogue. As a summons to a man to "own up," or confess, such a call maintains the posture of a "presentation of arms" characteristic of male oppressive behaviors: the terms of the encounter, in other words, remain the terms of war. I suggest that it is only by refusing the presentation of arms against arms, by disarming oneself and appealing to the other to do the same, that the peace of dialogical interaction can finally be affirmed.

In speaking of the "pseudo-question" of prerequisites to dialogue, however, I by no means wish to argue that the achievement of separation, advanced by many as just such a prerequisite, plays no role in the dialogical process. On the contrary, separation remains integrally and inextricably linked with relation. To say, however, that the separation is a *precondition* to dialogue is to raise new, though somewhat related, sets of issues. Yes, it is certainly the case that until oppressor and oppressed remove themselves from their respective forms of entrapment, it will remain unclear just "who" the participants in dialogue will be. Is it not the case that both interlocutors must first be able to speak, each in his or her own name, before they can speak to one another in what would constitute a genuine dialogue? If such a speaking in one's own name has not occurred, are we not merely talking to one another as functions of the systems to which we, often without awareness, belong? Where are we to turn in order to seek a form of separation that accords with the politics of the spirit?

In the endeavor to demystify the term "separation" and, in so doing, to call into question knee-jerk reactions to it on the part of many women and most men, we can look for initial guidance to Frye's discussion of female separation in her essay entitled "On Separatism and Power." According to Frye: "Feminist separation is . . . separation of various sorts or modes from men and from institutions, relationships, roles and activities which are male-defined, male-dominated and operating for the benefit of males and the maintenance of male privilege—this separation being initiated or maintained, at will, *by women*."[25] Separation is a theme running through such seemingly diverse behaviors as divorce, the establishment of lesbian communities, and the avoidance of sexist communications initiated by the media.[26] One who identifies herself as a "separatist" is merely one who "practices separation consciously, systematically, and probably more generally than the others and advocates thorough and 'broad-spectrum' separation as part of the conscious strategy of liberation."[27]

The first thing to be noted here is that if it is true that any and all partners to dialogue must be empowered selves, selves who warrant, in any meaningful sense, the name "partner," all the more is it true that female potential partners to dialogue with men must endeavor to separate themselves from the full range of patriarchal structures in order to become so empowered. Speaking of only one of the many female separation activities that arise in response to male oppression, Frye claims that:

The woman-only meeting is a fundamental challenge to the structure of power. It is always the privilege of the master to enter the slave's hut. The slave who decides to exclude the master from her hut is declaring herself not a slave. . . . When we start from a position of total accessibility there must be an aspect of no-saying (which is the beginning of control) in every effective act and strategy.[28]

A second element to be noted in Frye's words is her refusal to define the separation practiced by separatists as any form of political dogmatics; Frye takes great pains to distinguish separatism from any theory or doctrine. And, indeed, if such separation is to accord with the concept of a spiritual politics—the sole context, I have argued, in which a liberating dialogue can occur—then separatism must be an "ism" in name only; it must avoid that congealing-into-dogma which is the true contrary of dialogue. A separatism cut off from its living roots in dialogue would dry up, constituting the mere reverse of what is, in Reuther's words, "male hierarchalism," thus "making women normative humanity and males 'defective' members of the human species."[29]

What is to be avoided, in other words, is the reification of separation as an activity ultimately sufficient unto itself. Separation and relation are but two moments of the *same* dynamic. To speak of separation in any other fashion is to risk driving a wedge in the dialogical process between its inextricably and organically linked movements of self-definition and the extending-of-the-self-toward-the-other. In Buber's terms, my becoming who I am as a whole person and my entering into dialogue with a Thou constitute a circle that I can enter at any point; what is crucial here is the linkage of these movements to one another: "Concentrating and fusion into the whole being can never take place through my agency, nor can it ever take place without me. I become through my relation to the Thou; as I become I, I say Thou."[30] I cannot meet a Thou unless I am a self-defined "I"; yet I cannot be such a self-defined individual until I have met my Thou!

A word of caution with regard to the concept of separation is thus in order: to speak of separation as a "precondition" of dialogue, as a "strategy" toward liberation, is to risk its isolation from relation, is to risk the raising of the by now familiar question how separate is separate enough? At what juncture are practitioners of separation ready enough, on principle, to enter into the drawing-together mode of dialogue? To say with Buber, however, that becoming whole as an "I" and entering into dialogue are but two mutually dependent aspects of one human activity is not to say that female separation fails to maintain an integrity of its own. To see separation as part and parcel of the ontology of relation is not to see it as any less vital in its significance as an empowering act, any less whole in its movement to free women from the massive system of oppression that is patriarchy. Nor should it be thought that the linkage between separation and relation signifies that there will be no time lag between acts of separation and those of relation: as temporal beings our healings take place across the temporal dimension. To link separation and relation ontologically is not necessarily to link them in a single temporal moment: an oppressed group will undoubtedly require time to gather itself, to recollect itself, into a body that owns its existence.

Yet paradoxically, those very moments at which the authentic wrenching away from patriarchal structures is being accomplished are also the moments at which lines of relation—only now able to be fully realized—must be affirmed in principle, if not in fact. To become separatist, in the sense in which I am using this word, is to become a (authentically) relational being. One separates "in order to" come together—although this "in order to" must never be understood as that which is *merely* instrumental, thus compromising the integrity of such separation and making it some attenuated or token "no-saying." What is at issue here is no means-end relationship, but rather a dynamic, a living organism, which refuses any movement on the part of either of its modes to congeal into an ideological, and thus spurious, existence. Separation and relation exist in creative tension with one another, a tension that gives the lie to any pretense on the part of either to claim sufficiency unto itself. If we avert our eyes from the paradoxical nature of this so-called creative tension, we will be forced to make do, on the one hand, with an "I" that is less than a (empowered) self, and, on the other, with a relation between the sexes that, as less than fully dialogical in nature, is ultimately no different in kind from individual relationships under patriarchy.

If, furthermore, we fail to realize this paradox in our lives, we will fail to arrive at the truly radical core of feminist protest. To achieve a rebellion that is authentic is to avoid both reified separation and reified relation; it is, rather, to enter the Buberian "between" as the sole locus for redemptive political action. Healing cannot take place within a sterile separation, as it could not under the sterile relations between the sexes under patriarchy. The criterion according to which it is determined whether or not a protest is radical is not the presence of separation *as such*, as Frye seems to suggest,[31] but rather the "hallowing" of both separation and relation achieved in realizing the paradox of their inextricable linkage.

CONCLUSION: MALE INITIATIVES FOR DIALOGUE

Dialogue does not preclude—indeed, it demands—a uniqueness of response on the part of all parties to its realization. Although the dialogical encounter between men and women will be greater than the sum of its parts, and although no preconceived ideas of what either partner will say or do can ever be faithful to its enactment, it is nonetheless the case that, given a history of patriarchy, men can and must be asked about the quality of their dialogical initiative. In a chapter given over to arguments for the removal of *narrowly conceived* feminist concerns about the possibility of dialogue between men and women, the time has come for me as a male to speak about the nature of men's contribution to inaugurating the dialogue so envisioned. More specifically, I must turn, as I did above, to the question of separation—this time, a male separation—as part of the dialogical encounter.

As those who have oppressed women, or as those in whose name women have been oppressed, men have already practiced a spurious form of separation. In distinguishing feminist from masculist separation, Frye defines the latter as "the partial separation of women from men and male domains at the will of men."[32] Willy-nilly, men have separated themselves from women as part of a process by which the latter have been excluded from most of the arenas in which humans live and enjoy their lives in the course of becoming empowered beings.

How might the replacement of this pseudo-separation by one that is authentic be begun? Men must utilize the "signs of address" all around them—the protests of women, the kindred awarenesses of other men—in coming to the realization that there exist entangling webs that have been spun in their name to entrap women. Such activity—traditionally spoken of as consciousness-raising—inaugurates *genuine* separation. And just as women have spoken from their own experience (of oppression) and have employed (among others) traditionally defined "feminine" qualities in the service of their unique form of separation, so must men acknowledge their own experience as oppressors and proceed, not to reject wholesale, but to make fundamentally different use of (among other elements) that which has been traditionally attributed to "masculinity." Powers of analytic thinking and "self-assertion," for example—powers not, of course, exclusively or inherently male—must be "redeemed" from use as tools of oppression for use in the praxis of dialogue. It is not in the name of some abstract, and thus sexless, human "entity" that such an effort must be carried forth. Nor is it in the mode of *female* feminists—or in the mode of a superficial androgynous self still based on the male model of who is "really" human—that men must do their work of separation. Men must realize their solidarity with women in and through their being-as-men. Only by redemptively utilizing (among others) qualities often deemed to be distinctively theirs and most often employed in the service of oppression, will men enact the work of separation and its correlative, relation.

While it is the case, then, that men can only speak from a ground of "who they are" and where they have been, they must endeavor, we have argued, to transcend this givenness at the very moment it is acknowledged. Although the past grounds us as embodied beings, this past is always a past subject to present attitudes toward it. To escape the determining force of such a past, with all its fixity of sex roles, we must not pretend it has never existed; instead, in Buber's words, we must refuse to accept it as a "whirlpool of fate." This we do by living in a present that is not, in its primordial sense, a point posited on some continuum, but rather a "presentness-to": "The present arises only in virtue of the fact that the Thou becomes present."[33] Men must come through their embeddedness in history (and in a so-called "masculinity") to emerge as present-to-women.

This "presentness-to-women" must occur, moreover, across a full spectrum of behaviors ranging from the more apparently personal (for example, avoiding sexist language or sharing housework and childcare) to the more overtly political (for example, pursuing just economic legislative measures and legislation for women's reproductive rights). Furthermore, there is no (ultimate) choice to be made here regarding one area of concern to be addressed to the exclusion of others. We must not be content to do the work of dialogue merely at home, or merely in the workplace, or merely in the public political arena. We must work at dialogue at all places and all times! Men must separate themselves from their patriarchal legacy across the fullness of a "horizontal" dimension of human experience: all arenas of human endeavor must, on principle, be able to be addressed at once. In the face of a history of oppression we have no luxury of choosing to work only in one or the other of many realms. Moreover, we are reminded by radical feminists (among others) that the personal is, indeed, the political—just as we have reminded ourselves throughout this chapter that the (truly) political is the personal!

Nor must we men remain content with action across such a "horizontal" dimension: we must also learn to engage women as partners to dialogue in the fullness of the "vertical" dimension of time. Given the legacy of patriarchy, we must address these concerns—without respite—throughout the fullness of each day, and pass on this dialogical imperative to generations to come. There is no "time-out" from the healing work of dialogue: we must watch our words, our touch, our eyes, our gestures, our public postures—the whole of how we comport ourselves (including our silences) in a world in which women are oppressed in our name. The work of dialogue between men and women responds to a summons that is infinite and eternal.

And finally, just as men must go through and come out the "other side" of their guilt as oppressors, so must their facing of women be effected *and sustained* in the presence of women's anger at having been oppressed. To encounter a woman as a Thou is to encounter her in the fullness of who she is—with her anger also. As Maurice Friedman points out, "there is no measured rebellion."[34] Rebellion must not be regulated, as many men would have it, but rather sacramentalized by both men and women as that "showing of wounds" that demands a response in word and deed.

Given the nature of the male initiatives for dialogue sketched above, at least two lines of criticism can be anticipated. First, it may be argued that in proposing certain behaviors on the part of men as initiatives in reforming men's and women's relations, we have entered the realm of the good intentions of the liberal. On one level it would appear that nothing startlingly new or truly radical has been proposed—no initiatives strikingly different from those so often proposed in the writings of liberal feminists (male or female). Are we not, it may be asked, merely touching the surface of matters when we speak of such men's initiatives as consciousness-raising and the sharing of housework and childcare? A genuine liberation of women, radical feminists argue, is one that gets to the root causes of the malaise of patriarchy: the mere alleviation of symptoms constitutes the sole agenda for the meliorist philosophy of liberal strategists. Indeed, it can be argued that the measures undertaken by well-intentioned liberals are easily co-opted by those who would speak of an "equality" wholly derived from the (still) dominant male model of humankind. Other theorists, like Frye, speak, as we have noted above, of the presence of female separation *as such* as "one of the main things that guides or determines assessments of various theories, actions and practices as reformist or radical."[35] Frye goes on to claim that "the theme of separation is noticeably absent or heavily qualified in most of the things I take to be personal solutions and band-aid projects, like . . . liberal marriage contracts, improvements of the treatment of rape victims and affirmative action."[36]

Second, some radical theorists argue that inherent in heterosexual ideological tenets in general, and in the institution of marriage in particular, are sexist biases that leave no hope for the relief promised by the gradualist measures of liberal reformers. In the light of a built-in bias pervading heterosexual relations, are not such issues as those of childcare and equality of job opportunities a mere smokescreen, deflecting much-needed attention from the core issues at hand? A chapter that presumes to speak for a spiritual—and thus ultimately "radical"—politics must close by responding to these challenges.

A radical or root critique of patriarchy, I have argued here, lies not in the discovery of any one core element allegedly undergirding all other manifestations of patriarchy—whether such a core emerges from issues of control of women's bodies (as many radical feminists claim), issues of class (as socialist feminists argue), or issues of equal rights (as so-called liberal feminists contend). None of these pretenders to absolute status allows, in and of itself, for that change of levels, that shift in ontological dimensions from It to Thou, that is required by any claimant to such status. The truly radical revolution is one in which—*in* the struggle for women's control of their own bodies, *in* the struggle against capitalist structures as forms of male oppression, *in* the struggle for the enactment of equal rights—the primacy of dialogue is affirmed throughout! All, or none, of the elements alluded to above can play a role in the infinite task of realizing the Thou in the day-to-day encounters between men and women: what might look like a mere gesture or "band-aid"—male participation in housework or affirmative action projects, for example—can, if lived in the fullness of the endeavor to realize the other as a Thou by and through this concrete deed, serve as nothing short of the radical feminist praxis that is the object of our search.

Thus, what looked like a failure to propose radically new and sweeping initiatives by men may not be a failure at all. In addressing measures such as consciousness-raising, the sharing of what traditionally have been conceived to be women's tasks, and the pursuit of affirmative action, we may seem to have left everything as it is (in the literature of liberal feminism). Yet by acknowledging that each such activity must be invested with the Thou-saying of dialogue, nothing is untouched, nothing remains the same. That any such deed—like all human acts—remains (in the most obvious sense) limited is evident; that such an act can touch the depths of our humanity and thus send forth (genuinely) revolutionary reverberations throughout the human community must be seen to be evident as well. Such an act is thus both finite and infinite at once. In Buber's terms, a deed respecting the personhood of the other accomplishes nothing short of the planting of a "seed of redemption" in the field of troubled relations between men and women, and thus in the world at large.

In the face of this realization, then, the concept of separation chosen by Frye as a criterion for distinguishing between radical and reformist feminism may or may not be as central as she believes it to be. Whether or not such a separation is effected as an integrative aspect of a dialogical encounter will determine the presence or absence of a truly radical feminist praxis. In the same vein, no institution such as marriage can be labeled feminist or antifeminist in and of itself; rather, how it is lived, how it is borne witness to, determines its role in promoting or hindering liberation: heterosexual marriage is neither to be acclaimed nor condemned as such; rather, it is to be hallowed. It is this hallowing that constitutes the essence of liberation struggles in general, and of men's and women's liberation in particular.

To say the above, moreover, is to respond to a final challenge to the concept of a dialogical imperative as the foundation of men's and women's liberation. In his article "Male Feminism," alluded to in the opening paragraphs of this chapter, Heath makes the claim that men's relationship to feminism is an "impossible one," that "I am not where they are and . . . cannot pretend to be."[37] In saying this, Heath is certainly correct: I am not a woman and thus cannot, on principle, live her history, her life world. What must be stressed, however, is the ever-present possibility for both men and women to transcend our gendered being in and through our very acknowledgement of it. Yes, I, as a male, am not "where women are"; neither, however, in the most fundamental sense, are women where women are! We are all simultaneously both where we are (as embodied and thus gendered beings) and not where we are (as creatures capable of realizing a Thou-invested world). To be not where I am, however, is not to be in some "nowhere," some "never-never land." Rather, to acknowledge my ever-present possibility of transcending my fixity of role is to move toward encountering the other in the realm of the "between." This most concrete of all spaces—concrete because it is the one space to-be-witnessed-to, rather than to-be-posited—is the place where men and women can and must meet. It is here that the possibility of dialogue between the sexes, so often questioned throughout this chapter, is to be realized.

AUTOBIOGRAPHICAL POSTSCRIPT

I began this chapter with the claim that a male writing on the need for dialogue between men and women must step back from his enterprise in order to examine his own credentials for executing the task at hand. Such an examination of credentials refers not solely to an investigation of presuppositions that might play a role in the academic enterprise of "making a case," but also to a questioning of the presence or absence of that "personal witness"that any philosopher must bear to that about which he or she philosophizes. One "does" philosophy with the whole of one's being. To do philosophy is to stand naked before one's readers in the sense that, ultimately, what one has to say is a testimony to how one has lived one's life. The philosopher only (!) gives (hopefully thoughtful) expression to that which—in the course of his or her day-to-day life—cries out to be heard.

Having said this, let me proceed to sketch, briefly, some of the origins of my more personal involvement with the issues discussed at length in this chapter. The single most pronounced introduction on my part to these issues emerged during my years as the single parent of two children. Although I had paid lip service, and perhaps more, to breaking down traditional sex stereotypes during my early years as husband and father, it was only with the assumption of responsibility for the day-to-day care of a four and a six-year-old that certain visceral understandings of these matters came to be realized.

My initial reaction to my new role was nothing short of a fierce determination to be mother and father at once; without questioning the essence of a tradition of sex stereotyping, I tried to become what, in my limited vision, was a manifestation of "mom and dad" all rolled into one—and with a vengeance! By mechanically adding traditionally conceived feminine characteristics to masculine ones in my parenting, I believed I could be nothing short of "superparent"! Further, in the name of my young ones, I would effect a separation from those with whom I had experienced pain; in lieu of working to establish dialogical contact with women, I believed I could go it alone, incorporating that which was missing—femininity—into my (equally reified) conception of what it was to be a man. Walled-off from others—and especially from women—I would be both sexes in one. In this regard nothing could rile me more than an accusation, such as the one often leveled at me by my mother, to the effect that I did not know how to care for my daughter's hair; nothing upset me more than my mother's suggestion (within earshot of my children) that I hire a woman to take responsibility for rearing my children so that I could be free to attend to my properly male (professional) responsibilities. To learn to hem a piece of clothing became a task of critical importance.

Although I firmly believed I had learned a great deal about "how it was for women" during these years of playing at being superparent, the fact remained (as in retrospect it is so easy to perceive) that what I was doing, I was doing, of course, as a male. My emergence—and in some sense I'm still emerging—from all this began to take place as I started to attend to what was being said in the frequent praise, even acclaim, on the part of family and friends, regarding the mere fact that I was playing the role of primary parent to my children. In my world of relatives, friends, colleagues, acquaintances—many of whom I imagined would have known better—I heard, repeatedly, a chorus of encomiums:

"How can you manage as both parent and professor? What a dedicated individual you are! How do you do it?" Forgotten in all this was the brute fact that for untold centuries single mothers have assumed the traditional roles of mothering and fathering—seldom earning such expressions of wonderment and praise as I had experienced all around me. These encounters with one manifestation of a virulent sexism helped to sensitize me to feminist concerns.

Yet another set of insights emerged from this experience of single-parenting. Although I had expended much energy in the endeavor to combine feminine and masculine characteristics into being one parent, it soon became apparent to me that such a fierce effort to meld two sets of romanticized, and thus idealogically fixed, roles—coupled with a determination on my part to "go it alone" as the solitary hero-parent—was failing to bear fruit either for me or for my children: I would often quite self-righteously fall asleep in the evening, exhausted, at the same time as my children; and they risked forming much too dependent a bond with me as their "be-all and end-all." To be a truly liberated father who would be there for my children, I began to learn, was not to pile up alleged feminine skills and traits on top of masculine ones that were mine, I believed, by right of birth. Rather, the task at hand was to fashion myself as an authentic "I"— in this instance, an I as male parent—through that dialogical interaction with others that I was avoiding. To allow for my development as an honest parent was to "let the other in," to open myself to those encounters in which I could realize myself as parent (as well as lover, colleague, friend). This alone would allow me to become a "dad" worthy of the name. Only through dialogue, only through entering the "between," could there be that movement that allows, paradoxically, for some authentic approximation of the image of superparent to which I had previously aspired. The "superparent," I came to learn, is not one who combines some reified images of female and male in oneself, but one who becomes an empowered self through encounter with the other.

Finally, in later years of parenting—and co-parenting in a new relationship— it became clearer to me that the spiritual revolution in the world of men's and women's relations of which I had so often spoken—and whose prospect for realization forms the substance of this chapter—is one that is to be effected not only, or even most profoundly, on a "horizontal" level of breadth or scope. Rather, in passing down through the generations, largely through personal witness, an image of authentic dialogue between men and women, one sets in motion a hallowing of the world whose depth knows no fixed end. Through my experience of living closely with a new generation, I have no doubt but that a truly spiritual revolution is neither, in its essential or core moment, one that "merely" pervades one's own culture, or even one that crosses cultures; rather, it is an *inter-generational* teaching that will make its mark most pronouncedly in the advance of the human spirit in general and in the development of dialogue between men and women in particular. For this realization I am most thankful for my experience as parent.

NOTES

1. Steven Health, "Male Feminism," in Alice Jardine and Paul Smith, eds., *Men in Feminism* (New York: Methuen, 1987), 1.

2. Marilyn Frye, *The Politics of Reality: Essays in Feminist Theory* (Trumansburg, NY: Crossing Press, 1983), 4.

3. Ibid., 1–2.

4. Ibid., 10.

5. For the concept of "imperialism" used in this sense, I am indebted to Emmanuel Levinas, whose *Totality and Infinity,* trans. Alphonso Lingis (Pittsburg: Duquesne University Press, 1969), develops some of the ontological claims found implicitly in Buber's work. See especially p. 44.

6. Ibid., 46.

7. This term is used by Jean-Paul Sartre in *Being and Nothingness,* trans. Hazel Barnes (New York: Pocket Books, 1956), 243, to alert the reader to the synoptic quality of Hegelian metaphysics; here, I argue, it can well be used to describe Sartre's own ontology.

8. Ibid., 474–75.

9. Ibid., 394. It should be noted here that my interpretation of the impossibility of dialogue in Sartre's ontology has been most recently questioned by Betty Cannon's "Sartre's Idea of Community," in William Calder, Ulrich Goldsmith, and Phyllis Kenevan, eds., *Hypatia: Essays in Honor of Hazel E. Barnes* (Boulder: University of Colorado Press, 1985).

10. Martin Buber, "What Is Man?" in *Between Man and Man,* trans. Ronald Gregor Smith (New York: MacMillan, 1965), 184.

11. Quoted in Maurice Friedman, *The Hidden Human Image* (New York: Delacorte Press, 1974), 209.

12. Ibid.

13. Simone de Beauvoir, *The Second Sex,* trans. H. M, Parshley (New York: Vintage Books, 1974), 814.

14. Rosemary Radford Ruether, *Sexism and God-Talk: Toward a Feminist Theology* (Boston: Beacon Press, 1983), 20.

15. Martin Buber, "The Question to the Single One," in *Between Man and Man,* 68.

16. Martin Buber, "Genuine Dialogue and the Possibilities of Peace," in *Pointing the Way* (New York: Harper and Row, 1962), 238.

17. Quoted in Charlene Spretnak, ed., *The Politics of Women's Spirituality: Essays on the Rise of Spiritual Power Within the Feminist Movement* (Garden City, NY: Anchor Press, 1982), xxiii.

18. Martin Buber, *I and Thou,* trans. Ronald Gregor Smith (New York: Collier Books, 1987), 37.

19. Martin Buber, "Dialogue," in *Between Man and Man,* 10.

20. Ibid.

21. Buber, *I and Thou,* 27.

22. Conversation with Professor Ernest Sherman, Oct. 10, 1987.

23. Conversation with Diana Rivers, Dec. 28, 1987.

24. Buber, *I and Thou,* 18.

25. Marilyn Frye, "On Separatism and Power," in *The Politics of Reality,* 96.

26. Ibid., 97.
27. Ibid., 98.
28. Ibid., 104.
29. Ruether, *Sexism and God-Talk*, 231.
30. Buber, *I and Thou*, 11.
31. Frye, "On Separatism and Power," 96.
32. Ibid.
33. Buber, *I and Thou*, 12.
34. Friedman, *The Hidden Human Image*, 205.
35. Frye, "On Separatism and Power," 96.
36. Ibid.
37. Heath, "Male Feminism," 1.

9

Yeshua, Feminist and Androgynous: An Integrated Human

LEONARD SWIDLER

In a certain sense the whole of human life is a complex series of encounters on a variety of levels and in manifold directions: the encounter of the human being with its own self, with nature around it, with its fellow human beings, and with ultimate reality—in the Judeo-Christian tradition called God. This complex of encounters redound on and influence each other: whoever leaves the encounter of the human with ultimate reality aside, for example, will distort the human relationship to itself, to nature, and to fellow humanity. Only in the present day are we becoming fully aware that the encounter with our environment and nature is rapidly transforming the world into a place where humans can no longer meet each other in a human manner; indeed, we may soon no longer be able to exist at all if we do not succeed in reversing the pollution of our environment.

History is the story of the encounters of humans with themselves and their fellow humans—and it is too infrequently a joyful account. Often humans appear to flee from an encounter with their true selves and all too seldom really encounter their fellow humans; far too often they meet them as objects, but do not encounter them as persons. That means, of course, that they do not meet them as they really are. Still worse is the long history of the dehumanizing of humans by one another, a dehumanizing in various ways and in various degrees. Fortunately, one of the crassest forms of the exploitation of humans by other humans, slavery, has been largely eliminated. Even the elimination of economic slavery has made significant progress in recent centuries—although the remaining task in this area is still great.

However, even the complete elimination of economic exploitation in the customary sense would still leave half of the human race in conditions that systematically distort and degrade their humanity. Women are thought almost by nature to be submissive, subordinate, second-class—not as slaves in the usual sense, but rather as something perhaps even more unworthy: voluntarily submissive, willing slaves. They are often trained, programmed so that they are eager to be only half-humans, and specifically the "passive" half. Of course, as in every master-slave relationship, the humanness of the master is distorted as well as that of the slave. Men too are often trained, programmed to be half-humans, the "aggressive" half.

It is no solution, as one is wont to suggest, that the sexes naturally mutually complete each other so that a human whole is formed when the two half-humans are united, as, for example, in marriage. Even our colloquial speech tells us that this notion is false. To be "passive" is not normally thought of as virtuous, any more than being "aggressive" usually is. In the relationship of one human being to another the passivity of one does not complement the aggressiveness of the other, but encourages it. To be sure, all human beings must combine receptivity and assertiveness, softness and firmness, feeling and clear thinking. However, this combination must be present in *every* person. Every woman and every man must be receiving as well as giving, soft and firm, emotional and rational, in order to be a complete human. However, the structures of almost all societies tend to split the human person into two halves, the male and female, and even to insist that this is prescribed in natural law. Biology is transformed into ontology! But in fact women are no more constituted primarily by their sex than are men; they are primarily human, *persons*—just as men are.

Each religious tradition will have to draw on elements from its own heritage, while remaining in constant dialogue with all other traditions, to address these basic issues. Hence, I as a Christian must turn to my Christian roots. Christians are not distinguished from other people in that they try to be antihuman, unhuman, or superhuman. As all other people, Christians strive to be complete in their humanity, but they believe that they have found in the Jew Jesus (Yeshua, as he was called in his native Semitic tongue) the model of full humanity. Yeshua is the Christians' model of the encounter with God, nature, one's self, and one's fellow human beings, especially the oppressed, that is, the sick, the poor, the ignorant—and women. For centuries Christians have attempted to imitate Yeshua in all these encounters, except the last named one. And yet, the encounter between man and woman is the most basic and pervasive of all the exploitative encounters in the history of humanity. It is the encounter that most pressingly needs the liberating model of Yeshua. Perhaps because it is the most fundamental, final bastion of sinful humanity, that is, of egocentric, unfree humanity, it is the last to yield to the liberating grace in Yeshua.

Put in one word, the model that Yeshua provided, the burden of everything that he thought, taught, and wrought, was "liberation." According to Luke 4:18 he quoted Isaiah of himself: "He has sent me to bring the good news to the poor, and to proclaim liberty [*aphesin*]," and according to John 8:32, 36 he said, "If you make my word your home . . . you will learn the truth and the truth will make you free [*eleutherosei*]. . . . If the son makes you free, you will be free indeed." Fundamentally this liberation is a freeing from ignorance and hence from a bondage to a false self and a false perception of reality, that is, first of all of our fellow human beings, then all things around us, and through them the Source of all reality. Then the human being is free to reach out in love to her/his own true self, fellow humans, nature, and the Source of all.

If indeed the most exploitative encounter between human beings is that of men with women, and hence is most in need of Yeshua's liberating model, so too is the encounter with the self in a similar need in a very closely related manner. As the Jungian psychologist Hanna Wolff put it: "Jesus is the first male who broke through the androcentrism of antiquity. The despotism of the solely male values is deposed. Jesus is the first one who broke with the solidarity of men, that is, of non-integrated men, and their anti-feminine animus. Jesus stands before us as the first man without animus."[1] The so-called feminine and masculine characteristics were exemplified in Yeshua in integrated, liberating—"androgynous"—fashion, and he presented a similar mutual, liberating model in the encounter with nature and with God. It is on the first two of those encounters—men with women, and with self—that I will focus through the model Yeshua presented.

YESHUA WAS A FEMINIST

Perhaps today is the *Kairos* when this last rampart will finally yield to the power of the combination of the model of Yeshua and the grace of the moment, the contemporary secular movement toward a full, equal human development of women: feminism. What is the model of Yeshua's encounter with women? If we look at the Gospels not with the eyes of male chauvinism or the "eternal feminine," we will see that the model Yeshua presents is that of a feminist: Yeshua was a feminist. A feminist is a person who is in favor of, and who promotes, the equality of women with men, a person who advocates and practices treating women primarily as human persons (as men are so treated) and willingly contravenes social customs in so acting.

To prove the thesis it must be shown that, so far as we can tell, Yeshua neither said nor did anything indicating that he advocated treating women as intrinsically inferior to men, but that on the contrary he said and did things that indicated that he thought of women as the equals of men, and that in the process he willingly violated pertinent social mores.

The negative portion of the argument can be documented quite simply by reading through the four Gospels. Nowhere does Yeshua treat women as "inferior beings." In fact, it is apparent that Yeshua understood himself to be especially sent to the typical classes of "inferior beings," such as the poor, the lame, the sinner—and women—to call them all to the freedom and equality of the reign of God. But there are two factors that raise this negative result exponentially in its significance: the status of women in Palestine at the time of Yeshua, and the nature of the Gospels. Both need to be recalled here in some detail, particularly the former.

The Status of Women in Palestine

The status of women in Palestine during the time of Yeshua was decidedly that of inferiors. Despite the fact that there were several heroines recorded in the Hebrew scriptures, according to most Rabbinic customs[2] of Yeshua's time—and long after—women were not allowed to study scripture (Torah). One first-century Rabbi, Eliezer, put the point sharply: "Rather should the words of the Torah be burned than entrusted to a woman . . . . Whoever teaches his daughter the Torah is like one who teaches her lasciviousness."[3]

In the vital religious area of prayer, women were not given obligations of the same seriousness as men. For example, women, along with children and slaves, were not obliged to recite the *Shema,* the morning prayer, nor prayers at meals.[4] In fact, the Talmud states: "Let a curse come upon the man who [must needs have] his wife or children say grace for him."[5] Moreover, in the daily prayers of Jews there was a threefold thanksgiving: "Praised be God that he has not created me a Gentile; praised be God that he has not created me a woman; praised be God that he has not created me an ignorant man."[6] (It was presumably a version of this Rabbinic prayer that Paul controverted in his letter to the Galatians: "There is neither Jew nor Greek, there is neither slave nor free, there is neither male nor female; for you are all one in Christ Jesus"; Gal. 3:28.) Women were also greatly restricted in public prayer. They were not counted toward the number necessary for a quorum to form a congregation to worship communally (a *minyan*)[7]—they were again classified with children and slaves, who similarly did not qualify (there is an interesting parallel to the canon 93 of the 1917 *Codex Iuris Canonici* [CIC] of the Catholic Church—valid until 1983—which grouped married women, minors, and the insane). In the great temple at Jerusalem they were limited to one outer portion, the women's court, which was five steps below the court for the men.[8] In the synagogues the women were also separated from the men, and were not allowed to read aloud or take any leading function.[9] (The same is still true in many Orthodox synagogues today; also, canon 1262 of the 1917 CIC stated that "in church the women should be separated from the men.")

Besides the disabilities women suffered in the areas of prayer and worship, there were many others in the private and public forums of society. The "Proverbs of the Fathers" contain the injunction: "Speak not much with a woman." Since a man's own wife is meant there, how much more did this apply to the wife of another? The wise men said: "Who speaks much with a woman draws down misfortune on himself, neglects the words of the law, and finally earns hell."[10] If it were merely the too free intercourse of the sexes that was being warned against, this might signify nothing derogatory to women. But since a man was not allowed to speak even to his own wife, daughter, or sister in the street,[11] then only male superiority could have been the motive, for intercourse with uneducated company is warned against in exactly the same terms: "One is not so much as to greet a woman."[12] In addition, save in the rarest instances, women were not allowed to bear witness in a court of law.[13] Some Jewish thinkers, for example, Philo, a contemporary of Yeshua, thought women should not leave their households except to go to the synagogue (and then only at a time when most of the other people would be at home);[14] girls should not even cross the threshold that separated the male and female apartments of the household.[15]

In general, the attitude toward women was epitomized in the institutions and customs surrounding marriage. For the most part the function of women was thought of rather exclusively in terms of childbearing and rearing; women were almost always under the tutelage of a man, either the father or husband, or if a widow, the dead husband's brother. Polygamy—in the sense of having several wives, but *not* in the sense of having several husbands—was legal among Jews at the time of Yeshua, although probably not heavily practiced. Moreover, divorce of a wife was very easily obtained by the husband—he merely had to give her a writ of divorce; women in Palestine, on the other hand, were not allowed to divorce their husbands.

Rabbinic sayings about women also provide an insight into the attitude toward women: "It is well for those whose children are male, but ill for those whose children are female."[16] "At the birth of a boy all are joyful, but at the birth of a girl all are sad."[17] "When a boy comes into the world, peace comes into the world: when a girl comes, nothing comes."[18] "Even the most virtuous of women is a witch."[19] "Our teachers have said: Four qualities are evident in women: They are greedy at their food, eager to gossip, lazy, and jealous."[20]

The Nature of the Gospels

The Gospels are not the straight factual reports of eyewitnesses of the events in the life of Yeshua of Nazareth that one might find in the columns of the *New York Times* or the pages of a critical biography. Rather, they are four different faith statements reflecting at least four primitive Christian communities who believed that Yeshua was the Messiah. They were composed from a variety of sources, written and oral, over a period of time and in response to certain needs felt in the communities and individuals at the time; consequently, they are many-layered. Since the Gospel writer-editors were not twentieth-century critical historians, they were not particularly intent on recording the very words of Yeshua, the *ipsissima verba Christi*, nor were they concerned to winnow out all of their own cultural biases and assumptions. Indeed, it is doubtful that they were particularly conscious of them.

This modern understanding of the Gospels, of course, does not impugn the historical character of the Gospels; it merely describes the type of documents they are so their historical significance can be more accurately evaluated. Its religious value lies in the fact that modern Christians are thereby helped to know more precisely what Yeshua meant by the statements and actions reported by the first Christians in the Gospels. With this new knowledge of the nature of the Gospels, it is easier to make the vital distinction between the religious truth that is to be handed on and the time-conditioned categories and customs involved in expressing it.

Yeshua as Source and as Jew

When the fact that no negative attitudes by Yeshua toward women are portrayed in the Gospels is set side by side with the recently discerned "communal faith-statement" understanding of the nature of the Gospels, the importance of the former is vastly enhanced. For whatever Yeshua said or did comes to us only through the lens of the first Christians. If there were no very special religious significance in a particular concept or custom, we would expect that contemporary concept or custom to be reflected by Yeshua. The fact that the overwhelmingly negative attitude toward women in Palestine did not come through the primitive Christian communal lens by itself underscores the great religious importance Yeshua attached to his positive attitude—his feminist attitude—toward women: feminism, that is, personalism extended to women, is a constitutive part of the Gospel, the Good News, of Yeshua.

It should also be noted here that, although in the analysis that follows it is the image of Yeshua as it emerges from the four Gospels that will be dealt with, the feminist character that is found there is ultimately to be attributed to Yeshua himself and not to the church, the evangelists, or their sources. Basically the "principle of dissimularity" operates here. That principle, devised by contemporary New Testament scholars, states that if a saying or action attributed to Yeshua is contrary to the cultural milieu of the time, then it most probably had its origin in Yeshua. In this case the feminism of Yeshua could hardly be attributable to the primitive church. As is seen already in the later New Testament writings, the early church quickly became not only nonfeminist, but also anti-woman. For example: "The women should keep silence in the churches. For they are not permitted to speak, but should be subordinate, as even the law says" (1 Cor. 14:34); "Let a woman learn in silence with all submissiveness. I permit no woman to teach or to have authority over men; she is to keep silent" (1 Tim. 2:11–12). The misogynist slide continued after the New Testament: In the second century Tertullian, the "father of theology," said of woman: "You are the devil's gateway";[21] in the next century Origen wrote: "What is seen with the eyes of the creator is masculine, and not feminine, for God does not stoop to look upon what is feminine and of the flesh";[22] in the fourth century Epiphanius said: "The devil seeks to vomit out his disorder through women."[23]

As seen in some detail before, in the Jewish culture women were held to be, as the first-century Jewish historian Josephus put it, "in all things inferior to the man."[24] Since it was in that milieu that the evangelists were writing and from which they drew their sources, none of them could have been the source of the feminism found in the Yeshua of the Gospels. Its only possible source was Yeshua himself. In fact, given the misogynist tendency exhibited in both the Judaism of Yeshua's time and the early Christian church, there is every likelihood that the strong feminism of Yeshua has been muted in the Gospels, as can be seen for example by the fact that the story of the woman taken in adultery (John 8:2–11) is absent from the earliest Greek manuscripts and almost did not make it into the canon of the New Testament at all.[25]

A further word of caution is needed here. The Jewish culture of the time of Yeshua indeed treated women as inferior to men, as did also much of the surrounding cultures, and Yeshua did in this matter run counter to that culture.[26] In the case of women, as in that of other marginalized groups, Yeshua raised a powerful prophetic voice of protest. But it needs to be remembered that raising a prophetic voice was precisely a Jewish thing to do; in this Yeshua was not acting as a non-Jew, but specifically as a Jew. Moreover, after the first enthusiastic response of the women followers to this liberating feminist move by Yeshua, the Christian church quickly sank back into a nonfeminist, even misogynist morass until our time. There is no ground here for Christians to claim superiority over Jews, but rather just the opposite. Christians claim to be followers of Yeshua, whereas Jews do not. Christians therefore had far more reason to be, like Yeshua, feminists. But they failed miserably.

Women Disciples of Yeshua

One of the first things noticed in the Gospels about Yeshua's attitude toward women is that he taught them the Gospel, the meaning of the scriptures, and religious truths in general. When it is recalled that in Judaism it was considered improper, and even "obscene" to teach women the scriptures, this action of Yeshua was an extraordinary, deliberate decision to break with a custom invidious to women. Moreover, women became disciples of Yeshua not only in the sense of learning from him, but also in the sense of following him in his travels and ministering to him.[27] A number of women, married and unmarried, were regular followers of Yeshua. In Luke 8:1ff., several are mentioned by name in the same sentence with the Twelve: "He made his way through towns and villages preaching and proclaiming the Good News of the reign of God. With him went the Twelve as well as certain women. . . . who ministered to [*diekonoun*] them out of their own resources."[28] The significance of this phenomenon of women following Yeshua about, learning from and ministering to him, can be properly appreciated only when it is recalled that not only were women not to read or study the scriptures, but in the more observant settings they were not even to leave their household, whether as a daughter, a sole wife, or a member of a harem.

Women and Resurrection from the Dead

Within this context of women being disciples and ministers, the Yeshua of the Gospels quite deliberately broke another custom disadvantageous to women. According to the Gospels, Yeshua's first appearance after his resurrection to any of his followers was to a woman (or women), who was then commissioned by him to bear witness of the risen Yeshua to the Eleven (John 20: 11ff.; Matt. 28:9f.; Mark 16:9ff.). In typical male Palestinian style, the Eleven refused to believe the women since, according to Judaic law, women were not allowed to bear legal witness. Clearly this was a dramatic linking of a very definite rejection of the second-class status of women with a central element of the Gospel, the resurrection. The effort to connect these two points is so obvious—an effort certainly not attributable to the male disciples or evangelists—that it is an overwhelming tribute to male intellectual myopia not to have discerned it effectively in two thousand years.

The intimate connection of women with resurrection from the dead is not limited in the Gospels to that of Yeshua. There are accounts of three other resurrections in the Gospels—all closely involving a woman. The most obvious connection of a woman with a resurrection account is that of the raising of a woman, Jairus' daughter (Matt 9:18ff,; Mark 5:22ff.; Luke 8:41ff.). A second resurrection Yeshua performed was that of the only son of the widow of Nain: "And when the Lord saw her, he had compassion on her and he said to her, 'Do not weep' " (cf. Luke. 7:11ff.). The third resurrection Yeshua performed was Lazarus', at the request of his sisters Martha and Mary (cf. John 11). From the first it was Martha and Mary who sent for Yeshua because of Lazarus' illness. But when Yeshua finally came, Lazarus was four days dead. Martha met Yeshua and pleaded for his resurrection: "Lord, if you had been there, my brother would not have died. And even now I know that whatever you ask from God, God will give you." Then followed Yeshua's raising of Lazarus from the dead. Thus, Yeshua raised one woman from the dead, and raised two other persons largely because of women.

There are two further details that should be noted in these three resurrection stories. The first is that only in the case of Jairus' daughter did Yeshua touch the corpse—which made him ritually unclean. In the cases of the two men Yeshua did not touch them, but merely said, "Young man, I say to you, arise," or, "Lazarus, come out." One must at least wonder why Yeshua chose to violate the laws for ritual purity in order to help a woman, but not a man. The second detail is in Yeshua's conversation with Martha after she pleaded for the resurrection of Lazarus. According to John's Gospel, Yeshua declared himself to be the resurrection ("I am the resurrection and the life"), the only time he did so that is recorded in the Gospels. Yeshua here again revealed a central element in the Gospel—the resurrection—to a woman.

Women as Sex Objects

There are of course numerous occasions recorded in the Gospels where women were treated by various men as second-class citizens. There are also situations where women were treated by others not at all as persons but as sex objects, and it was expected that Yeshua would do the same. The expectations were disappointed. One such occasion occurred when Yeshua was invited to dinner at the house of a skeptical Pharisee (Luke 7:36ff.) and a woman of ill-repute entered and washed Yeshua's feet with her tears, wiped them with her hair, and anointed them. The Pharisee saw her solely as an evil sexual creature: "The Pharisee . . . said to himself, 'If this man were a prophet, he would know who this woman is who is touching him and what a bad name she has.' " But Yeshua deliberately rejected this approach to the woman as a sex object. He rebuked the Pharisee and spoke solely of the woman's human, spiritual actions; he spoke of her love, her unlove (i.e., her sins), her being forgiven, and her faith. Yeshua then addressed her (it was not "proper" to address women in public, especially "improper" women) as a person: "Your sins are forgiven. . . . Your faith has saved you; go in peace."

A similar situation occurred when the scribes and Pharisees used a woman reduced entirely to a sex object to set a legal trap for Yeshua (John 8:2–11). It is difficult to imagine a more callous use of a human person than the "adulterous" woman was put to by the enemies of Yeshua. First, she was surprised in the intimate act of sexual intercourse (quite possibly a trap was set up ahead of time by the suspicious husband) and then dragged before the scribes and Pharisees, and then by them before an even larger crowd that Yeshua was instructing: "making her stand in full view of everybody." They told Yeshua that she had been caught in the very act of committing adultery and that Moses had commanded that such women be stoned to death (Deut. 22:22ff.). "What have you to say?" The trap was partly that if Yeshua said "yes" to the stoning he would be violating the Roman law, which reserved capital punishment to Roman officials, and if he said "no" he would appear to contravene Mosaic law. It could also partly have been to place Yeshua's reputation for kindness toward, and championing of the cause of, women in opposition to the law and the condemnation of sin. Yeshua, of course, eluded their snares by refusing to become entangled in legalisms and abstractions. Rather, he dealt with both the accusers and the accused directly as spiritual, ethical human persons. He spoke directly to the accusers in the context of their own personal ethical conduct: "If there is one of you who has not sinned, let him be the first to throw a stone at her." To the accused woman he likewise spoke directly with compassion, but without approving her conduct: " 'Woman, where are they? Has no one condemned you?' She said, 'No one, Lord.' And Yeshua said, 'Neither do I condemn you; go, and do not sin again.' "

One detail of this encounter provides the basis for a short excursus related to the status of women. The scribes and Pharisees stated that the woman had been caught in the act of adultery and according to the Law of Moses was therefore to be stoned to death. Since the type of execution mentioned was stoning, the woman must have been a "virgin betrothed," as referred to in Deut. 22:23f. There provision is made for the stoning of *both* the man and the woman, although in the Gospel story only the woman is brought forward. However, the reason given for why the man ought to be stoned was not because he had violated the

woman, or God's law, but: "because he had violated the wife of his neighbor."
It was the injury of the man through the misuse of his property—wife—that was
the great evil.

Yeshua's Rejection of the Blood Taboo

All three of the synoptic Gospels insert into the middle of the account of
raising Jairus' daughter from the dead the story of the curing of the woman who
had an issue of blood for twelve years (Matt. 9:20ff.; Mark 5:25ff.; Luke 8:43ff.).
What is especially touching about this story is that the affected woman was so
reluctant to project herself into public attention that she "said to herself, 'If I
only touch his garment, I shall be made well.' " Her shyness was not because
she came from the poor, lower classes, for Mark pointed out that over the twelve
years she had been to many physicians—with no success—on whom she had
spent all her money. It was probably because for twelve years, as a woman with
a flow of blood, she was constantly unclean (Lev. 15:19ff.), which not only
made her incapable of participating in any cultic action and made her in some
sense "displeasing to God," but also rendered anyone and anything she touched
(or anyone who touched what she had touched!) similarly unclean. (Here was
the basis for the Catholic Church's not allowing women in the sanctuary during
Mass until after Vatican II—she might be menstruating, and hence unclean.)
The sense of degradation and contagion that her "womanly weakness" worked
upon her over the twelve years doubtless was oppressive in the extreme. This
would have been especially so when a religious teacher, a Rabbi, was involved.
But not only does Yeshua's power heal her, in one of his many acts of compassion
for the downtrodden and afflicted, including women, but Yeshua also makes a
great to-do about the event, calling extraordinary attention to the publicity-shy
woman: "And Yeshua, perceiving in himself that power had gone forth from
him, immediately turned about in the crowd, and said, 'Who touched my gar-
ments?' And his disciples said to him, 'You see the crowd pressing around you,
and yet you say, "Who touched me?" ' And he looked around to see who had
done it. But the woman, knowing what had been done to her, came in fear and
trembling and fell down before him and told him the whole truth. And he said
to her, 'Daughter, your faith has made you well; go in peace, and be healed of
your disease.' " It seems clear that Yeshua wanted to call attention to the fact
that he did not shrink from the ritual uncleanness incurred by being touched by
the "unclean" woman (on several occasions Yeshua rejected the notion of ritual
uncleanness), and by immediate implication rejected the "uncleanness" of a
woman who had a flow of blood, menstrous or continual. Yeshua apparently
placed a greater importance on the dramatic making of this point, both to the
afflicted woman herself and the crowd, than he did on avoiding the temporary
psychological discomfort of the embarrassed woman, which in light of Yeshua's
extraordinary concern to alleviate the pain of the afflicted, meant he placed a
great weight on teaching this lesson about the dignity of women.

Yeshua and the Samaritan Woman

On another occasion Yeshua again deliberately violated the then common code concerning men's relationship to women. It is recorded in the story of the Samaritan woman at the well of Jacob (John 4:5ff.). Yeshua was waiting at the well outside the village while his disciples were getting food. A Samaritan woman approached the well to draw water. Normally a Jew would not address a Samaritan, as the woman pointed out: "Jews, in fact, do not associate with Samaritans." But also normally a man would not speak to a woman in public (doubly so in the case of a Rabbi). However, Yeshua startled the woman by initiating a conversation. The woman was aware that on both counts, her being a Samaritan and being a woman, Yeshua's action was out of the ordinary for she replied: "How is it that you, a Jew, ask a drink of me, a woman of Samaria?" As hated as the Samaritans were by the Jews, it is nevertheless clear that Yeshua's speaking with a woman was considered a much more flagrant breach of conduct than his speaking with a Samaritan, for John related: "His disciples returned, and were surprised to find him speaking to a woman, though none of them asked, 'What do you want from her?' or, 'Why are you talking to her?' " However, Yeshua's bridging of the gap of inequality between men and women continued further, for in the conversation with the woman, according to John, he revealed himself in a straightforward fashion as the Messiah for the first time: "The woman said to him, 'I know that Messiah is coming'. . . . Yeshua said to her, 'I who speak to you am he.' "

Just as when, according to the Gospel, Yeshua revealed himself to Martha as "the resurrection," and to Mary as the "risen one," and bade her bear witness to the apostles, Yeshua here also revealed himself in one of his key roles, as Messiah, to a woman—who immediately bore witness of the fact to her fellow villagers. It is interesting to note that apparently the testimony of women carried greater weight among the Samaritans than among the Jews, for the villagers came out to see Yeshua: "Many Samaritans of that town believed in him on the strength of the woman's testimony." It would seem that John the Gospel writer deliberately highlighted this contrast in the way he wrote about this event, and also that he clearly wished to reinforce thereby Yeshua's stress on the equal dignity of women.

One other point should be noted in connection with this story. As the crowd of Samaritans was walking out to see Yeshua, he was speaking to his disciples about the fields being ready for the harvest and how he was sending them to reap what others had sown. He was clearly speaking of the souls of men and women, and most probably was referring directly to the approaching Samaritans. Such exegesis is standard. It is also rather standard to refer to others in general and only Yeshua in particular as having been the sowers whose harvest the apostles were about to reap (e.g., in the *Jerusalem Bible*). But it would seem that the evangelist also meant specifically to include the Samaritan woman among those sowers, for immediately after he recorded Yeshua's statement to the disciples about their reaping what others had sown, John added the above-mentioned verse: "Many Samaritans of that town had believed in him on the strength of the *woman*'s testimony."

Marriage and the Dignity of Woman

One of the most important stands of Yeshua in relation to the dignity of women was his position on marriage. His unpopular attitude toward marriage (cf. Matt. 19:10: "The disciples said to him, 'If such is the case of a man with his wife, it is not expedient to marry.' ") presupposed a feminist view of women; they had rights and responsibilities equal to men. It was quite possible in Jewish law for men to have more than one wife (though this was probably not frequently the case in Yeshua's time, there are recorded instances, e.g., Herod, Josephus), though the reverse was not possible. Divorce, of course, also was a simple matter, to be initiated only by the man. In both situations women were basically chattel to be collected or dismissed as the man was able and wished to; the double moral standard was flagrantly apparent. Yeshua rejected both by insisting on monogamy and the elimination of divorce; both the man and the woman were to have the same rights and responsibilities in their relationship toward each other (cf. Mark 10:2ff.; Matt. 19:3ff.). This stance of Yeshua was one of the few that was rather thoroughly assimilated by the Christian church (in fact, often in an over-rigid way concerning divorce, for here Yeshua was offering a goal ethic, not a minimum ethic—but how to understand the ethical prescriptions of Yeshua is another subject), doubtless in part because it was reinforced by various sociological conditions and other historical accidents, such as the then current strength in the Greek world of the Stoic philosophy. However, the notion of equal rights and responsibilities was not extended very far within the Christian marriage. The general role of women was *Kirche, Kinder, Küche*—and only a suppliant's role in the first.

The Intellectual Life for Women

However, Yeshua clearly did not think of woman's role in such restricted terms; she was not to be limited to being *only* a housekeeper. Yeshua quite directly rejected the stereotype that the proper place of all women is "in the home" during a visit to the house of Martha and Mary (Luke 10:38ff.). Martha took the typical woman's role: "Martha was distracted with much serving." Mary, however, took the supposedly "male" role: she "sat at the Lord's feet and listened to his teaching." (It should be noted that this is a technical term for being a disciple—which is even reflected in contemporary English speech when we say: I sat at the master's feet.) Martha apparently thought Mary was out of place in choosing the role of the "intellectual," for she complained to Yeshua. But Yeshua's response was a refusal to force all women into the stereotype; he treated Mary first of all as a person (whose highest faculty is the intellect, the spirit) who was allowed to set her own priorities, and in this instance had "chosen the better part." And Yeshua applauded her: "It is not to be taken from her." Again, when one recalls the Palestinian restriction on women studying the scriptures or studying with Rabbis, that is, engaging in the intellectual life or acquiring any "religious authority," it is difficult to imagine how Yeshua could possibly have been clearer in his insistence that women were called to the intellectual, the spiritual life, just as were men.

There is at least one other instance recorded in the Gospels when Yeshua uttered much the same message (Luke 11:27f.). One day, as Yeshua was preaching, a woman from the crowd apparently was very deeply impressed and, perhaps imagining how glad she would be to have such a son, raised her voice to pay Yeshua a compliment. She did so by referring to his mother, and did so in a way that was probably not untypical at that time and place. But her image of a woman was sexually reductionist in the extreme (one that largely persists to the present): female genitals and breasts. "Blessed is the womb that bore you, and the breasts that you sucked!" Although this was meant as a compliment, and although it was even uttered by a woman, Yeshua clearly felt it necessary to reject this "baby-machine" image of women and insist again on the personhood, the intellectual and moral faculties, being primary for all: "But he said, 'Blessed rather are those who hear the word of God and keep it!' " Looking at this text it is difficult to see how the primary point could be anything substantially other than this. Luke and the tradition and Christian communities he depended on must also have been quite clear about the sexual significance of this event. Otherwise, why would he (and they) have kept and included such a small event from all the months, or even years, of Yeshua's public life? It was not retained *merely* because he said blessed are those who hear and keep God's word (for the evangelist had already recorded that elsewhere), but because that was stressed by Yeshua as being primary in comparison to a woman's sexuality. Luke, however, seems to have had a discernment here, and elsewhere, concerning what Yeshua was about in the question of women's status that has not been shared by subsequent Christians (nor apparently by many of *his* fellow Christians), for, in the explanation of this passage, Christians for two thousand years did not see its meaning—doubtless because of unconscious presuppositions about the status of women inculcated by their cultural milieu.

WOMEN IN YESHUA'S LANGUAGE

Yeshua's attitude toward women is also reflected in the very language attributed to him in the Gospels. First, as seen, Yeshua often used women in his stories and sayings, something most unusual for his culture. Second, the images of women Yeshua used are never negative, but always positive—in dramatic contrast to his predecessors and contemporaries. Third, these positive images of women were often very exalted, at times being associated with the "reign of heaven," likened to the chosen people, and even to God herself! Fourth, Yeshua often taught a point by telling two similar stories or using two images, one of which featured a man and one a woman. This balance, among other things, indicated that Yeshua wanted it to be abundantly clear that his teaching, unlike that of other Rabbis, was intended for both women and men, which he obviously wanted to be clear to the men as well as the women, since he told these stories to all his disciples and at times even to crowds. These sexually parallel stories and images also confirm the presence of women among his hearers; they were used to bring home the point of a teaching in an image that was familiar to the women.

The sexually parallel stories and images used by Yeshua range from very brief pairings to lengthy parables. Their frequency in the synoptic Gospels is impressive—nine of them. For example, the reign of heaven was likened to a mustard seed that a man sowed and to leaven that a woman put in her dough (Matt. 13:31–33; Luke 13:18–21), or, in the final days one man of two in the field and one woman of two grinding corn will be taken (Matt. 24: 39–41).[29] The ultimate in sexually parallel stories told by Yeshua, however, was the one in which God was cast in the likeness of a woman.

God As a Woman

Yeshua strove in many ways to communicate the notion of the equal dignity of women and in one sense that effort was capped by his parable of the woman who found the lost coin (Luke 15:8ff.), for here Yeshua projected God in the image of a woman! Luke recorded that the despised tax-collectors were gathering around Yeshua, and hence the Pharisees complained. Yeshua, therefore, related three parables, all of which depicted God's being deeply concerned for that which was lost. The first story was of the shepherd who left the ninety-nine sheep to seek the one lost—the shepherd is God. The third parable was of the prodigal son—the father is God. The second story was of the woman who sought the lost coin—the woman is God. Yeshua did not shrink from the notion of God as feminine. In fact, it would appear that Luke's Yeshua included this womanly image of God quite deliberately at this point, for the scribes and Pharisees were among those who most of all denigrated women—just as they did the "tax-collectors and sinners."

There have been some instances in Christian history when the Holy Spirit has been associated with a feminine character, as, for example, in the third-century Syrian *Didascalia* where, in speaking of various offices in the church, it states: "The woman deacon however should be honored by you as the image of the Holy Spirit." It would make an interesting investigation to see whether these images of God presented here by Luke were ever used in a Trinitarian manner, Father, Son, Holy Spirit—thereby giving the Holy Spirit a feminine image. A negative result to the investigation would be as significant as a positive one, for this passage would seem to be particularly apt for a later Christian Trinitarian interpretation: the prodigal son's father is God the Father (this interpretation has in fact been quite common in Christian history); since Yeshua elsewhere identified himself as the Good Shepherd, the shepherd seeking the lost sheep is Yeshua, the Son (this standard interpretation is reflected in, among other things, the often-seen picture of Yeshua carrying the lost sheep on his shoulders); the woman who sought the lost coin should "logically" be the Holy Spirit. If such an interpretation has existed, it surely has not been common. Should such lack of "logic" be attributed to the general cultural denigration of women or the Christian abhorrence of pagan goddesses—although the Christian abhorrence of pagan male gods did not result in a Christian rejection of a male image of God?

From this evidence it should be clear that Yeshua vigorously promoted the dignity and equality of women in the midst of a very male-dominated society: Yeshua was a feminist, and a very radical one.

AN "ANDROGYNOUS" YESHUA

There is also, however, another message about Yeshua's attitude toward women and men to be found in the psychological image of Yeshua that is projected by the Gospels. That image is of an androgynous person, not in the sense of a combination of physical male and female traits, but rather the fusion and balance of so-called masculine and feminine psychological traits.

The notion that the significance of Yeshua lay in his humanity, rather than specifically in his maleness, is one that was stated clearly and even officially already in early Christianity. In the Nicene creed (325 A.D.) Christians said of Yeshua, "et *homo* factus est," "and he became *human*." They did *not* say, "et *vir* factus est," "and he became *male* (*vir*ile)." There was even a limited amount of Christian painting of Yeshua as physically androgynous, but it was not very fully developed. However, if it is asked whether the image of Yeshua in the Gospels reflects the psychologically so-called masculine or feminine traits, abundant material for an answer is at hand.

One of the humanly very destructive things our culture does is popularly to divide up various human traits into feminine and masculine ones, as if women naturally had one set and men the other. Such a division is scientifically unfounded; in fact, scientific data are piling up that tend to indicate that such an allegedly inborn division of traits is largely fallacious. Hence, even to continue to use the terms feminine characteristics and masculine characteristics tends to perpetuate the problem. So, until sexually neutral terms are developed and widely used, I will refer to these sets of traits as *so-called* feminine and masculine characteristics.

Certain ways of acting, thinking, speaking, etc., are popularly said to be specifically manly, and their opposites womanly: (1) men are supposed to be reasonable and cool—women are to be persons of feeling and emotion; (2) men are to be firm, aggressive—women, gentle, peaceful; (3) men should be advocates of justice—women, mercy; (4) men should have pride and self-confidence—women should have humility and reserve; (5) men are said to be the providers of security (food, clothing, shelter)—women, the ones who need security; (6) men are supposed to be concerned with organization and structure—women with persons, especially children. If we were to analyze the Gospel image of Yeshua in each of these categories we would find that Yeshua manifests both the so-called feminine and masculine traits in all six categories. Although this is not possible within the confines of this essay, we will analyze at least the first category.

Yeshua: Reasonable and Cool—With Feeling and Emotion

Yeshua had a large number of vigorous, at times even extremely vicious, enemies, both in debate and in life-and-death situations. In debate: after Yeshua criticized the chief priests and scribes, "they waited their opportunity and sent agents to pose as men devoted to the Law and to fasten on something he might say and so enable them to hand him over to the jurisdiction and authority of the governor. They put to him this question, 'Master, we know that you say and teach what is right; you favor no one, but teach the way in all honesty. Is it permissible for us to pay taxes to Caesar or not?' " They were a clever lot, for Israel was occupied by Roman troops and the Jews in general consequently hated everything Roman with a passion, and especially the publicans (native tax-collectors for Rome). If Yeshua said straight out to pay Roman taxes, he would have immediately lost his influence with the people, which would have suited his enemies. But if he said do not pay taxes, he would have immediately ended up in a Roman jail, or perhaps worse, which also would have suited his enemies.

"But he was aware of their cunning and said, 'Show me a denarius. Whose head and name are on it?' 'Caesar's,' they said. 'Well, then,' he said to them, 'give back to Caesar what belongs to Caesar—and to God what belongs to God.' " A most *reasonable* response: "As a result, they were unable to find fault with anything he had to say in public; his answer took them by surprise and they were silenced" (Luke 20:20–26).

In life-and-death situations: "When they heard this everyone in the synagogue was enraged. They sprang to their feet and hustled him out of the town, and they took him up to the brow of the hill their town was built on, intending to throw him down the cliff." Yeshua's reaction? "But he slipped through the crowd and walked away" (Luke 4:28–30). Real *cool*.

More examples could be given, but these would seem sufficient to place Yeshua in the "masculine" camp for category one.

On the other hand, once when Yeshua came to the little town of Nain he saw a funeral procession for a young man, "the only son of his mother, and she was a widow." The widow was in a desperate situation, for in that culture women had almost no legal or economic standing except through a man—father, husband, or son. Understandably the woman was weeping. A pitiable sight. But here Yeshua's reaction wasn't "cool." "When the Lord saw her he felt sorry for her. 'Do not cry' he said. Then he went up and put his hand on the bier and the bearers stood still, and he said, 'Young man, I tell you to get up.' And the dead man sat up and began to talk, and Jesus gave him to his mother'' (Luke 7:11–15). Yeshua responded with *feeling*.

Another time when Yeshua visited his friends Martha and Mary he learned that their brother Lazarus had died. Mary came to Yeshua and ''when Yeshua saw her weeping, and the Jews who had accompanied her also weeping, he was troubled in spirit and moved by the deepest emotions. 'Where have you laid him?' he asked. 'Lord, come and see,' they said. Yeshua began to weep, which caused the Jews to remark, 'See how much he loved him!' '' (John 11:33–36). Yeshua was clearly a person with deep emotions, and showed them publicly.

Hence, it is clear that in this category Yeshua had both the so-called masculine and feminine characteristics. A similar analysis for the other categories can be found in my *Biblical Affirmations,* pp. 281–290.

Conclusion

The evidence shows clearly that Yeshua had the full range of so-called feminine and masculine traits. What conclusion does that suggest? For one, it suggests that the division of characteristics by sex is quite artificial and false. Yeshua would have been less than a full human being if he had had only the so-called masculine set. In fact, if he had had any one of these supposedly separate sets exclusively, he would have been so lopsided as to have been less than human. Unfortunately, this sex role distortion has too often happened to the *image* of Yeshua in Christianity, past and present. At different times and places Yeshua has been seen solely as the great ruler of the world, a stern, just judge whose favor must be curried through his more sympathetic mother. At other times Yeshua has been projected as all-feeling, ''loving,'' or according to the ''Jesus freaks,'' as someone who ''saves'' without any just judgment involved. But Yeshua was not just so-called masculine or feminine. He was fully human.

The model of how to live an authentically human life, of how to attain ''salvation,'' that the Gospels' Yeshua presents is not one that fits the masculine stereotype, which automatically relegates the ''softer,'' ''feminine'' traits to women as being beneath the male—nor indeed is it the opposite stereotype. Rather, it is an egalitarian model. Thus the same message that Yeshua taught in his words and dealings with women—egalitarianism between women and men—was also taught by his own androgynous lifestyle.

What has often happened to the image of Yeshua in our society also tends to happen to most of us to a greater or lesser degree. Women are made to think they must cultivate only their ''womanly'' traits and avoid their ''manly'' ones, and the converse for men. But the liberating ''Good News'' of what Yeshua thought, taught, and wrought is that to be an authentic human we must reject the false division of traits by sex. Thus we will come to know, and love, our true, integrated self and will thereby be able to see our oneness with all our fellow humans (and most especially the oppressed), with all nature, and ultimately with the Source of all.

A PERSONAL REFLECTION

The example of Yeshua played an early role in starting me on the road to becoming a feminist, and it continues to play a reinforcing role for me. I first became sensitized to the pervasive and unjust inequality of women in society and religion in the early 1960s by seeing how my wife was treated at the university and in the church. As she began researching the subject, I was more and more drawn in, until in 1970 I decided to offer a course on women and religion at Temple University where I taught, since if I didn't, no such course would probably be offered there for years. In preparing for the course I found that there was an abundance of published material on Paul's attitude toward women—in fact, whole books—but an extraordinary dearth on Yeshua's attitude. I found this puzzling, but nevertheless, proceeded to do the obvious, namely, read through the four Gospels again, noting everything that had anything to do in any way with Yeshua and women. The results were quite stunning, as I have spelled out in detail above; Yeshua clearly was a feminist. Hence, I did not have to hesitate whatsoever in my Christian—or, at least, my Yeshua—commitment.

I sent off the limited results of this research (more limited than spelled out above) in popular form to the *Catholic World,* which published the essay in January 1971. Since that time it has been reprinted, sometimes by the millions, some three dozen times in at least twenty different countries in over half a dozen different languages—that I am aware of. Obviously, other Christians also found this "news" "Good News," just as I had, and felt confirmed and encouraged in their egalitarianism in regard to women and men by the model of Yeshua— that was there all the time in the Gospels.

I have come to understand quite well the feeling the little boy must have had who said out loud that the emperor had no clothes on. Or to shift the image, the evidence was so very obviously there, but apparently everyone was viewing it through male chauvinistically astigmatic lenses—mine fortunately had been broken by the sympathetic vibrations coming from Arlene Anderson Swidler's experiences of discrimination and subsequent reflection. And so, for me, and millions of other Christians, Yeshua, feminist and androgynous, has become the model of how to live an integrated human life.

The impression should not be given, however, that everyone enthusiastically accepted the arguments of my 1971 "Jesus Was a Feminist" article. Besides the positive response, by the overwhelming majority, there were at least two kinds of negative response.

One was by Christian feminist religious scholars. They tended to dismiss or downplay the argument that Yeshua was a feminist. Sometimes this took the form of claiming that we really cannot know what the historical Yeshua said and did, so we cannot know whether Yeshua was a feminist or not. I have tried to address that objection in these pages by pointing out that there was no other source for the clearly pro-woman sayings and actions attributed to Yeshua in the Gospels than Yeshua himself; the variant readings cited in note 26, accusing Yeshua of leading the Jewish women astray, reinforce the claim.

Some also argued that Yeshua really was not very feminist when, for example, he allowed Martha to continue to be busy about household matters rather than go into the kitchen himself to help her, since Mary did not. I could not bring myself to comment on such arguments, which completely overlook what could have been the purpose behind the remembrance and recording of the Martha and Mary story; it clearly was not to preen Yeshua as a feminist, but to document that he advocated and practiced allowing women to pursue the life of Torah-study just as men, if they so chose—in that culture, a very feminist thing to do.

A second major negative response was resistance to the idea that the lot of Jewish women was so restricted at the time of Yeshua. This negative response came first from Jewish male scholars, claiming that Jewish women were highly thought of in those ancient Rabbinic days, and that I was leaving out the evidence of this high Rabbinic evaluation of women; then usually a list of "for instances" would be proffered, beginning—but also always ending—with Beruriah, the early second-century wife of Rabbi Meir who was a significant Halakhist herself.

As a historian I felt chagrined and immediately began a long investigation of women in the Rabbinic period. I found that, with the exception of Beruriah, the lot of Jewish women at the beginning of the Common Era was actually more restricted and inferior than I had depicted in my article; this work resulted in my 1976 book on women in early Judaism.[30] In the process I also learned a great deal about the famous Beruriah, who was indeed a very admirable, and feminist, character. But not only did the list of significant Jewish women in the Rabbinic period begin and end with Beruriah, later Rabbinic and medieval Jewish tradition so resented her that it made her the object of character assassination.[31]

A "second wave" of this negative response developed, claiming that Christians were using the notion that "Jesus was a feminist" as a new club in their age-old Jew-bashing, and so they tried to argue that things were really not as restricted for Jewish women at the time of Yeshua as was made out in my article.[32] Subsequently a number of Christian feminist scholars attempted to sustain the position with further arguments and research, as, for example, that by Bernadette Brooten discussed above.

However, such defensive moves, understandable though they may be at times, do not, in my judgment, help the cause either of women or of Judaism. To be sure, as I stated above, Christians have no grounds to claim Christian superiority over Judaism because of the feminist Jew Yeshua, whom they refused to follow in his feminism; those who do, simply exemplify the adage "corruptio optimae pessima." Further, if it is proper and healthy for Christian feminist scholars to be searingly critical of the sexist dimensions of their tradition—and it is proper and healthy—then it is similarly proper and healthy for Jewish feminist scholars (both, of course, also eventually need to engage in the lifting up of the positive, humanizing elements of their traditions—"contribution history"). In this regard Jews, despite, and in a way because of, the history of antisemitism, need *glasnost* just as much as do the Soviets—and Christians. For Christian feminist scholars to support their Jewish colleagues is proper and admirable, but to be less frank and critical about the Jewish tradition than the Christian is simply another form of Christian patronizing of Jews—which of course is not intended, and definitely not needed.

As a male feminist, I have experienced two other types of negative responses from feminist women. Negative responses from the male sexist side pose no difficulty and cause no pain, but negative responses from feminist women do cause pain; I am quite willing to accept them, but that fact does not make them any less painful. Let me explain.

I have the sense that oftentimes my feminist scholarship is ignored by women feminists because it was done by a man. Had it been done by a woman, I suspect that in many cases it, and I, would have been "lionized" by a number of those women feminists who now ignore it. Women have for so long been shut out of scholarly prominence that there will undoubtedly be an awkward period of time until the imbalance can be righted.

In 1982 I was Visiting Professor for the summer semester at the University of Tübingen, West Germany; Professor Hans Küng had pleaded with me to conduct a seminar in his Ecumenical Institute on Women and Christianity. I resisted, arguing that it was long since time that women theological scholars should conduct such seminars. He countered that later that summer he was launching a huge research project within his institute, led by women scholars, on women and Christianity, with an international conference, but that for the moment there were no German-speaking women feminist theological professors available to his institute. I acceded with the proviso that a woman doctoral candidate in the institute, Jutta Flatters, co-chair the seminar with me, which she did.

What I feared would happen, did: The thirty women theology students in the seminar were just starting on the feminist road; they were at a stage of just becoming conscious of their oppression. So, for the first weeks I was a kind of lightning rod for their anger at men, despite my sincere endeavor to embrace a feminist perspective. Perhaps the fact of a feminist male being there as the lightning rod helped to bring critical issues out into the open. That fact, however, did not eliminate the pain for me.

However, as I have shared unasked in the "advantages" of being male, so then I shared unasked in the "disadvantages" of being male. Men are for the present and immediately foreseeable future quite properly cast in supporting roles to women who are working out their own liberation and independence. Eventually we will come to an egalitarian collaborative stage (which perhaps this book is helping to initiate), but until then men will just have to absorb a certain amount of pain. It's probably healthy for us, anyhow.

NOTES

1. Hanna Wolff, *Jesus der Mann* (Stuttgart: Radius, 1979), 80–81. While Dr. Wolff is very insightful regarding the psychological character balance of Yeshua and his lack of a hostile animus, she herself retains an extraordinary animus against all things Jewish. Moreover, she not only is aware of and rejects the work of Christian and Jewish scholars who are recovering the manifold dimensions of the Jewishness of Yeshua, she positively rails against them. Not being a scriptural scholar herself, or anything near it, she simply polemically insists that their work *must* be mistaken. In this she continues the age-old Christian anti-Judaism, and perhaps also the modern German anti-Jewish animus. As is well known, this animus is especially dangerous.

2. In Rabbinic writings, for example the *Mishnah* (codified 200 A.D.), the *Tosephta* (codified just afterward), the *Palestinian Talmud* (400 A.D.), and the *Babylonian Talmud* (500 A.D.), there are many references to persons and things as far back as 200 B.C. Thus in many matters we can know what the Rabbis of the time of Yeshua taught, even though caution must be exercised since later codifiers might have adjusted texts for their own purposes. Nevertheless, until cogent arguments and evidence are brought forth that substantial revision did occur in the pertinent passages, good scholarship dictates that the available texts be utilized with due care. For a broad treatment, see Leonard Swidler, *Women in Judaism. The Status of Women in Formative Judaism* (Metuchen, NJ: Scarecrow Press, 1976), and Leonard Swidler, *Biblical Affirmations of Women* (Philadelphia: Westminster Press, 1979).

3. *Mishnah*, Sota 3.4. It should be noted that in this citation and almost all of the following, the Rabbis to whom the sayings are attributed were all Tenaim, that is, from before, during, or relatively shortly after (maximum, somewhat over a century) the lifetime of Yeshua.

4. *Talmud*, bKid. 33b; *Mishnah*, Ber. 3,3.

5. *Talmud*, bBer. 20b.

6. *Tosephta*, Ber. 7.18; *Talmud*, pBer. 13b; bMen. 43b.

7. *Mishnah*, Aboth 3, 6.

8. See Josephus, *Antiquities*, trans. Ralph Marcus and Henry St. John Thackeray (Cambridge, MA, and London: Loeb Classical Library, Harvard University Press, 1963), 15:418f.; *Jewish War*, 5:5, par. 198–99.; *Mishnah*, Middoth 2,5.

9. See Eliezer L. Sukenik, *Ancient Synagogues in Palestine and Greece* (London: Oxford University Press, 1934), 47ff. See also Bernadette J. Brooten, *Women Leaders in the Ancient Synagogue* (Chico, CA: Scholars Press, 1982), in which the author raises serious questions about how early the physical division of men and women was reflected in synagogue architecture. By the nature of the issue, she cannot offer positive proof that there was no such architectural separation (which, as we know, definitely existed later and up to the present); she does, however, make the usual claims that it existed at the time of Yeshua less than certain. Nevertheless, looking at all the evidence, I am persuaded that it is more likely that women and men were separated in the synagogues at the time of Yeshua. Dr. Brooten also argues for some modicum of leadership roles for women in ancient Judaism, albeit as exceptions. Her scholarship is superb and her case is solid. But the exceptions that she adduces, important as they are as "usable history" for women, remain so much just that, that they become the proverbial "exceptions that prove the

rule"; the general description of ancient Jewish women as largely officially excluded from leadership roles still stands.

10. *Mishnah*, Aboth 1.5.

11. *Talmud*, bBer. 43b.

12. Ibid.

13. *Mishnah*, Shab. 4,1; *Talmud*, bB.K. 88a; Josephus, *Antiquities*, 4: 219.

14. Philo, *Flaccus*, trans. F. H. Colson (Cambridge, MA, and London: Loeb Classical Library, Harvard University Press and William Heinemann, Ltd, 1937), 89; *De Specialibus Legibus*, 3: 172.

15. Philo, *De Specialibus Legibus*, 3: 169.

16. *Talmud*, bKid. 82b; cf. also bSan. 100b.

17. *Talmud*, bNid. 31b.

18. Ibid.

19. *Mishnah*, Terum 15; *Talmud*, pKid. 4,66b, 32; Soferim 41a in A. Cohen, ed., *The Minor Tractates of the Talmud* (London: Soncino Press, 1971), 288.

20. *Midrash*, GnR. 45, 5.

21. Addressing all women, Tertullian said: "And do you not know that you are [each] an Eve? The sentence of God on this sex of yours lives in this age: the guilt must of necessity live too. You are the devil's gateway; you are the unsealer of that [forbidden] tree: you are the first deserter of the divine law: you are she who persuaded him whom the devil was not valiant enough to attack. You destroyed so easily God's image, man. On account of your desert—that is, death—even the Son of God had to die." *De Cultu Feminarum*, 1.1, in *The Fathers of the Church*, 40: 117f.

22. Origen, *Selecta in Exodus* XVIII.17, in Jacques Paul Migne, *Patrologia Graeca*, 12: cols. 296f.

23. Epiphanius wrote: "For the female sex is easily seduced, weak, and without much understanding. The devil seeks to vomit out his disorder through women. . . . We wish to apply masculine reasoning and destroy the folly of these women." *Adversus Collyridianos*, in Migne, *Patrologia Graeca*, 42: cols. 740f.

24. Josephus stated: "The woman, says the law, is in all things inferior to the man." *Against Apion*, 2: 201.

25. For a discussion of this "wandering" story of Yeshua and the adulteress, see Swidler, *Biblical Affirmations*, 185f., 250f., 275f.; there the evidence for its having first been recorded by a woman "evangelist" is discussed.

26. This whole essay, of course, attempts to present evidence sustaining this point. In this regard it is interesting to note that there are at least two early New Testament textual variants that directly accuse Yeshua of running counter to the culture and "leading women astray." In Luke 23:5, there is a variant manuscript reading attested to by the fourth-century Palestinian-born church father Epiphanius: The chief priests said to Pilate of Yeshua, "He is inflaming the people with his teachings all over Judea; it has come all the way from Galilee, where he started, down to here"—to which Epiphanius' attested text adds, "and he has turned our children and wives away from us for they are not bathed as we are, nor do they purify themselves [*et filios nostros et uxores avertit a nobis, non enim baptizantur sicut nos nec se mundant*]." The second text is even earlier, the first half of the second century, when some of the New Testament itself was still being written. It is attested to by Marcion (d. 160 A.D.) and occurs in Luke 23:2. "They began their accusation by saying, 'We found this man inciting our people to a revolt, opposing payment of the tribute to Caesar' "—to which Marcion's attested text adds,

"leading astray the women and the children [*kai apostrehonta tas gynaikas kai ta tekna*]."
For these variant texts and references see Eberhard Nestle, ed., *Novum Testamentum Graece et Latine* (Stuttgart: Privilegierte Württenbergische Bibelarnstalt, 1954), 221, and Roger Gryson, *The Ministry of Women in the Early Church* (Collegeville, MN: Liturgical Press, 1976), 126.

27. For a brief description of the implications of the Greek word used for "ministering," *diakoneo*, see Swidler, *Biblical Affirmations*, 194f. There is also a specific reference in the Acts of the Apostles to a woman by name as a disciple of Yeshua: "At Jaffa there was a woman disciple [*mathetria*] called Tabitha, or Dorcas in Greek" (Acts 9:36).

28. Cf. also Mark 15:40f. and Matthew 27:55f., where the women are also reported to have "ministered" [*diekonoun*] to Yeshua. A fascinating second-century Gnostic document refers to the seven holy women named in the Gospels as disciples on a par with the Twelve Apostles: "After he had risen from the dead, when they came, the twelve disciples [*mathetes*] and seven women who had followed him as disciples [*matheteuein*], into Galilee . . . there appeared to them the Redeemer." *Sophia Jesu Christ*, in E. Hennecke and W. Schneemelcher, *New Testament Apocrypha* (Philadelphia: Westminster Press, 1959), 1: 246. See Swidler, *Biblical Affirmations*, 195f., for further similar texts.

29. For further discussion of sexually parallel stories in the New Testament see Swidler, *Biblical Affirmations*, 164ff.

30. Leonard Swidler, *Women in Judaism. The Status of Women in Formative Judaism* (Metuchen, NJ: Scarecrow Press, 1976).

31. Leonard Swidler, "Beruriah: Her Word Became Law," *Lilith* 2 (Spring/Summer 1977): 9–12.

32. In a later issue of *Lilith*, Judith Plaskow ("Blaming the Jews for the Creation of Patriarchy," 7 [Fall 1980]) argued at length that the Christian claim that "Jesus Was a Feminist" was being used as an anti-Semitic tool in a way that implied that the proper response was for Christians to stop making such claims for Yeshua. In a still later issue of *Lilith*, Rabbi Nancy Fuchs (Letter to the Editor, 1981, p. 3) effectively rebutted Plaskow's line of thought.

Part IV

Educating for Dialogue between Men and Women

10

Sartre, Transcendence, and Education for Equality between the Sexes

BETTY CANNON

INTRODUCTION: SARTRE'S ONTOLOGY AS A "TESTIMONY OF SPIRIT"

When the editors of this volume asked me to contribute a chapter on Sartre, human liberation, and pedagogical principles, I hesitated for several reasons. This was not because a chapter on Sartre and men's and women's liberation would prove problematic. It would not. Nor would it prove exceedingly difficult to apply Sartre's ideas on human liberation to the educational scene. My hesitation came from the subtitle of the book, "Testimonies of Spirit," and my knowledge that other contributors would be looking at human liberation from the perspective of the world's five great religious traditions. How, I wondered, might one connect the ideas of an atheistic existentialist with the religious outlook of the other contributors? One can imagine Sartre himself shuddering at the thought. Furthermore, the world's great religions have had more than a passing share in providing justification for repressive patriarchal social mores—social mores from which Sartre would certainly wish to dissociate himself. I therefore puzzled about this request until I read the prospectus and several chapters of the book. If what is being sought after in the various chapters is an *ontological core* for a nonmaterialistic approach to relations between the sexes—an approach that allows for human transcendence—then Sartre's ontology might provide a basis for looking at these issues.

Although the word "transcendence" has no suprahuman connotation for Sartre, his ontology nonetheless provides a way of thinking about human reality as a going beyond present social and material conditions toward the creation of meaning and value—a different future. For Sartre, in fact, human reality is itself just such a transcendence or going beyond, which he describes as "transcendence transcending [objects in the world toward a different future].'' Such a description is certainly closer to the ontological core of religious experience than it is, say, to the scientific materialism of most modern atheistic thinkers. For example, Sartre is philosophically more in agreement with religious existentialists like Kierkegaard and Buber than with materialists like Freud and Marx in his utter rejection of a deterministic interpretation of human affairs.[1] Like the radical religious thinkers, Sartre would not accept the status quo (or some particular way of moving away from the status quo) as inevitable. He would instead insist that it requires human commitment and responsibility to make a better world— to, for instance, achieve equality between the sexes. In fact, since gender identification as we know it is, from a Sartrean perspective, not given but chosen, it is possible to do away with the distinctions that even today relegate women to less powerful positions with respect to their status in the world of politics and work. In this respect, Sartre is in consonance with what I take to be the ''spiritual'' core of world religions, which, like the Apostle Paul, often claim that ''in Christ [the spiritual world before it has been contaminated by human gender and other arrangements?] there is neither male nor female.'' The difference is that for Sartre, equality would be a desirable goal in *this* world rather than in the next world or, as has often been the case with world religions, in the religious as opposed to the secular order. Nonetheless, the religious idea of equality of human beings before their God has often been the only impetus toward any kind of equality in highly patriarchal societies. Because religions recognize the value of transcendence in the Sartrean sense, they implicitly recognize the revolutionary possibility of transcending rigid gender role arrangements as well.

This brings me to the second set of thoughts that I had in reading some of the other chapters of this book. It occurred to me that two things seem to happen in all religions and that they are not entirely at odds with Sartre's ontology. In fact, they may make better sense from a Sartrean perspective than from most others. First of all, an injunction to pursue meaning or value beyond the material exigencies of everyday living is characteristic of all major religions. Human beings, according to such a view, are uniquely valuable because they are value makers. Secondly, most religions provide spiritual practices or subscribe to ideas of conversion to an enlightened state or state of salvation where everyday concerns become less important or where one's relationship with the world is transformed in some way that is not understandable from a pragmatic perspective. An appreciation for the sacredness of life, especially human life, is a common form that such a conversion or achievement of enlightenment may take. In most religions, the spiritual path or the path of salvation is open to women as well as to men, even in societies that place the severest restrictions on women's roles in secular life.[2] The heart of such conversions or enlightenment states seems to be the desertion of an allegedly ''natural'' perspective on the world in favor of some ''higher'' or ''truer'' state.

Certainly, transformation themes and the hunger for value and meaning in most religions make sense from a Sartrean perspective. Nor does Sartre's ontology simply reduce them to an underlying materialist explanation. Rather, without invoking the divine, Sartre makes the urge toward and emphasis on transcendence and transformation in most religions explicable from an ontological perspective. Like those religions at their best (Sartre was more likely to take note of them at their worst), Sartrean existentialism embraces value making and transformation—particularly the kind of transformation that recognizes the value of human transcendence—as positive values. In fact, Sartre claims that the pursuit of value is a definition of being human, since the attempt to make a self in the world is co-equivalent to the pursuit of value. Transformation or radical change is possible from a Sartrean perspective because human beings are radically free, rather than determined by environmental and other circumstances.

Yet despite this common emphasis on value and transformation, there is a fundamental difference between Sartre and the majority of the world's religious thinkers. This difference lies in the propensity of most religions to encourage an essentialist, as opposed to an existentialist, approach to ultimate reality and to values. As Mircea Eliade declares in *Myth and Reality,* "For *homo religiosus* the essential precedes existence."[3] This "essential" may take the form of myths about the creation or origins of human life or the universe, a high god/s, revealed values or codes for living, or simply a path revealed by an esteemed leader or guru (as in many forms of Buddhism). Regardless of the form, there is an attempt to *find* or *return to* the essential rather than to create it. According to Sartre, on the other hand, the basic tenet of existentialism is that "existence precedes essence." This means that while Sartre would agree with religious thinkers that human beings are by definition seekers after meaning and value rather than simple searchers after pleasure or other sensual or material rewards, he would not agree that these meanings are given in advance—by gods, demons, gurus, established paths, or any religious decrees as to essential truths or values. Thus while there are existentialist strains in all religions, it is their admixture with essentialism to which Sartre would object as a sign of inauthenticity.

For Sartre, there are no *a prioris.* Individuals bear the whole responsibility for bringing meaning and value into the universe. Each of us must therefore accept responsibility for defining what it means to be human. In other words, we are not simply free to do or not to do the will of god/s or to follow the correct path, as most religions indicate. We are instead free to determine the path itself. Sartrean freedom is in this respect a fearful freedom. In fact, Sartre views the escape into theism of many religions as an effort in bad faith to avoid the implications of this radical freedom, in situation,[4] of every human being by calling on illegitimate guarantees that one's choices are valid. Sartre's philosophy is a radical testimony to the human spirit as the only origin and arbiter of values. It is therefore, perhaps, as a representative of a tough brand of humanism—which, nonetheless, has much in common with the living core of many spiritual traditions—that Sartre ultimately deserves to be included in the present volume. If, as Sartre believes, existence precedes essence, then the responsibility for defining what it means to be a person of the male or female gender rests squarely on the shoulders of men and women. Sexism is without excuse. Neither narrowly understood religious decrees nor biological determinism can decide on "natural" relations between the sexes, since these are *chosen* rather than *given*.

In line with this idea, we find that a Sartrean view of positive relations between the sexes (or positive interpersonal relations in general) is based on a "conversion" experience that is the opposite of most religious conversions understood in their narrowest dogmatic sense. This conversion is not to, but away from essentialism in all its forms. For Sartre, the proposition that essence (whether defined as God, human nature, individual character, *a priori* values, or the determinative facticity of materialist science) precedes existence is a lie designed to obscure the ontological truth that one is radically free. This form of "bad faith," however, is a constant lure for most of us because the fundamental human project of establishing value seduces us into longing for established values. Especially, we would like to view ourselves as "being somebody" (to use a popular phrase) in the substantive sense—that is, as having solidity and absolute definition like other objects in the world. To this end, we are likely to try to use both material objects and other people. Other people are especially alluring since they, as other transcendences, are able to objectify us within their consciousnesses. Thus arises that fundamental struggle between people that Sartre, in the section of *Being and Nothingness* entitles "Concrete Relations with Others," describes as "the conflict of consciousnesses."[5] Simone de Beauvoir,[6] applying Sartre's description to relations between the sexes, further views this conflict in the sexual sphere as a conspiracy to make woman an object and witness to man's enterprises as subject and doer. Obviously, wherever this struggle occurs, it is a conflict, the aim of which is the subjection or incorporation of the other's freedom into one's own or one's own into the other's. The ultimate aim of this struggle, however subtle or seductive a form it may take, is the use of the other to create a substantive self.

Many writers, including Haim Gordon in the companion chapter to this one, have regarded this description of interpersonal hostility as Sartre's final statement about what is possible in interpersonal relations. In doing so, they ignore Sartre's own later statements to the contrary,[7] together with an elusive footnote to "Concrete Relations" that suggests an entirely different possibility for relating to others. In this footnote, Sartre comments that the foregoing description of human conflicts does not preclude a "radical conversion" to "an ethics of deliverance and salvation [from the sado-masochistic circle described there]."[8] I think the religious metaphor that Sartre uses here is not accidental, since he is precisely talking about the kind of radical transformation of all one's past experience that is most commonly met with in religious experience. The form that this "conversion" leading to "salvation" must take is not hard to guess in the light of Sartre's description in other sections of the book of the differences between good and bad faith, authentic and inauthentic living. The conversion that Sartre envisages is a conversion from an essentialist attempt to establish a substantive self to an existentialist acceptance of oneself—and others—as value makers whose "nature" (always behind one) is carved out in existence. No one can give me that sense of solidity of Being that I so passionately desire, since to do so would deprive me of that freedom that defines being human. I must instead learn to face and accept what the title of a recent novel refers to as the "unbearable lightness of being."[9] Toward the end of *Being and Nothingness* Sartre positively states that the purpose of "existential psychoanalysis" as he sees it is to evoke such a conversion from essentialism to existentialism.[10] Similarly, I might add from the evidence of Sartre's psychobiographical studies, that the "normal" movement from infancy to maturity is a movement from essentialism to existentialism, a point to which I shall return in discussing the psychological and pedagogical implications of Sartre's ontology.

In the interpersonal sphere, the existentialist "conversion" involves giving up the struggle to incorporate, coerce, or manipulate other people into conferring substance on oneself. Only giving up the illusion that other people can be useful in this enterprise, Sartre tells us, will allow one to offer genuine love and respect to the other as another transcendence. As long as the other's freedom remains a temptation and a threat to my sense of identity, I will attempt to tyrannize over the other (sadism) or to allow him or her to tyrannize over me (masochism) as a means to establishing that identity. Or, disillusioned with the sado-masochistic circle, I will withdraw into an uneasy indifference that leads me to pretend that the other has no power to see and name me. A genuine love relationship or friendship, on the other hand, will involve recognizing my involvement with and vulnerability before the other at the same time that I grant and encourage the other's freedom. In the following passage from *The Second Sex*, Simone de Beauvoir describes what such a genuine love relationship would be like:

Genuine love ought to be founded on the mutual recognition of two liberties; the lovers would then experience themselves as both self and as other; neither would give up transcendence, neither would be mutilated; together they would manifest values and aims in the world. For the one and the other, love would be a revelation of self by the gift of self and enrichment of the world.[11]

Sartre himself in a late interview commented that he wrote *Saint Genet* to suggest similar distinctions between real love and the inauthentic variety described in "Concrete Relations."[12]

So far, Sartre's ontology allows us to understand why people are inclined to engage in sado-masochistic relationships and how such relations can be transcended through recognizing and embracing one's own and the other's freedom. What Sartre has not explained—and what Beauvoir only partially accounts for— is the ontological origins of sexism. Why, in other words, should the conflict of consciousnesses, so persistent and pervasive throughout human history and across human cultures, have taken the form of enhancing one sex at the expense of the other? I believe that at least part of the answer to this question lies in

Sartre's own description of the impact of the original others on the developing child. Since the first consistent other whom the child encounters is almost always a woman, this could be supposed to have an enormous influence on relationships with other persons of her gender. This is exactly what I propose in the following section, where I also consider the possibility that since only a few people apparently succeed in escaping from the illusion of substantive freedom to any significant extent, the greater or lesser subjugation of women is a rather cruel concomitant of their confinement to the sphere of the nursery in the first place.

A SARTREAN PERSPECTIVE ON HUMAN DEVELOPMENT
AND THE ORIGINS OF SEXISM

While some psychologists may regard the idea of an existentialist developmental theory to be contradictory, I think it is possible to view human development not simply in terms of "natural" stages, like the growth of a tree, but in terms of existential crises. Such a view would not deny that the human being as a biological organism undergoes various physical and cognitive growth processes. But it would add to this a view of personal history as a series of choices, rather than as the inevitable outcome of hereditary and environmental forces combined with psychobiological development. In such a view, the ontological plight of the human infant would be considered, as well as his or her psychobiological needs and desires. Building on the discussion in the preceding section, we can guess what that ontological plight is. First of all, the infant is thrust into a universe that does not have *a priori* meaning and value. Within such a universe, he or she must begin to make sense and create meaning in the world. A very significant part of that universe and of the young child's meaning-creation will revolve around the original significant others.

Unfortunately, as I will attempt to show, the fact that the "first parent" is almost always a woman frequently greatly affects a child's later view of the place of women in the world. What we might say of the male child is that it is because a woman first "placed" the infant in the world, not simply in terms of his biological birth but even more significantly in terms of seeing and naming him, he may well develop a need to "put her in her place" as a way of escaping her original power. And his sister, only slightly less afraid because she somehow senses that she embodies in her person that same mysterious power, will help him to do so. While ideal development would allow both the young boy and the young girl to transcend this position in transcending their needs for substantive freedom, ideal development rarely takes place. Concomitantly, genuinely equal relations between the sexes are relatively rare—though they have always existed.

If the reader is dubious about this scenario, I think a look at the "mirroring" needs uncovered by many contemporary psychoanalytic theorists as they have worked with infants and young children and more deeply disturbed patients may help to clarify matters. As I argue at length in *Sartre and Psychoanalysis*,[13] the need for accurate and emphatic mirroring from the earliest days of infancy—

noted by psychoanalytic theorists as different as Harry Stack Sullivan,[14] D. W. Winnicott,[15] Margaret Mahler,[16] Mahler, Fred Pine, and Anni Bergman,[17] and Heinz Kohut[18]—finds no adequate elucidation in traditional Freudian metatheory. The bridge between drive gratification and human valuation is simply not there. Sartre's ontology, on the other hand, can both help to clarify and provide for an expansion of these important findings of contemporary psychoanalytic theorists. In *Being and Nothingness* Sartre proposes that basic human relatedness cannot be reduced to an external materialist assumption like Freud's pleasure principle, but that relatedness is rather an outgrowth of a fundamental internal experience of the other that Sartre calls the "look." The other's look elicits my awareness of myself as an object for another consciousness—an awareness that produces a shudder of shame or terror (and later also a feeling of pride) in my being. This happens because I recognize that of all the objects in the world, only the other is able to see and judge me from the outside—that only the other (and not myself) can establish my object status as a transcendence transcended. Nor is my experience of the other as another consciousness a mere surmise; on the contrary, the look provides an experience of "apodictic certainty" similar to the Cartesian certainty about myself as an experiencing subject (I think, therefore I am). Once I have felt the other's gaze upon my flesh, I cannot doubt his or her presence as another consciousness. Nor can I resist, at least for a time, the urge to use the other to create a substantive sense of self referred to in the preceding section.

It is this burning power of the look that, I believe, explains the mirroring needs described by the psychoanalytic theorists. I think it also explains why women, who are usually the most consistent source of that first powerful look, must be kept in subordinate positions—why it is almost universally felt that the "hand that rocks the cradle" must never in reality be allowed to "rule the world." Let us look more carefully at why this should be so. Sartre is as aware as contemporary psychoanalytic theorists that a child must have adequate mirroring from his or her parents in order to develop a healthy self-regard. In fact, his psychobiographies describe varous ways in which inadequate mirroring or mirroring gone astray produces psychopathology.[19] In the first volume of his biography of Flaubert, Sartre describes the need for "valorization" through parental love that every child experiences:

a child must have a *mandate to live,* the parents are the authorities who issue the mandate. A grant of love enjoins him to cross the barrier of the moment—the next moment is awaited, he is already adored there, everything is prepared for his joyful reception, the future appears to him as a vague and gilded cloud, as his mission. . . . If later on with a little luck he can say: "my life has a purpose, I have found purpose in my life," it is because the parents' love, their creation and expectation, creation for future delight, has revealed his existence to him as a movement toward an end; he is the conscious arrow that is awakened in mid-flight and discovers, simultaneously, the distant archer, the target and the intoxication of flight . . . [if this happens] living will be the *passion*—in the religious sense—that will transform self-centeredness into a gift; experience will be felt as the *free exercise of generosity*.[20]

The recognition and love of the parents, their willingness to make the child feel like he or she is the center of the universe, guarantee the valorized child a sense of mission—a mission that "becomes a sovereign choice, permitted and evoked in the subjective person by the sense of self worth."[21] Where the child is not valorized, Sartre tells us, a sense of malaise—as though one's existence were senseless or wrong—develops.

In a certain sense, what the loved child experiences is the illusion of substance described in the preceding section. Yet Sartre does not recommend confronting the child with the gratuitousness of mere existence in itself (without the addition of human meaning) too soon. Instead he tells us that the "ethical-ontological" truth that one must create one's own value (rather than having it handed to one through the parents' valorization) "must be revealed slowly" at the "end of a long vagabond delusion."[22] Without the presence of such an illusion of self-justification, Sartre tells us, the child will develop an even more dangerous illusion—the idea of the unloved child that life does not simply lack *a priori* justification but that there is no possibility for creating a meaningful life at all. Thus we could say that the parental mandate of the loved child is a true lie since it allows him or her to assume the task of creating meaning, while the too early confrontation with the gratuitousness of simple existence in itself of the unloved child is a lying truth since it robs him or her of a viable future. The task of the unloved child as an adult is much more difficult: he or she must somehow overcome the early sense of emptiness and malaise and learn to create meaning out of an existence that has never hitherto seemed meaningful. The loved child, on the other hand, must face the existential crisis that the unloved child faced far too early: he or she must come to understand that there are no *a priori* justifications, that one must *create* rather than find meaning and purpose.

Sartre thus envisages a movement from essentialism to existentialism in his account of optimal human development. He recognizes, of course, that such development often does not take place, since the majority of the world's children are not loved in the sense of having their genuine choices validated.[23] This fact, in itself, could help to account for the prevalence of sexism—since the movement to genuine autonomy, with its concomitant relinquishment of the dream to use the other to create a substantive self, would not be likely to take place for such children. Woman as a special kind of (transcendent) object and witness would therefore be needed to console and absolve man of his object status, as Beauvoir has shown. Also, having never achieved the kind of sense of self-worth that Sartre says the loved child develops, such a person would be much more likely to engage in the "conflict of consciousnesses," simply because he or she would find it difficult if not impossible to face the anguish of his or her freedom. Girls who grew up in such a fashion could then be expected to collude with men in disparaging the once all-powerful mother in themselves and other women. Since it is only the person who undergoes the "radical conversion" to an acceptance of his or her freedom who is able to abandon the essentialism of fixed roles and assigned character, including gender roles and the personality characteristics associated with these, it seems likely that most mother-raised children (not having received optimal love) would grow up to be sexist.

Actually, some psychoanalytic theorists have themselves seen the connection between the fact that the mother is the first parent and sexism, though few have suggested that it is possible to change this scenario—either in childhood or through the later development of an autonomy that transcends sex roles. D. W. Winnicott, for example, points out that the refusal of world-making power to women dates back to their personal power in the nursery:

In psychoanalytic and allied work it is found that all individuals (men and women) have in reserve a certain fear of *woman*. Some individuals have this fear to a greater extent than others, but it can be said to be universal. This is quite different from saying that an individual fears a particular woman. This fear of *woman* is a powerful agent in society structure, and it is responsible for the fact that in very few societies does a woman hold the political reins. It is also responsible for the immense amount of cruelty to women, which can be found in customs that are accepted by almost all civilizations.[24]

Winnicott attributes this fear to "fear of the mother who had absolute power at the beginning of the infant's existence to provide, or to fail to provide, the essentials for the early establishment of the self as an individual."[25] Unfortunately, Winnicott accepts this regrettable situation as simply the way things are. Just as there is no true accounting for mirroring needs in orthodox psychoanalytic theory, there is likewise no way to radically transform gender identification, once it has jelled around one's earliest experience. The psyche, for Freud and for Winnicott, is a psychic entity with substance and structure. Even for a neo-Freudian feminist theorist like Dorothy Dinnerstein,[26] the only possible solution to the problem of sexism deriving from women's presence as first parents is to have men share equally in infant care—a possibility that is made problematic by the fact that most mother-raised men have a great reluctance to do so.

For Sartre, since psychological substance and structure are illusions maintained in bad faith, it is possible to transcend them and in doing so to transcend the inauthentic search for ontological security that rigid gender roles represent. And although this might be easier for valorized than for unvalorized children, it is always possible even for an unvalorized child to overcome both the sense of malaise that such a situation promotes and the sexism that provides him or her with some sense of security and power against the all-powerful first parent. For valorized children, even where the first parent was a woman, it ought to be much easier to promote a loosening of the bonds of false identity that sex roles and other rigid identifications represent and to facilitate a movement in the direction of a mature acceptance of oneself as a free value-making being. Since it can be argued that the second most important place where children and young adults can learn to free themselves from rigid gender roles is the schools, I will now consider how a Sartrean perspective on the depth psychological underpinnings of sexism can aid in contemporary efforts to understand and overcome sexism in the schools.

A SARTREAN PERSPECTIVE ON SEXISM IN PEDAGOGICAL THEORY AND PRACTICE

While it may be possible to overcome sexism in the schools, this will not be a simple matter of removing offending passages from textbooks and admonishing teachers to encourage the talents of all students regardless of sex. No doubt, much progress has been made in avoiding sex-role stereotyping in the schools since the days when first-grade readers depicted father going to work, mother staying home, and Dick and Jane and Sally behaving according to traditional gender roles. A perusal of three different series of contemporary first through fifth grade readers[27] provided this writer with a pleasant surprise. First of all, children and adults of all colors and cultures are represented, along with handicapped children and adults. These changes, I am told by elementary school teachers, preceded the changes in sex role stereotyping, which are also quite striking. In the pages of these readers, both men and women perform all types of occupations, including the traditional ones, and boys and girls seem untrapped either by traditional dress or traditional pursuits. For example, a second-grade reader asks the question, "What Could You Be?" The answer seems to be that you could be whatever you want to be and have the talent, skill, and interest to be. One picture portrays a woman as a nurse, but there is also a woman doctor. Another woman is portrayed as a veterinarian and still another as a computer programmer, while various men are portrayed working in a factory, growing plants in a greenhouse, teaching, and working as a policeman. Within the pages of these readers, there are Moms who carry mail and Dads who bake bread and get junior ready for a walk. Obviously things have changed radically since Dick and Jane.

On the other hand, if sexism has its origins in earliest relations with mother, then it could not be expected to disappear in its more subtle forms as a result of surface correctives. In fact, much current educational research indicates that subtle sexism is not disappearing. And while many useful suggestions about what to do about the subtler forms of gender-role stereotyping have come out of this literature, which is highly influenced by behavioral and cognitive learning theory approaches, I think there is still some failure to understand the depth issues that lie behind the stubborn persistence of sexism in education on the part of both male and female teachers and students. My Sartrean approach to sexist pedagogy would contribute two insights: (1) overcoming sexism in the schools will require both teachers and students to confront their deepest fears and most stubborn avoidances of the mythical power of woman as first witness, and (2) nonsexist education will require teachers to be sensitive to developmental issues at the same time that they provide older students with encouragement to develop beyond the illusion of substantive freedom in order to establish truly equal relationships. Before considering the significance of these two insights (both of which draw on an understanding of transcendence that lies at the core of this volume) on contemporary pedagogy, I would like to take a brief look at some aspects of the contemporary educational scene in the United States. Increasingly, as more and more women work to support or to help support their families, day care facilities, preschools, and kindergartens become as important or more important influences on child development than the years of formal subject-oriented schooling from grade school through college.

Recent studies of sex-role socialization in the schools have shifted from more blatant examples of sex-role stereotyping in textbooks, teacher behavior, and educational materials to the subtler forms of teacher-student interaction patterns, peer group pressures, student attitudes toward self and other, gender-related toys and play, and general social conditioning. Many of these studies reveal social-ization processes of which teachers themselves are unaware. For example, Lisa Serbin[28] observed in fifteen classrooms at four preschools that aggressive behavior is encouraged in boys and discouraged in girls by teachers who note (often in a negative way) such behavior in boys while ignoring similar behavior in girls. On the other hand, teachers subtly and without awareness reinforce dependent behavior in girls by paying attention to them in direct relationship to their closeness to the teacher; boys receive attention and interaction regardless of their distance from the teacher. Serbin also found that this tendency could be coun-teracted by having teachers change their characteristic patterns of paying attention to children. She also found that if female teachers make an effort to spend more time in so-called masculine enterprises, such as playing with blocks and trucks, then little girls will follow suit; similarly, male teachers can model opportunities for boys to engage in play that is usually considered the prerogative of girls, such as playing with dolls or cooking. Teachers can also encourage cross-sex play simply by noting it when it naturally occurs, as in the following statement, "John and Cathy are building a very high tower with blocks." All of this, of course, attests to the continuing power of the look to influence children's be-havior.

Since dolls are in the preschool classroom to encourage the learning of nur-turing and blocks to promote eye-hand coordination and spatial learning devel-opment, a society free of sex roles will want to encourage children of both sexes to engage in both kinds of play. Indeed, as Roger Hart[29] points out, "The different amounts of self-directed spatial exploration and opportunities for free manipu-lation of the environment that seem to characterize girls and boys, especially as they become older, quite probably has serious consequences for the development of certain cognitive abilities [i.e., the superiority that males demonstrate in spatial abilities and mathematics by adolescence]." The seeming differences between males and females in this respect, it might be surmised, may have more to do with sex-role socialization than genetic endowment. So may the discouragement of nurturing attitudes in men.

Obviously, the effects of subtle socialization processes in the earliest extra-familial social settings that children encounter are significant—and changes like those suggested by the educators discussed above are certainly salutary. Quite possibly, women would be more likely than they are today to enter highly lucrative scientific and technological fields if they had been encouraged as early as preschool to develop their abilities to manipulate the environment as well as to nourish other people—and men might be more enthusiastic about taking on early child care roles if they felt more comfortable with the role of nurturer.[30] At the same time that we acknowledge the enormous effect of early schooling, however, we must also keep in mind that children by the age of two or three may already have fairly fixed ideas about sex roles—so much so that a three-year-old may refuse to play with a toy that has been designated as appropriate for the opposite sex. Even children from homes where mothers work are likely to make fairly stereotypic distinctions between the sexes. Nor do attempts at positive intervention always work.

For example, Marcia Guttentag[31] reports an experiment in which teachers were instructed in methods designed to ''stimulate psychological androgyny'' in three age groups of children—kindergarten and grades five and nine (the three grades were chosen because of their correspondence to the three cognitive stages—preoperational, operational, and formal operational—as defined by Jean Piaget). A nonsexist curriculum in English and social studies combined with attempts to present a variety of different possibilities for boys and girls in the areas of occupation, family roles, and socioemotional roles produced a surprising result in the boys whose mothers worked: they became *more* stereotyped following the intervention, with ninth-grade boys becoming especially more sexist as a result of the intervention. It would seem that this result suggests a limitation to the social learning-theory and cognitive development models that have pervaded most feminist attempts to restructure school curricula. And while the reluctance to use a psychoanalytic model can be easily understood in the light of Freud's many well-known antifeminist statements and the definition of rigid sex roles as characteristic of ''normal'' development in orthodox psychoanalytic theory,[32] I would suggest that a revised look at sex roles and education from the perspective of existential psychoanalysis might provide a much-needed supplement to the other models. We must consider the roots of sexism as well as its perpetuation in contemporary pedagogical behavior and environmental pressures if we are to intervene in useful ways in the development of rigid gender roles in our children.

One recent large-scale study of gender-role socialization in the schools in-advertently indicates the need for an existential analytic perspective on why sexism in its more subtle forms seems so hard to overcome in our schools. Myra and David Sadker[33] conducted a five-year study on the differences between perceived and actual participation of boys and girls in the classrooms of the

1980s. What they found was that at all grade levels, in all communities and in all subjects, boys dominated classroom communication at a ratio of three to one and that teachers (male and female alike) encouraged this. Nonetheless, teachers themselves perceived that the girls in a particular class were talking more than the boys. Nor did viewing films of the classes dissuade them. In fact, even experienced researchers were only able to discover the discrepancy by coding the children's actual contributions. What, we ask, was the source of this disturbing perceptual distortion? The Sadkers suggest that stereotypes of garrulous women may have influenced these misperceptions. This, however, is only to beg the question, since it leaves the question of the origins of the stereotype of the overly talkative woman itself unexplored.

Perhaps our earlier discussion of the power of the mother as first witness can help us to understand this odd phenomenon. It may be that girls are *perceived* as dominating the classroom when they talk at all, just as mother dominated the nursery. Whatever girls have to say in such a situation, it is already "too much" from this perspective. Obviously this lack of equal participation is likely to have a powerful impact on the educational future of girls, since researchers have also discovered that when students participate in classroom discussion they hold a more positive attitude toward school and that this in turn enhances learning.[34] Perhaps this is part of the reason why girls, who are originally ahead of boys in reading and basic computation in the lower grades, have lower SAT scores in both areas than boys by the time they graduate from high school. Perhaps it also helps to explain why other girls, despite grades and achievement test scores that are as high as those of boys, have by high school become less committed to careers than their male counterparts.

Nor do matters apparently improve for women students if they do choose to go on to college and graduate school.[35] A study by Alexander W. Astin concludes that "even though men and women are presumably exposed to a common liberal arts curriculum and other educational programs during the undergraduate years, it would seem that these programs serve more to preserve, rather than to reduce, stereotypic differences between men and women in behavior, aspirations and achievement."[36] Roberta Hall and Bernice Sandler (1982) comment that while this trend may have moderated somewhat, it is still evident. Part of the problem, they believe, may be subtle issues related to "classroom climate." Classroom climate is more often favorable to men than to women. Like elementary school teachers, college teachers tend to call on men students more, to interrupt them less, and to take their remarks more seriously. Add to this the fact that the greater majority of college teachers—especially in the traditionally male professions—are men, and you have a situation where women students are discouraged both in interaction and in the provision of role models. Often the style of argumentation in the college classroom is more traditionally "male" than "female"—with hard points and competitiveness gaining the edge over open-ended questioning and concerns with affiliation. Indications are that the scenario gets worse if the young woman goes on to graduate or professional school.[37]

Actually, it seems that as a female student climbs the educational ladder, the internal[38] and external obstacles to success—laid down in preschool, grade school, and high school—grow stronger. This would make sense from the existential psychoanalytic perspective that we have been developing here, since it would seem that as she advances in school, the female student comes closer and closer to attaining a position in the world comparable to that of men. The fact that so few women actually do achieve such positions is perhaps a negative tribute to the need of both sexes to keep "Mom" out of the world-making arena. On the other hand, inhibiting a woman's full development, both educationally and otherwise, reinforces both the fear and the hostility that are inherent in the old gender stereotypes.

What can be done pedagogically to combat this situation? Our discussion thus far would suggest that promoting awareness of the more subtle issues leading to sexual discrimination is of primary importance if children and young adults are to be encouraged to develop their talents along lines unlinked to gender. Ideally this would involve an awareness of the "depth" psychological issues, which could then be confronted more directly by educators and college-age students. Even without directly confronting the origins of sexism, it is possible that much can be done on a purely behavioral level to mitigate sex-role stereotyping in the classroom. For example, the Sadkers found that four days of training provided sixty teachers with the necessary awareness to allow them to eliminate classroom bias in favor of boys. It is interesting that overall teaching also improved as teachers changed their gender favoritism. Similarly, Serbin found that the subtle sex-role socialization that she found in her study could be counteracted by training teachers to respond differently. On the other hand, Serbin also concludes that the "process of freeing children from stereotypes will have to counter children's own tendencies to stereotype."[39] It is also possible that without more understanding of the roots of sexism in each of our personal histories that the results of changes in teacher behavior will be short-lived, and one would like to see long-range studies on the effects of teacher training for nonsexist classroom interaction. In any case, one still has to deal with the disturbing idea, suggested by Guttentag's study, that interventions do not always produce the desired results—for example, that increasing awareness on the part of some boys leads to an intensified sexist outlook.

What I believe existential psychoanalysis can contribute to the whole pedagogical endeavor to overcome sexism is a new understanding of "children's own tendencies to stereotype." Of course, Piaget[40] and Kohlberg[41] have dealt with this issue in their accounts of cognitive and moral development. But I think they fail to get to the heart of the matter, which is the ontological process that lies behind such stereotyping. If we are correct in our assumptions thus far, the origin of stereotyping lies in the desire to create a substantive self. And the sexist nature of much stereotyping derives from the fact that the original version of that substantive self took shape beneath the gaze of a witness who is almost always female. Without the addition of this phenomenological fact to the prior ontological truth, stereotyping might occur but it would probably not be sexist. An amusing example of how this might happen can be seen in Carole Joffe's account[42] of her observations of children at a progressive preschool. These children used "boys only" and "girls only" stereotypes in order to try to settle space and property disputes. The only problem with this ideology was that it was never accepted by the group that stood to lose by accepting it. Apparently, such attempts at "behavior control" were unsuccessful in an environment that did not promote the usual sex-role stereotypes.

Even more to the point is the possibility that stereotypes will either fail to appear or dissolve sooner in a situation where children are recognized and respected by parents and schools as having an "identity" based on individual merit rather than membership in a particular sex (or other category)—and where such "identity" is conferred by both parents from the beginning of life. Yet even where co-parenting does not exist, it is highly possible for adequately validated children to outgrow their need for using others to create a substantive self—and with it their need to subjugate others or themselves to this enterprise. Recognizing that the dissolution of stereotypes—including gender-role stereotypes—is a normal function of maturity can be an important pedagogical principle, one that colleges in particular ought not to overlook. Perhaps we do not have to wait until midlife, as psychologist Carl Jung[43] thought, to begin to develop the other gender possibilities in ourselves—or to drop gender expectations for ourselves and others altogether. After all, from a Sartrean perspective, we are much more active partners in our own "socialization" than most psychological or social learning theories admit. And the kind of "radical conversion" to a philosophy of freedom that would render obsolete the "conflict of consciousnesses," as it so persistently occurs in the field of gender relations, is always possible. One cannot help thinking that teachers and schools, as well as parents, can facilitate the realization of this possibility by recognizing and encouraging the kind of personal/social development that would include working through this existential crisis. It is, in fact, in this ontological sense that the idea that the liberation of the two sexes goes hand in hand is most true—since men as well as women would be freed from the false "security" of rigid gender roles to explore new possibilities for living and relating.

Obviously, what I am suggesting here does not contradict many of the attempts to transcend gender-role socialization that are currently being tried in the schools. What an existential psychoanalytic perspective does make clear is that the problem is more complex than the mere learning, unlearning, and modifying of social roles. It has its roots in ontology and our basic choices of ways of being human— a quest that can well be named eternal—as we live these choices in the context of particular personal histories. By understanding the significance of the look of the first parent, we can both reevaluate our current parenting practices and look more deeply and perceptively at the subtler forms of sexism among teachers and students—forms that defy explanation unless we understand their purpose as nothing less than overcoming (on the part of both male and female teachers and students) the ontological power of the first witness. And by understanding that we are nonetheless free, both as individuals and as members of groups, to transcend that history in the direction of a different future, we can begin to remake ourselves and our world along nonsexist lines. In the schools, this would obviously have to begin with teacher awareness and change—just as in the home it would have to begin with parent awareness and change. From an existential psychoanalytic perspective, such change is possible—just as it is possible from the perspective of the other "testimonies of spirit" in this volume. I do not see how it is possible from the point of view of scientific determinism—whether this takes an orthodox psychoanalytic, behaviorist, or cognitive development perspective. Nor do I see how any of those perspectives can lead to a fully nonsexist pedagogy, since they ignore the ontological core of the problem. The specifics of an existentially oriented pedagogy would, of course, have to be worked out by teachers and researchers aware of that ontological core.

CONCLUSION

This recommendation for the development of an existentially oriented peda- gogy brings us full circle. According to our analysis, the more subtle failures to overcome sexism in the schools are related to a failure to understand the ontological basis of sexism in the desire to ceate a substantive self in the presence of a first witness who is almost always female. Materialist science or its social science derivatives cannot help us to understand this matter, since materialism denies human transcendence. Nor can materialism propose a viable solution, since that solution lies in the renunciation of the attempt to use the other to create a substantive self in favor of an acceptance of and respect for one's own and the other's freedom. Perhaps as teachers and older students begin to understand this ontological truth, not simply on an intellectual level but on the deeply personal level of one's most intimate relations, they will feel less of a need to promote in subtle ways the maintenance of gender-role stereotypes. And perhaps they will then consequently be more able to open themselves to fostering optimal development, regardless of gender or any other characteristic.

Sartrean existentialism, as we noted in the introduction, stands with the re- ligious testimonies represented in the rest of this volume as a nonmaterialistic view of human reality. Sartre's ontology also helps to make explicable the emphasis in world religions on meaning making or value creation, and on the possibility of radical change leading to enlightenment or salvation—without reducing these to an underlying materialist thesis. Yet Sartre's ontology is ex- istentialist, where most of the world's religions have engaged in varying com- binations of essentialism and existentialism. As a pervasively existentialist view, Sartre's philosophy allows the freedom to look at and remake relations between the sexes without the encumbrances of tradition and religious authority. At the same time, there is no reason why humanists with a Sartrean perspective should not join radical religious revisionists in calling for a respect for both sexes based on a respect for each other as other "transcendences." Sartre's particular point of view on human relations allows for a transcendence of the fundamental conflicts between people on which all "master-slave" relations (including relations between the sexes) are based. It also allows for an understanding of human development that will give us a perspective on what is needed educationally if sexism in its subtle and overt forms is to be overcome in the schools.

NOTES

1. Actually, Sartre's relationship with Freud and Marx is more complicated than this. Obviously, Sartre's version of "existential psychoanalysis" would have been inconceivable without the prior development of Freudian psychoanalysis. On the other hand, as Sartre points out in his discussion of existential psychoanalysis in *Being and Nothingness* (trans. Hazel Barnes [New York: Philosophical Library, 1956], 557–75), he approaches psychological metatheory with an entirely different set of philosophical premises than the assumptions Freud drew from nineteenth-century natural science. As for Marx, though Sartre gives him great credit in *Search for a Method* (trans. Hazel Barnes [New York: Vintage, 1963] and *Critique of Dialectical Reason* (trans. Alan Sheridan-Smith [London: Verso, 1982]) as the originator of the only socially viable philosophy of our time, he is nonetheless highly critical of Marxist materialism.

2. See Katherine Young, in her introduction to *Women in World Religions*, ed. Arvind Sharma (Albany: State University of New York Press, 1987). See also *Women Saints: East and West*, Swami Ghanananda, and Sir John Stewart-Wallace, eds. (Hollywood: Vedanta Press, 1979).

3. Mircea Eliade, *Myth and Reality* (New York: Harper and Row, 1975), 92.

4. It is important to note that for Sartre freedom is always situated, since some have mistakenly equated his philosophy with arguments concerning free will as a gratuitous act. For Sartre, because there is an intimate and indissoluble connection between consciousness and the world (consciousness, Sartre tells us, is always "intentional"—it is always consciousness of), there can be no such thing as an unmotivated act in the sense of an act that is totally without relationship to its context. On the other hand, all acts are uncaused in the sense of deterministic causality. In other words, choices are always made on the face of a particular world, which must be taken into account if we want to understand the actions of others. There is no such thing as ungrounded freedom any more than there is (in the deterministic sense) unfree groundedness.

5. Jean-Paul Sartre, *Being and Nothingness*, trans. Hazel Barnes (New York: Philosophical Library, 1956), 361–430.

6. Simone de Beauvoir, *The Second Sex*, trans. H. M. Parshley (New York: Alfred A. Knopf, 1970).

7. Sartre later remarked, for instance, that all of the relations in "Concrete Relations with Others" were examples of bad faith. In an interview at the age of seventy, he went so far as to argue for the desirability of utter "transparency" between people, a situation that is inconceivable if one takes hostility as the basic relationship between people. The "payoff" for such transparency, Sartre tells us, is greater self-understanding, since "this dark region that we have within ourselves, which is at once dark for us and dark for others, can only be illuminated for ourselves in trying to illuminate it for others." (See *Life / Situations*, trans. Paul Auster and Lydia Davis [New York: Pantheon Books, 1977],

11–12). Actually, the later Sartre is quite emphatic in seeing positive reciprocity as the basis not only for intimacy between the sexes but for a positive sense of community, a point on which I have elaborated in my article on "Sartre's Idea of Community" in William Calder, Ulrich Goldsmith, and Phyllis Kenevan, eds., *Hypatia: Essays in Honor of Hazel E. Barnes* (Boulder: University of Colorado Press, 1985).

8. Sartre, *Being and Nothingness*, 412.

9. Milan Kundera, *The Unbearable Lightness of Being*, trans. Michael A. Heim (New York: Harper and Row, 1984).

10. Sartre, *Being and Nothingness*, 626.

11. Beauvoir, *The Second Sex*, 628.

12. In this interview Sartre says that he has changed his position somewhat since writing *Being and Nothingness* and that he sees more possibilities for "positivity in love." According to Sartre, *Saint Genet: Actor and Martyr* (trans. Bernard Frechtman [New York: Beorge Braziller, 1963]), was written "to try to present a love that goes beyond the sadism in which Genet is steeped and the masochism that he suffered." (Paul Arthur Schilpp, ed., *The Philosophy of Jean-Paul Sartre*, Library of Living Philosophers Series [La Salle, Ill.: Open Court, 1981], 13.) In a passage from *Saint Genet* that resembles the passage from Beauvoir's book quoted above, Sartre contrasts Genet's solipsism with real love, pointing out that "in order to be completely true, a love must be shared; it is a joint undertaking in which the feeling of each is the substance of that of the Other. Each of the two freedoms addresses the Other, captivates it, tempts it, it is the Other's love of me that is the truth of my love: if my passion is solitary it becomes a cult or a phantasmagoria." (pp. 327–28).

13. Betty Cannon, *Sartre and Psychoanalysis: An Existentialist Approach to Clinical Metatheory* (Lawrence: University Press of Kansas, 1991).

14. See Harry Stack Sullivan, *Conceptions of Modern Psychiatry* (New York: W. W. Norton and Company, 1953); idem, *The Interpersonal Theory of Psychiatry* (New York: W. W. Norton and Company, 1953).

15. See D. W. Winnicott, *The Family and Individual Development* (London: Tavistock Publications, 1984); idem, *The Maturational Process and the Facilitating Environment* (New York: International Universities Press, 1965); idem, *Playing and Reality* (London: Tavistock Publications, 1985).

16. See Margaret S. Mahler, *The Selected Papers of Margaret S. Mahler*, Vols. 1 and 2 (New York and London: Jason Aronson, 1979).

17. See Margaret S. Mahler, Fred Pine, and Anni Bergman, *The Psychological Birth of the Human Infant* (New York: Basic Books, 1975).

18. See Heinz Kohut, *How Does Analysis Cure? Contributions to the Psychology of the Self*, eds. Arnold Goldberg and Paul Stepansky (Chicago and London: University of Chicago Press, 1984); idem, *The Restoration of the Self* (New York: International Universities Press, 1977).

19. Actually, there are various forms that the "look" takes in these discussions. In my book *Sartre and Psychoanalysis*, I designate these as the *look* (in the sense of the actual physical viewing), the *touch*, and the *word*. The look should require no further explication at this point. As for the touch, Sartre considers the origin of Flaubert's psychopathology to be his mother's dutiful but unloving way of handling him when he was an infant, leading to the development of a passive personality. (*The Family Idiot*, Vol. 1, trans. Carol Cosman [Chicago and London: University of Chicago Press, 1981], 47.) For Genet, the origin was the word "thief," pronounced on the young foundling

who for complex psychological reasons found himself stealing from the Morvan peasants into whose care he had been given; for Genet, Sartre tells us, this provided the starting point of a life project of attempting to "be the thief they said I was" (*Saint Genet: Actor and Martyr*, 17–58). In my own experience as a therapist, I find that the actual way in which the parents looked at the child often proves to be critical in uncovering the origins of a client's difficulties, and I frequently ask people to imagine the "look in your mother's or father's eye" when this or that happened. I also am concerned with early experiences of touching and the words that first told the child who he or she was.

20. Sartre, *The Family Idiot*, 133–34.

21. Ibid., 135.

22. Ibid., 136.

23. Ibid., 135.

24. Winnicott, *The Family and Individual Development*, 164.

25. Ibid.

26. Dorothy Dinnerstein, *The Mermaid and the Minotaur: Sexual Arrangements and Human Malaise* (New York: Harper and Row, 1977).

27. The three series that I examined were by Scott Foresman and Company (Glenview, IL), Houghton Mifflin Company (Boston), and D. C. Heath and Company (Lexington, MA, and Toronto). All were published in 1986 and 1987. The second-grade reader referred to is *Discoveries* by Houghton Mifflin. My thanks go to Lee Tapley, who is a second-grade teacher, for providing me with the books to examine and for her enlightening conversation concerning the changes in grade school materials and classes over the last twenty years.

28. Lisa Serbin, "Teachers, Peers and Play Preferences: An Environmental Approach to Sex Typing in the Preschool," in Barbara Sprung, ed., *Perspectives on Non-Sexist Early Childhood Education* (New York and London: Columbia University Press, 1978).

29. Roger Hart, "Sex Differences in the Use of Outdoors Space," in Barbara Sprung, ed., *Perspectives on Non-Sexist Early Childhood Education*.

30. Cross-cultural studies actually show that boys who take care of younger siblings tend to grow up to be more nurturing and less aggressive than their counterparts who do not.

31. Marcia Guttentag, "The Social Psychology of Sex-Role Intervention," in Barbara Sprung, ed., *Perspectives on Non-Sexist Early Childhood Education*.

32. See Eli Sagan, *Freud, Women, and Morality: The Psychology of Good and Evil* (New York: Basic Books, 1988), for a view of Freud's position on women that is both respectful to Freud and critical of his limitations. For an alternative view that sees Freud's ideas as not fundamentally antithetical to feminism, see Juliet Mitchell, *Psychoanalysis and Feminism* (New York: Random House, 1975).

33. Myra and David Sadker, *Sex Equity Handbook for Schools* (New York: Longman, 1982); idem, "Sexism in the Schoolroom of the 80's," *Psychology Today* (March 1985): 54–57; idem, *Teachers Make the Difference: An Introduction to Education* (New York: Random House, 1988).

34. See David A. Karp and William C. Yoels, "The College Classroom: Some Observations on the Meanings of Student Participation," *Sociology and Social Research* 60, no. 4 (July 1976): 421–39. See also Roberta M. Hall and Bernice R. Sandler, *The Classroom Climate:A Chilly One for Women?* (Washington, D.C.: Association of American Colleges, 1982).

35. See Alexander W. Astin, *Four Critical Years: Effects of College on Beliefs,*

Attitudes, and Knowledge (San Francisco: Jossey-Bass Publishers, 1977); Mary Hughes and Mary Kennedy, eds., *New Futures: Changing Women's Education* (New York: Methuen, 1985); Pamela Perun, ed., *The Undergraduate Woman: Issues in Educational Equity* (Lexington, MA: Lexington Books, 1982); Barbara M. Solomon, *In the Company of Educated Women: A History of Women and Higher Education in America* (New Haven: Yale University Press, 1985); M. E. Tiball, "Of Men and Research: The Dominant Themes in American Higher Education Include Neither Teaching Nor Women," *Journal of Higher Education* 47, no. 4 (1976): 373–89; and Frank J. Till, *Sexual Harassment: A Report on the Sexual Harassment of Students* (Washington, D.C.: The National Advisory Council on Women's Educational Programs, August 1980).

36. Astin, *Four Critical Years: Effects of College on Beliefs, Attitudes, and Knowledge*, 75.

37. Sue Vartuli, ed., *The Ph.D. Experience: A Woman's Point of View* (New York: Praeger, 1982).

38. Matina Horner's work ("Toward an Understanding of Achievement-Related Conflicts in Women," in Judith Stacey, Susan Bereaud, and Joan Daniels, eds., *And Jill Came Tumbling After* [New York: Dell, 1974]) is, of course, well-known; it is further buttressed by studies like one conducted by Philip Goldberg ("Are Women Prejudiced Against Women?" *Trans-Action* [1968], 23–30). In this study women rated the same article more highly if it appeared to be written by a man instead of a woman. We have also seen in various studies that women teachers are no less likely than men to promote the perpetuation of sex-role stereotypes and to pay more attention to boys than to girls (this was less true of women teachers at the college and university level).

39. Lisa Serbin, "Teachers, Peers and Play Preferences: An Environmental Approach to Sex Typing in the Preschool," Barbara Sprung, ed., *Perspectives on Non-Sexist Early Childhood Education*, 91.

40. See Jean Piaget, *The Construction of Reality in the Child*, trans. M. Cook (New York: Basic Books, 1954); idem, *The Equilibration of Cognitive Structures: The Central Problem of Intellectual Development*, trans. Terrance Brown and Kishore Trampy (Chicago: University of Chicago Press, 1985).

41. See Lawrence Kohlberg, "A Cognitive-Developmental Analysis of Children's Sex-Role Concepts and Attitudes," in Eleanor Maccoby, ed., *The Development of Sex Differences* (Stanford: Stanford University Press, 1966); idem, *Child Psychology and Childhood Education: A Cognitive-Development View* (White Plains, NY: Longman, 1987).

42. Carole Joffe, "As the Twig Is Bent," in Judith Stacey, Susan Bereaud, and Joan Daniels, eds., *And Jill Came Tumbling After*.

43. Carl Jung, "The Stages of Life," in *Modern Man in Search of a Soul* (New York and London: Harcourt Brace Jovanovich, 1933).

11

Men's and Women's Sharing of Freedom: The Educational Task

HAIM GORDON

These past few years I have been teaching a course entitled "Education for a Life of Democracy," in which one section is devoted to women's liberation. I explain at length the ways men enslave and degrade women, be it by excluding them from economic decision making or equal participation in religious life, or in the way many doctors view a woman's body—as an object to be healed, not as the embodiment of a person. I cuss out male-domineering decisions that one finds almost daily in the Israeli press; in short, I passionately demand changes so that men and women may live together as free persons. The response to my attack on male chauvinism is often enthusiastic—about sixty percent of the students are women. But I suspect that few, if any, begin working for men's and women's liberation.

My students' inaction is an affirmation of the old truism that awareness need not necessarily lead to action. It is probably also an expression of their fear of freedom, which would require that they assume new responsibilities, give up ingrained habits, and reject accepted dogmas. Yet perhaps my impressions of my students are wrong. Perhaps they are merely a projection of my groping for a way to live, as a male educator, with feminism. Elements of this groping will, no doubt, emerge in the following pages.

The educational challenge of men's and women's liberation could begin with teaching people to live a life of dialogue and love. This challenge is not new; think of Jesus' message of love, or of Martin Buber's belief that at the core of each religion one finds the dialogical experience. But Moses as a person of dialogue or Jesus as a teacher of love can seem hazy, especially since the society that nurtured them oppressed and enslaved women, and in many of their statements and deeds they themselves, at least partially, accepted this degradation of women. Contemporary writers rarely fill this lack. Consider Doris Lessing's short stories, or her fascinating description of Anna Wulf's struggle for freedom in *The Golden Notebook*. Nowhere does she depict a joyful, dialogical, loving relationship that I could advise my students to emulate. On the other hand, the macho-portrayer Hemingway did show moments of true love and dialogue in *For Whom the Bell Tolls*.

The lack of models is indicative. We lack a clear positive direction in educating for men's and women's liberation, although there are some good models of women who lived their freedom creatively—Isak Dinesen, Beryl Markham, Georgia O'Keeffe, and Simone de Beauvoir come to mind. The goals of men's and women's liberation have been formulated so often that they often sound banal. On the personal level men and women should live together in freedom, in dialogue, in love. On the social and political levels there should be mutual respect, equal opportunities, and equal responsibilities. Granted, these goals do not seem to present a concrete vision of human existence in which men and women live together in freedom. One reason is that today, presenting a concrete vision often sounds simplistic, naive; too many people are addicted to seeking out the complexity of any change they may face. But addiction to complexity and to seeking out the details of any possible difficulties stifles much of the spontaneity of joyfully accepting a direction for development. Hence, in what follows I shall accept the above goals as a background and purposely evade complexities. Like any vision-seeking, groping educator I shall indicate a simple direction, knowing that complexities may arise, but also knowing that with courage one can struggle to cope with them. Such a struggle, at times, will also bring glory to those engaged in it.

Not only glory. At the core of this book is the belief that dialogue is essential to human existence, including one's ability to develop a meaningful relationship to transcendence. But without the possibility of dialogue on the personal level, without simplicity in one's intimate relations, it may be extremely difficult to relate dialogically as a person of faith, as an educator, as a friend. Here is an ontological aspect of men's and women's liberation that one can perceive, for instance, in the marriage relationship. When a man and a woman live together in dialogue and love, their entire manner of being-in-the-world differs from when a man and a woman live together in compromise, or in mutual toleration, or in despair.

Consider an example that I used in my book *Make Room for Dreams*.[1] In the commentaries on Genesis there is much discussion of Jacob's sin when he stole Esau's blessing. I do not remember any commentary on why Rivca, Jacob's and Esau's mother, decided to deceive her husband Isaac, thus to ensure that Jacob be blessed. It seems that the male commentators wished to overlook the fact that if dialogue had prevailed between Isaac and Rivca, perhaps none of these sins would have occurred. The commentators seem to have never entertained the thought that Rivca could share with Isaac the decision as to which of their sons was worthy of being blessed; neither did Rivca herself envision this possibility. Thus, Isaac's unwillingness to share his reservations and deliberations concerning the passing on of Abraham's blessing, coupled with his relating to Rivca as an object, created an atmosphere of trickery, delusion, and deceit. In short, since he was unable or unwilling to seek dialogue with Rivca, Isaac fled into a manner of being-in-the-world characterized by mendacity.

The crucial test for a movement of liberation is: Can it be transformed into a movement for freedom? I grew up when socialism, and to some extent Soviet communism, were regarded by many as great movements of liberation. In the Western democracies, socialist parties had proudly helped liberate workers from extended hours of exhausting labor at minimum compensation. But these proud socialists ignored the fact that many of these liberated workers, who suddenly had some leisure and some affluence, could not find in socialism any guidance on how to live as free human beings. They espoused consumerism, without recognizing that this was merely a new manner of being alienated. Dependent on Marx, these socialists never distinguished between liberation and freedom.

Marx taught us all that a liberated person no longer submits to the yoke of economic enslavement and alienation. But he did not acknowledge that such is only a first step. Being free also requires acting creatively, giving of oneself; that is why only free persons may lead a spiritual existence. Hence, if liberated women merely become similar to men, without men and women changing their manner of relating to each other and to the world, men and women will be reenslaved by the various contemporary idols, such as Mammon, consumerism, pursuit of power, and nationalism.[2] The opportunity for establishing a new manner of being-in-the-world will vanish.

Grabbing and lust characterize many persons' manner of being-in-the-world; such ontic relations are manners of being enslaved. Frequently they are results of oppression. In contrast, free persons can establish a manner of being-in-the-world based on passion and sharing. Why not love and dialogue? Moments of genuine dialogue are rare, and moments of love seem even rarer. These are moments of grandeur, of relating with one's whole being to another person, but they are fleeting moments, and as such can partially guide our daily manner of being-in-the-world.

One cannot reach dialogue with every person, even if one strives to do so. But one can relate to other persons and to oneself as sojournors on this earth who wish to share one's life and the bounty of this earth with each other. The joys, the living profoundly, the possibilities of enlightenment that accompany such a sharing have been vividly described by Dostoyevski, Tolstoy, Faulkner, and many others. Often one learns to share after experiencing a passionate love or a profound moment of dialogue. For Dimitri Karamazov, the loving relationship with Grushenka led to a vision of sharing. Like Dimitri, for many persons the most intimate loving relationship is that between a man and a woman; it can often serve as a bedrock upon which an ontology of sharing rises.

An ontology of sharing is based on passion, not lust. In fulfilling a passion, a person is satisfying a desire, but is also giving of oneself. Acts of lust are merely a grabbing to oneself. Language upholds this distinction. We can say: she has a passion for opera, or for mountain climbing, or for Graham Greene's novels. We wouldn't say: she has a lust for opera, or mountain climbing, or certain novels. One has lust for sex, or for money, or for power; in short, lust is incarnated in greed.

An ontology of sharing seems to underlie many aspects of human existence. Education is a sharing of knowledge, living actively in the political realm is a sharing of freedom, and any act of creativity is an attempt to share with other persons one's manner of giving form to a portion of reality. A closer look reveals, though, that creativity is rare, that much of what occurs in the political realm is motivated by lust for power and blatant greed, and education very often has more to do with individual achievement than with the sharing of knowledge.

It need not be so. In many faiths living a spiritual existence means constantly striving to rejuvenate and revitalize the ontology of sharing. Like the appearance of other spiritual movements in human history, the emergence of the women's movement opens an entire new realm in which the ontology of sharing can prevail. It is not only that once women attain freedom, men and women will equally share this world, with its delights, opportunities, and difficulties. It is not only that when women and men freely share their bodies and minds with each other, the dialogue, love, and harmony that may emerge between them may also become a spiritual relationship. It is also that when women can act and live as free human beings, both men and women will be able to live much more creatively, lovingly, and courageously.

For instance, I hold, although it is beyond the scope of this chapter to prove, that much of the hatred and violence that currently prevails between Jews and Arabs in the Middle East is sustained by the Jewish and Muslim macho-oriented social norms, religious establishments, and prevailing culture. Let us look briefly at the religious establishments. Both the Jewish and the Muslim religious establishments encourage and support oppression of women; hence, a true male believer must live as a master, and a true female believer must live as a servant. Religious leaders project this dialectic—this manner of being-in-the-world that violates freedom, diminishes dialogue, and rejects the integrity of the other—onto other relations. Hence, both the Jewish and Muslim (male dominated) religious establishments are much more concerned with conquest and with vanquishing non-believers than with sharing with other human beings the enlightening insights of their religions. A change from within, whereby oppression of women would vanish—which I admit is today a dream—could change much of the external enslaving policies adopted by these religious administrations. Religious leaders (among them women) could then concentrate on conveying the message of love, creativity, and courage that is at the core of their religions.

But let us turn to education, the main concern of this chapter. Of course, the sharing of knowledge and skills is central to all education, but such a sharing need not lead pupils to share with each other. They can be taught that knowledge has to be grabbed and lustfully guarded, or acquired by trading away something insignificant, much as Jacob traded some lentil soup for Esau's birthright. They can view the acquisition of knowledge merely as an escalator to a higher social or economic level, or as a manner of attaining power. In short, the sharing of knowledge in education seems to have little to do with educating persons to share this world with each other.

How can one educate for an ontology of sharing? I'll briefly sketch a two-step process. First, one must go beyond the objectifying look of the other that Sartre described in *Being and Nothingness*; next, one must live some of Plato's thoughts in *Theaetetus*.

Sartre holds that the appearance of another person in "my universe" adds an "element of disintegration" to that universe. "The Other is first the permanent flight of things toward a goal which I apprehend as an object at a certain distance from me but which escapes me inasmuch as it unfolds about itself its own distances."[3] Hence, with the appearance of the other, and with his or her look at me and my universe, "suddenly an object has appeared which has stolen the world from me."[4] I have no doubt that in many, if not most encounters between two persons, Sartre is right; the appearance of the look of the other creates "a kind of drain hole in the middle of its [the world's] being and that it is perpetually flowing off through this hole."[5] But I also have no doubt that there are encounters between persons in which the look of the other is a look of sharing, in which one person's look does not steal the world from another person, but rather supports the world of the other person, contributes to it, enlarges it. A look of love is one such example. Not the love that Sartre describes, which is an act of consciousness based on one's grasping the look of the other as creating a hemorrhage in one's own world (think of Swann's love for Odette in Proust's *Remembrance of Things Past*)—but rather a look of love that, to borrow a metaphor from Nietzsche's Zarathustra, is like an invitation to dance together through life. And one cannot dance together without sharing the music and sharing the world while harmoniously responding to one's dancing partner.

I agree with Sartre that men and women very often consider each other as objects. Women, especially, are often related to as objects-to-be-enslaved, not as whole persons. But, to borrow from Gershwin, "It ain't necessarily so." Only persons who are obsessively committed to the objective world and to the world of objects cannot learn to look at other persons as possible partners to the music of life. But wait. Isn't it possible that Sartre's continual regarding of the look as making other persons into objects and his judgment that "man is a useless passion"[6] stem from a rationality whose origin might be linked to male domination? I strongly suspect that this is indeed the case and that with the elimination of male domination, there will be much more sharing in this world. The glory of women and men being able to courageously give of themselves will then be celebrated. But how does one learn to share?

In *Theaetetus* Socrates compares himself to the midwives who bring forth children:

Well, my art of midwifery has, in general, the same characteristics as theirs, but it is different in that I attend men, not women, and in that I watch over minds in childbirth, not bodies. And And the greatest thing in my art is this: to be able to test, by every means, whether it is an imitation and a falsehood that the young man's intellect is giving birth to, or something genuine and true.[7]

A true sharing of the world with another person means being midwives to each other. Each person helps his or her partner to give birth, to be creative in that realm in which a person chooses to give of oneself. Being a midwife, as Socrates points out, also means testing the genuineness of the product that has emerged; it means accepting the person whose mind gave birth, but, when needed, criticizing the product of his or her creativity. It may mean convincing that person that the result of his or her birthpangs is not worth much and should be discarded. Sharing includes the sadness and suffering involved in learning about one's limitations.

A person who lives a relationship of sharing is also willing to criticize and direct the way of life of one's partner. Sharing is not only a meeting of minds, but a meeting of modes of existence. In much the same way as one dancer can and should suggest to his or her partner how to respond in greater harmony or how to give oneself to the music—lean back and float on the melody, when you are dancing a waltz—a sharing of one's life can and should lead to working with one's partner in learning how to live more courageously, more creatively. One can always dance through life alone. But dancing in harmony with one's partner is much more enhancing, fulfilling, and gratifying.

What I have described sounds poetic, simpleminded, utopic, in short, unrealistic. I don't care. What is important is that such a possibility exists. Another person's look need not necessarily be a manner of stealing the world from me; it can also be an invitation to share the world with that person. My passion for a woman's body can lead to my giving myself to that woman and her giving herself to me. We can learn to live with each other as sharers of this world and of life, not as exploiters and oppressors of each other. But in order to share, men and women must live in freedom, and they must be courageous persons.

In endeavoring to educate people to live an ontology of sharing, the educator should remember that at its core, the religious experience is a sharing, albeit there are moments when a person confronts God or transcendence alone. It is a sharing because central to the religious experience—as lived by Abraham, Moses, Jesus, Muhammad, Buddha, and many others—is the belief that each person should live as a sojourner upon earth, whose journey through life can be worthy if it is based on a courageous pursuit of freedom while nurturing a relationship to transcendence.

Two points need to be made before briefly discussing educational praxis. First, as Nietzsche stressed in *Thus Spoke Zarathustra* and *On the Genealogy of Morals*, sharing a way of life should not allow the weakness of each partner in the sharing process to enfeeble the other partner or partners. When such occurs, people begin to live mediocre lives. Creativity disappears. Resentment triumphs. Sharing without the courage advocated by Socrates in *Theaetetus*, without the courage to criticize and point out to another person his or her weaknesses, while demanding that he or she change—all of this leads to a herd mentality, which as Nietzsche pointed out, has characterized much of human history.

The establishing of women's groups, so that women could discover themselves and their mutual plight through each other, was an act of courage and creativity. For many women this act of sharing led to a new acceptance of themselves as persons who can be courageous, free, creative, joyful, and loving. And this new acceptance of themselves led to additional acts of sharing. Thus consciousness-raising groups as a form of living together can be an initial and important stage in developing an ontology of sharing.

Unfortunately, in some groups women merely basked in sharing their frustrations and rage concerning the injustice and the details of men's domination and oppression. Justified as these frustrations may be, basking in them leads to a new mediocrity, a new herd mentality. Because Nietzsche was right. Resentment cannot lead to a joyful human existence. People who constantly identify with each other's weaknesses and merely develop resentment of those who are joyful and free will not be creative; and a brooding awareness of one's difficult situation cannot lead to love of life and to an ability to dance one's existence. As Plato intimates in *Theaetetus* and other dialogues, a courageous sharing helps a person develop one's soul and one's virtue, and such occurs when courageous persons share with each other their difficulties in seeking for things that are worthy in themselves, be it knowledge, the Good, or love. Only a courageous sharing can be the basis of the ontology that I have been advocating.

The second point also has to do with courage, which is generally considered to be a political or a military virtue. A host of thinkers who discussed courage—among them Machiavelli and Nietzsche—did not discern, probably because of their chauvinism, that dialogical relations between men and women can be a source of courage. When one acts courageously, one's whole being is involved, and in a dialogical relationship one is also relating as a whole being. In dialogue one confronts the other person, which requires courage, and this confronting can lead to a deeper knowledge of that person, to a profound relationship to what Buber called the "dynamic center" of that person. The opposite is also true. Those persons who relate naturally to the "dynamic center" of another person, who genuinely confront other people, will also have the courage to share their lives and this world with fellow human beings.

These points indicate where one can begin in educational practice. The teacher who wishes to develop an ontology of sharing in the classroom cannot begin from a sharing of weaknesses (much as is encouraged in those "group-dynamic" groups in which persons merely give vent to their frustrations, hang-ups, and personal problems and seek empathy and identification). As Buber once noted in a similar context, one must begin from above—from our ability to share our potentials, our moments of enhancement, our love of life, our passion for this worldly existence, justice, and beauty. Very often such a sharing is an act of courage, or is linked to acts of courage. Furthermore, such as sharing must be expressed not only in one's pronouncements, but also in the details of one's existence. And when men and women, or boys and girls, participate in such a learning experience, they are also learning to share the world with each other as equals.

But, while teaching math, or botany, or English, how can one relate as a courageous sojourner who is willing to share with others one's life and the bounty of the world? Only by going beyond the means-end dialectic, or the problem-solving approach. If one teaches math merely as a subject in which pupils acquire problem-solving skills, if one does not convey what Bertrand Russell once called the cold indifferent beauty of mathematics, a beauty well worth comprehending and sharing, then, of course, the pupil will view math merely as a tool that might help a person carve out one's place in the world. If one teaches botany merely as a systematic identifying of plants, without sharing one's wonder at the varieties of flora in our world, or one's response to the arresting beauty of an individual flower, then one can hardly hope that the pupil will view plants as live beings that share this world with us, nourish us not only physically but also spiritually, and hence are worthy of being related to, not merely exploited.

But that is the easier part of education. More difficult is showing the students that sharing is central to living a full life. Or, in educational terms, achievement is not a rejection of sharing. Quite the opposite. The reason one should wish to "achieve" is to be able to share one's knowledge, one's discoveries, one's capabilities with others. The successful mathematician, or botanist, or flute player, or swimmer wants other people to appreciate his or her excellence, to respond to it, to share in one's happiness at having presented a high level of proficiency, or of art, or of originality. In short, as the Greeks of antiquity indicated, sharing can be a way of establishing an appreciation of excellence in our shared universe, and of sharing the glory that accompanies excellence.

The difficulties of presenting excellence are also worthy of being shared; they can be sources of learning. But such requires that the teacher view education as more than a sharing of certain structures of knowledge, or a conveying of facts and data, which the pupil must learn and be able to present in an exam. Education is a learning to struggle for excellence, for justice, for knowledge, for beauty, and for other things that are worthy in themselves, in order to share them with one's fellow sojourners upon the earth. Educators must be people who share while struggling for excellence in their own lives. And as already mentioned, one crucial realm where one can learn to share is the living together, in equality, of men and women.

Equality is a necessary condition for sharing; as such it should prevail in all human relations. Inequality of women should be rejected on every level. But the educator should constantly remember that equality is not itself sharing. Persons in a mob are equal, yet they do not share with each other. In other words, in pursuing the necessary conditions, the educator must not lose sight of the goals.

Similarly, arousing awareness, which is an important stage in liberation, and can become a form of freedom, can also become a hindrance to the freedom required for sharing. In *The Golden Notebook* and other writings, Doris Lessing poignantly shows—what the women's movement has since painfully learned—that awareness is not freedom. Awareness occurs in one's mind, not in the political realm or in those interpersonal relations where freedom is realized. While quite a few psychological approaches perceive the acquiring of awareness as an important stage in a person's development, educators, in a role that requires results, should constantly demand that their pupils surpass that stage. Doing is what counts in learning, not awareness. Much as there is a gap between understanding and knowing that can only be bridged by learning, there is a great gap between being aware and doing that can only be bridged by performing, by acting. And the educator is the person who must demand that pupils bridge the gap between understanding and knowing and the gap between being aware and doing. In other words, educating for equality and sharing means educating men and women to participate together in the making of history.

How can the educator encourage a bridging between awareness and doing? Once again consider *Theaetetus*. The dialogue deals with the question: What is knowledge? From the beginning of his discussion with Socrates, Theaetetus understands that defining knowledge is no simple task. He doesn't know how to deal with the question except by suggesting a general answer: knowledge is perception. Socrates leads him beyond understanding to the knowledge that they both do not know what knowledge is. This result, though, is less significant than the process of sharing one's beliefs, which demands courage, especially the courage to recognize that those beliefs may be totally invalid. Socrates is not only revealing to Theaetetus their mutual limitations in defining knowledge, he is also teaching him that such limitations can only be identified by going through a process that demands confronting issues and persons. (At a certain point in the dialogue Socrates changes roles and confronts himself by assuming the role of Protagoras, who has died; in that role he responds as Protagoras would have responded to the attack of Socrates on the assertion, presented by Protagoras, that knowledge is perception.) In short, bridging the gap between understanding and knowing or between awareness and doing demands confronting persons and issues.

Women may have a somewhat different way of confronting issues and persons than men. One might term it a more accepting mode of confronting. This appears in the writings of such women novelists such as Doris Lessing, Isak Dinesen, and others, and is currently being studied, marginally I suspect, in some of the comparative studies of men and women.[8] What is significant is that the classroom in which there is a confronting of issues and of persons straightforwardly can help lay the basis for an ontology of sharing. The educator must constantly remember that the arousing of mere awareness and understanding can lead to a basking in impotence. Thus, in my work on educating Jews and Arabs to relate dialogically to each other,[9] in which I constantly confronted the participants and painful issues, I had greater success in encouraging persons to act and to share, than I have had in my lectures on "Education for a Life of Democracy," where I merely confronted issues before an audience of fifty students.

While educating for sharing should be expressed in the way of life of the educator, it is much easier to educate for sharing when one teaches in conditions that facilitate the confronting of issues and of persons. Here many of the well-known suggestions for openness in education can be the first step: small discussion groups, tutorials, joint reading of texts in the classroom, the encouraging of dialogue in the classroom setting, promoting individual research by pupils, etc. To such openness, though, one must persistently add the demand that pupils assume responsibility for what is happening around them in the world they share equally with others, and the demand that each one assume responsibility for his or her development as a person. But again, only a teacher who has the courage to confront issues and persons will be able to use these methods to encourage authentic sharing among pupils.

Three points still need to be made. First, the ontology of sharing that I have briefly sketched is also an ontology of responsibility toward the world, other human beings, and transcendence. Thus the educator who is educating his or her pupils to share the world with others as a sojourner is also educating them to act responsibly in this world. Describing the linkage between an ontology of sharing and personal responsibility is beyond the scope of this essay; but it should be stressed that an important outcome of women and men living as free human beings and sharing their freedom can be that both will assume greater responsibility in their daily lives.

Second, educating for sharing often means not accepting certain tenets in the text that is at the basis of one's religion, or not accepting certain interpretations of that text. I believe that the core of the Bible is a chronicle of freedom, of the encounter between the People of Israel, as free persons, and God. This chronicle should not become a new manner of enslavement. In short, men and women must read the Bible as free persons. They must be willing to reject sections that impose on human freedom. On the basis of this belief, I vehemently reject all Biblical sources that view women as property, or as impure, or as unable to share in freedom, or in any way unequal to men. The saying "one man among a thousand I have found; but a woman among all those have I not found" (Eccles. 8:28) is unworthy of the Bible; it diminishes the import of the encounter between God and the men and women of Israel.

Furthermore, although interpretations of the Bible may differ, valid interpretations are those that demand of the Jew and Jewess, or of any other reader, that one live as a free human being. Thus, interpretations that degrade women must be vigorously rejected, for instance, the verse from the Sayings of the Jewish Fathers, "Whoever speaks much with a woman will inherit Gehenna" (Sayings of the Jewish Fathers 1: 5). Put otherwise, the confronting of issues and persons mentioned above should also guide one's reading, including the reading of holy texts and their interpretations.

Third, educating for an ontology of sharing is also educating for interfaith dialogue. We share this world with persons of other faiths, who are sojourners, much as each one of us is. We may be unable to comprehend their manner of relating to God or to transcendence, but we must accept them and share with them, knowing that our inability to comprehend may be rooted in our own way of life. Any rejection, or murder, or oppression of the other on the basis of one's own faith is an undermining of the ontology of sharing and of that faith. And I believe that one of the best places to educate oneself and others for an ontology of sharing is in the realm of relations between men and women.

NOTES

1. Haim Gordon, *Make Room for Dreams: Spiritual Challenges to Zionism* (Westport, CT: Greenwood Press, 1989), 67.

2. Some feminists are still trying to combine socialism with feminism, basing their analysis on Marx, and are thus losing the spiritual dimensions of the women's movement. See Juliet Mitchell and Ann Oakley, eds., *What Is Feminism?* (New York: Pantheon, 1986).

3. Jean Paul Sartre, *Being and Nothingness,* trans. Hazel E. Barnes (London: Methuen, 1957), 255.

4. Ibid.

5. Ibid., 256.

6. Ibid., 615.

7. Plato, *Theaetetus,* trans. John McDowell (Oxford: Clarendon, 1973), 13.

8. See, for example, Carol Gilligan, *In a Different Voice: Psychological Theory and Women's Development* (Cambridge: Harvard University Press, 1982).

9. My main book on this subject is: Haim Gordon, *Dance, Dialogue, and Despair: Existentialist Philosophy and Education for Peace in Israel* (University: University of Alabama Press, 1986). I also address these topics in my essays in: Haim Gordon and Leonard Grob, eds., *Education for Peace: Testimonies from World Religions* (New York: Orbis Books, 1987).

Selected Bibliography

Astin, Alexander W. *Four Critical Years: Effects of College on Beliefs, Attitudes, and Knowledge*. San Francisco: Josey-Bass Publishers, 1977.

Atkinson, Clarissa, Constance Buchanan, and Margaret Miles, eds. *Immaculate and Powerful: The Female in Sacred Image and Social Reality*. Boston: Beacon Press, 1985.

Beauvoir, Simone de. *The Second Sex*. Translated by H. M. Parshley. New York: Alfred A. Knopf, 1970.

Belenky, Mary Field, et al. *Women's Ways of Knowing*. New York: Basic Books, 1986.

Buber, Martin. *Between Man and Man*. New York: Macmillan, 1965.

———. *I and Thou*. New York: Collier Books, 1987.

———. *The Knowledge of Man*. New York: Harper and Row, 1965.

———. *Pointing the Way*. New York: Harper and Row, 1957.

Buckley, Mary, and Janet Klavens, eds. *Women's Spirit Bonding*. New York: Pilgrim Press, 1984.

Calder, William, Ulrich Goldsmith, and Phyllis Kenevan. *Hypatia: Essays in Honor of Hazel E. Barnes*. Boulder: University of Colorado Press, 1985.

Cannon, Betty. *Sartre and Psychoanalysis: An Existentialist Approach to Clinical Metatheory*. Lawrence: University Press of Kansas, 1991. New York and London: Columbia University Press, 1978.

———. "Sartre's Idea of Community." In *Hypatia: Essays in Honor of Hazel E. Barnes*, edited by William Calder, Ulrich Goldsmith, and Phyllis Kenevan. Boulder: University of Colorado Press, 1985.

Carmody, Denise Lardner. *Feminism and Christianity: A Two Way Reflection*. Nashville: Abingdon Press, 1982.

Crawford, Janet, and Michael, Kinnamon, eds. *In God's Image*. Geneva: World Council of Churches, 1983.

Christ, Carol P., and Judith Plaskow, eds. *Womanspirit Rising—A Feminist Reader in Religion*. New York: Harper and Row, 1979.

Dinnerstein, Dorothy. *The Mermaid and the Minotaur: Sexual Arrangements and Human Malaise.* New York: Harper and Row, 1977.

Eliade, Mircea. *Myth and Reality.* New York: Harper and Row, 1975.

Falk, Nancy, and Rita Gross, eds. *Unspoken Words: Women's Religious Lives in Non-Western Cultures.* New York: Harper and Row, 1980.

Fiorenza, Elisabeth Schussler. *Bread Not Stone: The Challenge of Feminist Biblical Interpretation.* Boston: Beacon Press, 1984.

————. *In Memory of Her.* New York: Crossroads, 1985.

Frye, Marilyn. *The Politics of Reality: Essays in Feminist Theory.* Trumansburg, N.Y.: The Crossing Press, 1983.

Ghanananda, Swami, and Sir John Stewart-Wallace, eds. *Women Saints: East and West.* Hollywood: Vedanta Press, 1979.

Gilligan, Carol. *In a Different Voice: Psychological Theory and Women's Development.* Cambridge: Harvard University Press, 1982.

Goldberg, Philip. "Are Women Prejudiced Against Women?" *Trans-Action* 5 (1968): 23–30.

Goldenberg, Naomi. *The Changing of the Gods: Feminism and the End of Traditional Religions.* Boston: Beacon Press, 1989.

Gordon, Haim. *Dance, Dialogue, and Despair: Existentialist Philosophy and Education for Peace in Israel.* University: University of Alabama Press, 1986.

————. *Make Room for Dreams: Spiritual Challenges to Zionism.* Westport, CT: Greenwood Press, 1989.

Gray, Elizabeth Dodson. *Patriarchy as a Conceptual Trap.* Wellesley, MA: Roundtable Press, 1982.

Guttentag, Marcia. "The Social Psychology of Sex-Role Intervention." In *Perspectives on Non-Sexist Early Childhood Education,* edited by Barbara Sprung. New York and London: Columbia University Press, 1978.

Hall, Roberta M., and Bernice R. Sandler. *The Classroom Climate: A Chilly One for Women?* Washington, D.C.: Association of American Colleges, 1982.

Hart, Roger. "Sex Differences in the Use of Outdoors Space." In *Perspectives on Non-Sexist Early Childhood Education,* edited by Barbara Sprung. New York and London: Columbia University Press, 1978.

Heyward, Isabel Carter. *The Redemption of God: Toward a Theology of Mutual Relation.* Washington D.C.: University Press of America, 1982.

Horner, Matina. "Toward an Understanding of Achievement-Related Conflicts in Women." In *And Jill Came Tumbling After,* edited by Judith Stacey, Susan Bereaud, and Joan Daniels. New York: Dell, 1974.

Hughes, Mary, and Mary Kennedy, eds. *New Futures: Changing Women's Education.* New York: Methuen, 1985.

Jardine, Alice, and Paul Smith, eds. *Men in Feminism.* New York: Methuen, 1987.

Joffe, Carole. "As the Twig is Bent." In *And Jill Came Tumbling After,* edited by Judith Stacey, Susan Bereaud, and Joan Daniels. New York: Dell, 1974.

Jung, Carl. *Modern Man in Search of a Soul.* New York: Harcourt Brace Jovanovich, 1933.

Karp, David, A., and William C. Yoels. "The College Classrooms: Some Observations on the Meanings of Student Participation." *Sociology and Social Research* 60, no. 4 (July 1976): 421–39.

Kohlberg, Lawrence. *Child Psychology and Childhood Education: A Cognitive-Development View*. White Plains, N.Y.: Longman, 1987.

———. "A Cognitive-Developmental Analysis of Children's Sex-Role Concepts and Attitudes." In *The Development of Sex Differences,* edited by Eleanor Maccoby. Stanford: Stanford University Press.

Kohut, Heinz. *How Does Analysis Cure?: Contributions to the Psychology of the Self.* Edited by Arnold Goldberg and Paul Stepansky. Chicago and London: University of Chicago Press, 1984.

———. *The Restoration of the Self*. New York: International Universities Press, 1977.

Kristeva, Julia. *In the Beginning Was Love: Psychoanalysis and Faith*. New York: Columbia University Press, 1988.

Kundera, Milan. *The Unbearable Lightness of Being*. Translated by Michael A. Heim. New York: Harper and Row, 1984.

Mahler, Margaret S. *The Selected Papers of Margaret S. Mahler*. Vols. 1 and 2. New York and London: Jason Aronson, 1979.

Mahler, Margaret, Fred Pine, and Anni Bergman. *The Psychological Birth of the Human Infant*. New York: Basic Books, 1975.

Marks, Elaine, and Esabelle de Courtivron, eds. *New French Feminisms: An Anthology*. New York: Schocken Books, 1981.

Massey, Marilyn Chaplin. *Feminine Soul: The Fate of an Ideal*. Boston: Beacon Press, 1985.

Matsuda, Mizuho, et al. *Reading the Bible as Asian Women*. Singapore: Christian Conference of Asia, 1986.

McFague, Sallie. *Models of God*. Philadelphia: Fortress Press, 1987.

Mitchell, Juliet. *Psychoanalysis and Feminism*. New York: Random House, 1975.

Mitchell, Juliet, and Ann Oakley, eds. *What Is Feminism?* New York: Pantheon, 1986.

Mollenkott, Virginia R. *The Divine Feminine*. New York: Crossroads, 1981.

Oduyoye, Modupe. *The Sons of the Gods and the Daughters of Men: An Afro-Asiatic Interpretation of Genesis 1–11*. New York: Orbis, 1984.

Parvey, Constance F. *Ordination of Women in Ecumenical Perspective*: Geneva: World Council of Churches, 1980.

———. ed. *The Community of Women and Men in the Church*. Geneva: World Council of Churches, 1983.

Perun, Pamela, ed. *The Undergraduate Woman: Issues in Educational Equity*. Lexington, Mass.: Lexington Books, 1982.

Piaget, Jean. *The Construction of Reality in the Child*. Translated by M. Cook. New York: Basic Books, 1954.

———. *The Equilibration of Cognitive Structures: The Central Problem of Intellectual Development*. Translated by Terrance Brown and Kishore Trampy. Chicago: University of Chicago Press, 1985.

Pobee, John S., and Barbel von Wartenberg-Potter. *New Eyes for Reading: Biblical and Theological Reflections by Women from the Third World*. Geneva: World Council of Churches, 1987.

Robins, Wendy S., ed. *Through the Eyes of a Woman*. Geneva: World YWCA, 1986.

Ruethen, Rosemary R. *New Woman/New Earth: Sexist Ideologies and Human Liberation*. New York: Seabury Press, 1975.

———. *Religion and Sexism*. New York: Simon and Schuster, 1974.

———. *Sexism and God Talk*. Boston: Beacon Press, 1983.

————. *Womanguides: Readings Toward a Feminist Theology*. Boston: Beacon Press, 1985.

————. *Women-Church*, New York: Harper and Row, 1985.

Russell, Letty. *Becoming Human*. Philadelphia: Westminster Press, 1982.

————, ed., *Feminist Interpretation of the Bible*. Philadelphia: Westminster Press, 1985.

————. *Household of Freedom*. Philadelphia: Fortress Press, 1987.

Russell, Letty, et al., eds. *Inheriting Our Mothers' Gardens*. Philadelphia: Westminster Press, 1988.

Sadker, Myra, and David Sadker. *Sex Equity Handbook for Schools*. New York: Longman, 1982.

————. "Sexism in the Schoolroom of the 80's." *Psychology Today* (March 1985): 54–57.

————. *Teachers Make the Difference: An Introduction to Education*. New York: Random House, 1988.

Sagan, Eli. *Freud, Women, and Morality: The Psychology of Good and Evil*. New York: Basic Books, 1988.

Sartre, Jean-Paul. *Being and Nothingness*. Translated by Hazel Barnes. New York: Philosophical Library, 1956.

————. *Critique of Dialectical Reason*. Translated by Alan Sheridan-Smith. London: Verso, 1982.

————. *The Family Idiot*. Vol. 1. Translated by Carol Carman. Chicago: University of Chicago Press, 1981.

————. *Life/Situations*. Translated by Paul Auster and Lydia Davis. New York: Pantheon Books, 1977.

————. *Saint Genet: Actor and Martyr*. Translated by Bernard Frechtman. New York: George Braziller, 1963.

————. *Search for a Method*. Translated by Hazel Barnes. New York: Vintage, 1968.

Scanzoni, Letha D., and Hardesty, Nancy A. *All We Were Meant to Be*. Rev. ed. Nashville: Abingdon, 1986.

Serbin, Lisa. "Teachers, Peers and Play Preferences: An Environmental Approach to Sex Typing in the Preschool." In *Perspectives on Non-Sexist Early Childhood Education*, edited by Barbara Sprung. New York and London: Columbia University Press, 1978.

Solomon, Barbara M. *In the Company of Educated Women: A History of Women and Higher Education in America*. New Haven: Yale University Press, 1985.

Sprung, Barbara. *Perspectives on Non-Sexist Early Childhood Education*. New York and London: Columbia University Press, 1978.

Stacey, Judith, Susan Bereaud, and Joan Daniels. *And Jill Came Tumbling After*. New York: Dell, 1974.

Stendahl, Drister. *The Bible and the Role of Women: A Case Study in Hermeneutics*. Philadelphia: Fortress Press, 1966.

Sullivan, Harry Stack. *Conceptions of Modern Psychiatry*. New York: Norton, 1953.

————. *The Interpersonal Theory of Psychiatry*. New York: Norton, 1953.

Swartley, Willard M. *Case Issues in Biblical Interpretation of Slavery, Sabbath, War and Women*. Scottdale, PA: Herald Press, 1983.

Tiball, M. E. "Of Men and Research: The Dominant Themes in American Higher Education Include Neither Teaching Nor Women." *Journal of Higher Education* 47, no. 4 (1976): 373–89.

Till, Frank J. *Sexual Harassment: A Report on the Sexual Harassment of Students.* Washington, D.C.: The National Advisory Council of Women's Educational Programs, August 1980.

Trible, Phyllis. *God and the Rhetoric of Sexuality.* Philadelphia: Fortress Press, 1978.

————. *Texts of Terror: Literary-Feminist Readings of Biblical Narratives.* Philadelphia: Fortress Press, 1984.

Vartuli, Sue, ed. *The Ph.D. Experience: A Woman's Point of View.* New York: Praeger, 1982.

Wartenberg-Potter, Barbel, von. *By Our Lives: Stories of Women Today and in the Bible.* Geneva: World Council of Churches, 1985.

Webster, John C., and Ellen Low Webster. *The Church and Women in the Third World.* Philadelphia: Westminster, 1985.

Weidman, Judith L., ed. *Christian Feminism: Visions of a New Humanity.* San Francisco: Harper and Row, 1983.

Wilson, Patricia. *Faith, Feminism, and Christ.* Philadelphia: Fortress Press, 1983.

Winnicot, D. W. *The Family and Individual Development.* London: Tavistock Publications, 1984.

————. *The Maturational Process and the Facilitating Environment.* New York: International Universities Press, 1965.

————. *Playing and Reality.* London: Tavistock Publications, 1985.

Young, Katherine. "Introduction." In *Women in World Religions,* edited by Arvind Sharma. Albany: State University of New York Press, 1987.

Index

About the Editors and Contributors

BETTY CANNON is Associate Professor of Humanities and Social Sciences at the Colorado School of Mines. She has published extensively in the areas of existential philosophy, existential psychology, and peace education. In 1984 Dr. Cannon co-edited a volume devoted to the life and work of Mahatma Gandhi. Her new book, *Sartre and Psychoanalysis: An Existentialist Challenge to Clinical Metatheory,* will be published in 1991.

TIKVAH FRYMER-KENSKY is Director of Rabbinical Studies at the Reconstructionist Rabbinical College in Philadelphia. She is the author of numerous articles in Bible studies, Assyriology, and Women's Studies. Works in progress include *In the Wake of the Goddesses,* a study of the function of goddesses in Mesopotamian religion and how these functions are filled, in the absence of goddesses, in Biblical monotheism.

HAIM GORDON is Senior Lecturer in the Department of Education at Ben Gurion University of the Negev, Beersheba, Israel. He is the author of numerous books and articles in such areas as existential philosophy, Arab-Israeli dialogue, and Zionism. His most recent books are *Naguib Mahfouz's Egypt: Existential Themes in His Writings, Make Room for Dreams: Spiritual Challenges to Zionism* (Greenwood Press, 1990 and 1989, respectively), and *The Other Martin Buber.*

LEONARD GROB is Chairperson of the Philosophy Department and Director of the University Core Curriculum Program at Fairleigh Dickinson University. He is the co-editor of *Education for Peace: Testimonies from World Religions,* and has written in the area of the philosophy of Martin Buber. His articles have appeared in *Journal of Jewish Studies, Judaism,* and *Educational Theory.*

RITA M. GROSS is Associate Professor of Comparative Studies in Religion at the University of Wisconsin-Eau Claire. Her numerous publications include *Unspoken Worlds: Women's Religious Lives*, co-edited with Nancy Auer Falk. Currently she is president of the Society for Buddhist-Christian Studies. Her articles on women in Buddhism have been published in journals such as *Eastern Buddhist*, *Buddhist-Christian Studies*, *Tibet Journal*, and *Journal of Feminist Studies in Religion*.

RIFFAT HASSAN is Associate Professor of Religion at the University of Louisville. For the past fifteen years she has been a scholar of feminist theology in Islam, and she is the author of numerous articles and two books on the Muslim thinker Allama a Muhammad Iqbal. Dr. Hassan is currently completing *Equal Before Allah?* a study of issues relating to woman-man equality discussed in light of the Qur'an and the Judeo-Christian-Islamic traditions.

KANA MITRA is a part-time member of the faculty in the Department of Religious Studies at Villanova and La Salle Universities. She is also Associate Editor of the *Journal of Ecumenical Studies*. Dr. Mitra has written in the area of women in Hinduism; her latest book is *Catholicism-Hinduism: Vedantic Investigation of Raimundo Pannikkar's Attempt at Bridge Building*, published in 1987.

CONSTANCE F. PARVEY is pastor of the Evangelical Lutheran Church in America, presently serving a parish, Good Shepherd Lutheran Church, in Jericho, Vermont. She has served as a pastor in Cambridge, Massachusetts, and as chaplain at Harvard and MIT. She taught at the Lutheran Theological Seminary in Philadelphia, Bryn Mawr College, and Temple University. She was director of the World Council of Churches Community of Women and Men in the Church Study, 1978–82; she has published three books and over a hundred book chapters and articles.

MYRA SHAPIRO is a poet. She was the winner of the Dylan Thomas Award from the New School, and she has been awarded two fellowships from the MacDowell Colony. Her poems appear in *The Poetry Miscellany*, *Painted Bird Quarterly*, *Calliope*, and *The Ohio Review*. She is presently at work on a manuscript of poems entitled "The Third Seduction."

LEONARD SWIDLER is Professor of Catholic Thought and Interreligious Dialogue at Temple University. He is co-founder and Editor of the *Journal for Ecumenical Studies*. Dr. Swidler is the author or editor of over forty books, including *Women in Judaism, Jewish-Christian-Muslim Dialogue, Biblical Affirmations of Women*, and *Bursting the Bonds? A Jewish-Christian Dialogue on Jesus and Paul*.

DATE DUE

HIGHSMITH   # 45220